Wednesdays in Mississippi

Wednesdays in Mississippi

PROPER LADIES WORKING FOR RADICAL CHANGE,

FREEDOM SUMMER 1964

Debbie Z. Harwell

UNIVERSITY PRESS OF MISSISSIPPI

JACKSON

www.upress.state.ms.us

Designed by Peter D. Halverson

The University Press of Mississippi is a member of the Association of
American University Presses.

Page ii: National Council of Negro Women president Dorothy Height with
Wednesdays in Mississippi team members Billie Hetzel, Flaxie Pinkett, Peg-
gy Roach, Justin Randers-Pehrson, and Marie Barksdale. Photo courtesy
of National Park Service, Mary McLeod Bethune Council House National
Historic Site; DC-WaMMB; National Archives for Black Women's History.
Unknown photographer.

First printing 2014
∞
Library of Congress Cataloging-in-Publication Data

Harwell, Debbie Z.
Wednesdays in Mississippi : proper ladies working for radical change,
Freedom Summer 1964 / Debbie Z. Harwell.
pages cm
Includes bibliographical references and index.
ISBN 978-1-62846-095-7 (cloth : alkaline paper)
— ISBN 978-1-62846-096-4 (ebook) 1. Wednesdays in Mississippi (Orga-
nization) 2. African American women political activists—Mississippi—
History—20th century. 3. African American women civil rights work-
ers—Mississippi—History—20th century. 4. African Americans—Civil
rights—Mississippi—History—20th century. 5. Civil rights movements—
Mississippi—History—20th century. 6. Mississippi Freedom Project—History. 7. Mississippi—Race relations—History—20th century. I. Title.
E185.93.M6H37 2014
305.48'896073076209034—dc23   2014001977

British Library Cataloging-in-Publication Data available

To my husband, Tom, who supported and encouraged me along every step of this journey.

To the women of Wednesdays in Mississippi, whose vision and selfless determination made the world a better place to live.

Contents

Preface

SOMETIMES THE SIMPLEST CHOICES CAN CHANGE YOUR LIFE'S TRAJECTORY
in unexpected ways. The assignment for my first graduate school class involved selecting a book of my choice and reporting back to the class on what
I had learned from it. As I walked through the stacks at the University of
Memphis, I noticed the picture of a young professional woman staring back
from the cover of a book that had been left lying on a shelf. I remembered
seeing her on television a couple of years earlier and had wanted to read the
book but never did. I grabbed it and went home. The book, *Open Wide the
Freedom Gates*, was the autobiography of Dorothy Height, president of the
National Council of Negro Women. While I found many parts of her life
interesting, my thoughts kept returning to the single chapter about an interracial, interfaith group of middle-aged, middle-class women who traveled
to Mississippi during Freedom Summer to work behind the scenes for civil
rights. They called the program Wednesdays in Mississippi (WIMS), and it
was unlike anything I had ever heard about the civil rights movement.

I had entered graduate school planning to study midlife women's changing roles in the family as part of the sandwich generation, but I could not
stop thinking about how different the WIMS women were from the women
in my own family. As southerners, my mother, her sisters, and her friends
did not subscribe to such liberal ideals, and they certainly would *never* have
volunteered for such a mission. What made the Wednesdays women so different from the women I had known growing up in the 1960s? Why were
these northern women willing to risk their lives for the rights of others, for
people they did not even know? What happened to them? I had to know. I
surrendered myself to finding the answers and have never once regretted it.
The fiftieth anniversary of Freedom Summer offers the perfect opportunity
to learn more about these women and what their trips meant to them and
those they met.

Abbreviations

AAUW	American Association of University Women
ABC	American Broadcasting Corporation
AFSC	American Friends Service Committee
AME	African Methodist Episcopal
CBS	Columbia Broadcasting System
CDF	Children's Defense Fund
CDGM	Child Development Group of Mississippi
COFO	Council of Federated Organizations
CORE	Congress of Racial Equality
CWU	Church Women United
EOA	Economic Opportunity Act of 1964
FBI	Federal Bureau of Investigation
KKK	Ku Klux Klan
LCDC	Lawyers' Constitutional Defense Committee
LWV	League of Women Voters
MFDP	Mississippi Freedom Democratic Party
MPE	Mississippians for Public Education
NAACP	National Association for the Advancement of Colored People
NBC	National Broadcasting Corporation
NCC	National Council of Churches
NCCW	National Council of Catholic Women
NCJW	National Council of Jewish Women
NCNW	National Council of Negro Women
OEO	Office of Economic Opportunity
SCLC	Southern Christian Leadership Conference
SNCC	Student Nonviolent Coordinating Committee
WIC	Women's Inter-organizational Committee
WICS	Women in Community Service
WIMS	Wednesdays in Mississippi
WSCS	Women's Society of Christian Service
YWCA	Young Women's Christian Association

Wednesdays in Mississippi

CHAPTER ONE

Peering Behind the Cotton Curtain

*"Prejudice feeds on prejudice whereas brotherhood nourishes brother-
hood. Hate is forever corrosive."*

—RABBI CHARLES MANTINBAND[1]

FIVE MIDDLE-AGED, MIDDLE-CLASS WOMEN, THREE OF THEM WHITE AND
two black, stepped off an airplane and into the summer heat at the Jackson,
Mississippi, airport late Tuesday afternoon, July 7, 1964. They pretended to
be strangers even though they knew each other well—this was part of their
plan to come into town undetected. By some Mississippians' standards, these
women represented the lowest of the low. They were civil rights workers, but
no one would have guessed it based on their appearance. They had joked
cavalierly during the flight down that they would not speak again until they
returned home to New York, but the reality upon arrival was not so amusing.
After the white women headed off to their hotel, the two black women were
left to locate their luggage and their ride. Marian Logan said of that moment,
"It struck me ... how alone we really were."[2] That summer, forty-eight women
from cities across the North and upper-Midwest flew into Jackson in similar
interracial, interfaith teams with the same mission. Some were frightened,
but all had resolved to show their support for the civil rights movement by
meeting with their southern counterparts.

What propelled these women to join the civil rights struggle in Mississippi
just as hostility against the movement was reaching its peak? Why did they
come dressed to blend in with the southern ladies? And what could they possibly hope to accomplish in such small groups?

Earlier in the year, black and white women leaders from Jackson had
asked Dorothy Height, president of the National Council of Negro Women
(NCNW), to send representatives to their community to act as a "ministry
of presence," and NCNW volunteer Polly Cowan conceived a plan to honor
that request. The women would fly into Jackson on Tuesdays, on Wednesdays

3

they would travel to nearby communities to visit the Freedom Summer projects and meet with local women, and on Thursdays they would return home. The NCNW called the program Wednesdays in Mississippi (WIMS); and for seven weeks in July and August, WIMS conducted weekly visits to the southern women to act as a calming influence during this volatile time.

The women who came together that summer were a study in diversity: black and white; from the North and the South; from the largest cities and smallest towns; privileged and disadvantaged; Protestant, Jewish, and Catholic; PhDs and those from the "school of hard knocks." Yet, despite such divergent backgrounds, they shared a common bond as women who desired to bridge the widening racial divide.

Participants in this unique program worked woman-to-woman, encouraging black and white women to communicate their concerns to one another and by so doing to realize that they actually shared common goals for their families and their communities. The WIMS organizers believed that this kind of understanding would ultimately achieve an integrated society. While the teams met with women from a wide socioeconomic spectrum, the NCNW recognized that its overarching goal could not be accomplished without gaining the support of the southern white middle class. No other national group of men or women worked with the specific goal of opening lines of communication between black and white middle-class women to facilitate acceptance of integration and black enfranchisement in Mississippi, let alone across the South.[3]

Historians have written a great deal about the high-profile civil rights organizations and their leaders; however, other organizations and support systems, frequently composed of women and often overlooked, worked behind the scenes, serving as a backbone to the larger movement. Wednesdays in Mississippi was one such organization. Working outside the power structures of the national civil rights organizations and of Mississippi's political elites, black and white team members employed the intersecting identities of their gender, class, and age to open doors that remained closed to younger, more "radical" protestors. In an unusual and quintessentially feminine approach, WIMS employed the normative rules of southern protocol for black and white middle-class women as both their vehicle and their protection in the South.[4]

WIMS was the only civil rights program organized by women, for women, as part of a national women's organization. The NCNW served as leader of the coalition of national women's organizations under which WIMS was conceived and implemented. The coalition included the Young Women's

Christian Association (YWCA), the National Council of Jewish Women (NCJW), the National Council of Catholic Women (NCCW), Church Women United (CWU), the League of Women Voters (LWV), and the American Association of University Women (AAUW).[5]

Other national women's organizations—including Alpha Kappa Alpha, Business and Professional Women, Delta Sigma Theta, the General Federation of Women's Clubs, the Girl Scouts, Hadassah, the National Association of Colored Women, and the Women's International League for Peace and Freedom—lobbied for, funded, and publicly supported civil rights. They primarily worked in cooperation with non-gender-specific, male-led organizations. The two oldest of these male-led groups, the National Association for the Advancement of Colored People (NAACP, 1909) and the Brotherhood of Sleeping Car Porters (1925), had formed to secure political, social, and economic rights for blacks, primarily working through the legal system to achieve their goals. The Congress for Racial Equality (CORE, 1942) and the Southern Christian Leadership Conference (SCLC, 1957) followed, stressing nonviolence, interracial cooperation, and the spiritual nature of the civil rights movement. Young people in the SCLC formed the Student Nonviolent Coordinating Committee (SNCC, 1960) to engage in nonviolent direct action under their own leadership, but soon found that escalating activity in the South required better organization. To address this need, the leaders of SNCC, CORE, and the NAACP formed the Council of Federated Organizations (COFO, 1962) as an umbrella organization to oversee the expansion of voter education and registration drives in Mississippi. None of these groups, however, initiated civil rights projects reaching out to women.

Despite their distinctive focus, WIMS and the NCNW remain largely absent from the written histories of women in the civil rights movement and of Freedom Summer. Still, WIMS played a vital role in initiating a change in race relations between Mississippi women. Through WIMS, the NCNW engaged in the civil rights effort. WIMS team members did this by introducing and fostering relationships between community members of very different views on civil rights in order to open lines of communication where the larger movement had failed.

WIMS operated on the premise that achieving equal rights required people of extreme differences to accept and respect each other as equals, which could not happen if prejudice prevented normal interaction. The WIMS teams served as catalysts for change by initiating dialogue across race, region, and religion; and their gender, age, and class, rather than acting as barriers, enabled them to accomplish this goal. Historical texts and images tend to portray Freedom Summer activists as northern students, poor local blacks, and SNCC members trying to force unwanted change on white Mississippians. The story of the summer of 1964 is more complicated than that contained in these traditional narratives. Additionally, the absence of WIMS from the larger civil rights chronicle is not surprising; WIMS successfully worked behind the scenes to advance civil rights by employing a quiet, non-threatening approach directed toward white middle-class Mississippi women, who began taking the first steps towards integration.

The Wednesdays women faced an uphill battle as they worked to overcome the barriers to interracial communication that had built up for over a century. To be effective, team members had to take into consideration the state's long history of racial customs, as well as secular and religious influences that dictated how Mississippians, based on their own race and class, viewed civil rights. Fear acted as a stumbling block—fear of retribution and fear generated by the doomsday racist diatribes warning that integration would lead to society's downfall. This rhetoric was persuasive because it came not only from men in white sheets and hoods but also from elected officials, the news media, community leaders, and ministers to whom Mississippians looked with respect. The struggle also played out in the churches, with segregationists often overruling ministers in matters of doctrine, policy, and moral teaching. For the local women who opposed civil rights, the churches' stance justified their thinking and made persuading them to change all the more difficult for the WIMS teams. All of these elements played a role in the thinking of the Jackson women and determined how the Wednesdays women approached their southern counterparts when meeting for coffee and conversation.

After Reconstruction, southern legislatures created the Jim Crow laws, which the courts upheld, and which institutionalized separation of the races, causing the South's social climate to become more hate-filled. The consequences of segregation went beyond relegating blacks to inferior public facilities, however. Sociologist Barbara Ellen Smith explains that Jim Crow "encompassed customs of racial deference designed to ritualize whites' privileged claim to public space." By enforcing physical separation and racializing public space, the laws effectively encoded "race as extreme biological difference," creating a society in which "blackness was contamination."[6] Even as southern whites drew boundaries for public interaction, they paradoxically lived in close proximity to blacks, and black servants prepared food and cared for the physical needs of white families.[7] This degree of intimate contact, complicated by the racial hierarchy, was an important difference between black-white relations in the North and South.[8] Blacks in the South were rarely on an equal footing with whites, and black parents taught children the rules of appropriate interaction with whites from an early age. Many southern whites in the 1960s blamed the civil rights movement for damaging congenial race relations, misinterpreting earlier dutiful behavior by blacks as friendship.[9] Nevertheless, they believed that blacks remained happy with segregation and that love flowed across the color line—albeit mostly between employers and their maids or nannies.[10]

Mississippi sat at the heart of the Deep South geographically and exemplified what Charles Payne calls "systematic racial terrorism" born of hate and bigotry.[11] Lynchings, cross burnings, bombings, and beatings of blacks and their white supporters were common, as was abuse by law officers. The state had the highest number of lynchings, with 581 reported between 1882 and 1968. White supremacists threatened individuals physically and economically for attempting to register to vote or for participating in civil rights meetings and demonstrations; and rarely, if ever, were perpetrators brought to justice.[12] For example, in 1961, Mississippi state representative E. H. Hurst murdered farmer and NAACP member Herbert Lee after Lee helped Bob Moses register black voters for SNCC. Hurst went free, yet white supremacists habitually harassed Louis Allen, who had identified Hurst as the murderer. Out of fear, Allen made plans to move north, but on the eve of his departure, he too was killed. No one was charged.[13]

Racial divisions became more pronounced as the state's population grew and shifted. In 1900, blacks comprised 59% of Mississippi's 1.5 million people, and 75% of the population of Hinds County in which Jackson is situated. By 1960, the number of Mississippi residents increased to 2,178,141; but the number of blacks remained almost constant, dropping to 42% of the state's inhabitants and 40% of the population of the Jackson metropolitan area.[14]

Even though blacks had gone from a significant majority to a minority, racial divisions, while uncomfortable, were not impossible to navigate. Black Methodist women in Meridian, for instance, held interracial church meetings and often met with white women to share meals and speak at white churches.[15] The racial lines hardened, however, after the Supreme Court called for desegregation of the University of Mississippi in 1962 and a federal judge ordered the Mississippi public schools to comply with the *Brown* decision in 1964. Segregationists warned both would lead to "mongrelization" and "destruction" because "there is no such thing as token integration."[16]

In a sermon delivered after James Meredith was admitted to the University of Mississippi, a white minister highlighted the seriousness of passing down this racist alarmism from generation to generation. He recalled leading a church youth group in which students called for Meredith's murder. One "especially pretty little girl" repeated several times, "Kill him—niggers who want to go to school with whites ought to be killed." The minister found this distressing because each of the teenagers had once been an "innocent, loving, unsuspecting baby who loved everyone from the Negro maid who probably helped rear him to his parents" who had baptized him and promised to reflect unconditional love through Christ. "But NO!" he continued, "seventeen or more years of listening to their parents and friends, reading the state's newspapers and listening to the radio and TV stations of our state has filled their hearts, minds, emotions and to some extent their actions with hate, vengeance and contempt for justice so much so that murder is mentioned with glee and the new 'messiahs' are those defended by the state who carry out such actions. . . . We have left our youth a tragic inheritance—HATE."[17] An important and more nebulous goal of the civil rights movement targeted changing the ingrained mindset of hate and white privilege that was condoned in the South and impeded progress. Projects like WIMS that were part of Freedom Summer stood out as important steps to overcoming the psychological destruction wrought by racial oppression. Only in taking those initial steps could freedom become a reality.

Myrlie Evers, wife of Jackson NAACP field secretary Medgar Evers, wrote that "the change of tide in Mississippi" began with the 1961 sit-ins by Tougaloo College students at the Jackson Public Library, which started a trend of young blacks across the state openly confronting white supremacy.[18] Prior to that time, blacks and whites met on the campus of the historically black school, which integrated in 1962. Tougaloo had close connections to several local white churches whose members taught there, white bishops sat on the college's board, and white bankers granted Tougaloo building loans. This relationship had been possible, Tougaloo College chaplain Ed King argued, because "everything was in its place." It changed when the civil rights movement intensified, and Tougaloo students and faculty began working closely with SNCC and COFO. In 1963 students sat in at the Jackson Woolworth's lunch counter, where they were beaten and covered in salt, sugar, mustard, and ketchup by a white mob, as police and FBI agents watched.[19] This event carried an important symbolic meaning for the black masses, according to Ed King.[20]

Representing the state's capital, Jackson city officials had a chance to play a leadership role by setting a positive example in response to racial unrest. The day of the Woolworth's protests, a group of black and white students, faculty, and community members assembled to walk down Capitol Street calling for a biracial committee to help resolve the city's racial issues. The demonstration lasted just seventeen seconds, however; and Mayor Allen Thompson boasted about the protesters' speedy arrests.[21] Ed King thought that most white Mississippians agreed with the mayor's actions and believed themselves when they said, "Change will never take place," and if God wanted blacks to be served in Woolworth's, he would not have created a segregated lunch counter. Everything reinforced their prejudice because they heard no voice of moderation advocating change, nor did judges or the federal government take action to protect the demonstrators' constitutional rights.[22]

In a television address to the nation on June 11, 1963, President John F. Kennedy responded to increasing racial tensions and announced that he would call on Congress to pass civil rights legislation, stating, "It ought to be possible, in short, for every American to enjoy the privileges of being American without regard to his race or his color." Just a few hours later, an assassin shot Medgar Evers in front of his Jackson home as he returned from an NAACP meeting. His assailant, too, escaped punishment.[23]

Despite the violence in Mississippi, it took nationally televised images of Birmingham commissioner of safety Theophilus Eugene "Bull" Connor with his boot on the neck of a black woman, of children being washed away with fire hoses, and of protestors being attacked by police dogs for the larger public to take notice. The events caused President Kennedy to comment at a 1963 meeting attended by Attorney General Robert Kennedy and Martin Luther King Jr. that "Bull Connor has done more for the civil rights movement than anyone in this room." Demonstrating that the actions and sentiments of white supremacists had gone too far, these bold transgressions against civil liberties ironically had a galvanizing effect, bringing sympathetic people together to stand up for the rights of others.[24]

Southern extremists carried on with their terrorist tactics, nevertheless. On September 15, 1963, congregants gathered at the Sixteenth Street Baptist Church in Birmingham, Alabama, for Youth Day to hear a sermon, "The Love That Forgives." As children entered the room, a bomb exploded, killing four young girls. Rather than focus on the criminals, local law enforcement moved in to contain the black population.[25]

White southerners heard from the media and political leaders that the racial unrest was what Jason Sokol terms the "brainchild of distant enemies": of communists, the NAACP, northern liberals, and the federal government.[26] The State of Mississippi had taken action to fight the communist menace and cement in the minds of its citizens the connection between civil rights and communism when it created the Mississippi State Sovereignty Commission in 1956 as "a permanent authority for maintenance of racial segregation."[27] In doing so, however, it generated the kind of police-state environment it claimed to abhor. Southern politicians banked on Cold War hysteria to enable themselves to equate communism with racial justice and to frighten the public. This tactic became so prevalent, historian Linda Reed notes, that one person appearing before the House Un-American Activities Committee remarked that Senator James Eastland (D-MS) saw a "Red behind every black."[28] Further, many white southerners believed that blacks lacked the capability or desire to organize on their own. Communism, therefore, explained the unrest, enabling southern whites to hold onto their myths about the southern way of life.[29]

Accusations of Communist Party connections carried serious consequences for people's careers and personal lives, causing many to disavow any association with those labeled communists, accurately or not.[30] Minister Clay Lee stated, "All you had to do was mention the word 'communist.'"[31] The term had effectively lost its original meaning and become a catchall pejorative. The broad definition increased the word's power because the accusation could stick against those who clearly did not belong to the Communist Party or subscribe to its economic or anti-religious tenets.

Segregationist-controlled media ingrained misconceptions in the minds of the state's residents. In these early years of television, the networks limited national news to fifteen-minute broadcasts, although they ran longer documentaries. *The CBS Evening News* went to thirty minutes on September 2, 1963; the next week, NBC expanded *The Huntley-Brinkley Report.* The *ABC Evening Report* followed suit four years later.[32] Extending the broadcasts should have in theory improved exposure to national news—assuming local stations broadcast it. But during the summer of 1964, local stations often experienced mysterious blackouts at the precise moments when news about Mississippi came on national programs, limiting civil rights coverage.[33]

Getting news from print media presented similar challenges since Jackson's primary daily newspaper, the *Clarion-Ledger*, also tainted the picture of important events. Mississippian Patt Derian wrote that the biggest barrier to communication was the Jackson newspaper: "Everyone is afraid of it . . . it is autonomous . . . conscienceless . . . I suppose that it is evil . . . it is racist . . . dishonest . . . all obstructive. It is not the only problem but it is the most crucial and the least likely to be rectified."[34]

Local community leaders owned these newspapers, and Mississippi residents trusted what they read in them. The Hederman family controlled one of Jackson's two television stations, the *Clarion-Ledger*, the *Jackson Daily News,* a radio station, and one of the city's largest printing companies. Robert and Tom Hederman Jr., staunch segregationists, ran the companies and sat on the boards of Jackson's electric company, banks, thrifts, colleges, and public schools. They held leadership positions at the state's largest Baptist church, Baptist hospital, and Baptist college.[35]

The one newspaper that did report on the civil rights movement was Hazel Brannon Smith's *Northside Reporter,* published from 1954 to 1973. Smith, a white woman, received multiple awards, including the Pulitzer Prize in 1964, for her "steadfast adherence to her editorial duties in the face of great pressure and opposition."[36] Despite outside recognition, she was the target of cross burnings, bombings, ostracism, and threats. Nevertheless, Smith criticized white silence, claiming, "The haters, bombers, lynchers, and murderers could not operate in a society where the overwhelming weight of public opinion [was] openly expressed against them."[37]

John Morley Goodwillie, the father of WIMS staffer Susan Goodwillie, realized that such silence and inaction across the country had created the current situation. When his own father instructed him to stop Susan from going to Mississippi to settle someone else's problem, John replied, "For a hundred years it's been wonderfully convenient to shove the whole thing under the rug with the statement that the [N]egro problem is the [N]egro's problem. Well, it never has been, and it surely isn't today. . . . It is precisely because you and I have persisted in this approach for all these years that the thing has busted out in 1962, busted out still further in 1963, and is about to really break loose in 1964. I think we've sown the seeds of our crop with our own indifference. . . . Now [we] find ourselves in the dreadful position of having Susie, whether we like it or not, compelled to pick up the pieces."[38] John Goodwillie recognized that by opting out of support for the civil rights movement in the past, passive whites had in effect taken action. Their silence sustained white privilege and its invisibility.[39] Rabbi Charles Mantinband, one of two Mississippi rabbis fighting for civil rights, found that a "conspiracy of silence" existed in middle-class society, so that only the "blatant, raucous segregationists" were heard, while the sensitive, timid souls were drowned out or never voiced their protests.[40] To change things, those who had remained silent in the past needed to approach the problem proactively and get involved.

For both blacks and whites, fear proved to be the greatest obstacle to publicly supporting civil rights, though not always in the same way. The whole state appeared paralyzed by fear, with everyone afraid of something.[41] As one white Mississippi woman put it, "We are afraid of ourselves."[42] One black woman explained that white citizens fell into two categories—those who re-fused to aid African Americans in any way and those who wanted to help but were afraid to act. No one wanted to be categorized as either segregationist or integrationist, preferring to remain "mid-road." It proved equally difficult to engage other blacks to fight for the cause.[43] I. S. Sanders, a black school prin-cipal and husband of a local WIMS supporter, contended that fear was the greatest obstacle, because it was "inbred into everyone" for so long that they no longer waited for an actual threat. Rather, they anticipated it, hampering their ability to act.[44]

The threat of reprisals—both economic and physical—haunted everyone. As a result, many of the Mississippi women who took part in WIMS did so anonymously, and the project's records reflect that.[45] Civil rights activists, such as the COFO students, faced the most violent reprisals, from beatings and arrests to bombings and shootings.[46] Local white women who operat-ed openly received threatening phone calls and letters, had crosses burned in their yards, were ostracized socially, or had their own or their husbands' jobs threatened; rarely, though, were they physically harmed.[47] Janet Purvis, a white Jackson woman who was active in CWU, the YWCA, and Mississip-pians for Public Education, and whose husband was the first Jackson doctor to integrate his waiting room, felt that as long as she did not demonstrate, she could go to meetings at black churches or homes without a problem.[48] By contrast, the husbands of LWV members had their jobs threatened, as did the husband of the chair of the Mississippi Committee for Civil Rights, Jane Schutt, who consequently resigned.[49]

Black women did not fare as well. Historians differ on whether black women faced fewer risks than black men in the movement. Accounts abound of black women activists being beaten and jailed. Charles Payne argues that women who took part placed their whole families in jeopardy, since drive-by shootings, arson, and bombings targeted the family home. None of the wom-en he interviewed claimed to have joined the movement because it was safer for them than for the men.[50] Nevertheless, some women did find it easier to negotiate the rough terrain. Victoria Gray, a force in the Hattiesburg move-ment and the Mississippi Freedom Democratic Party (MFDP), said, "Women were out front as a survival tactic. Men could not function in high-visibility, high-profile roles . . . because they would be plucked off."[51] Martin Harvey, dean of students at Southern University in Baton Rouge, Louisiana, told his wife, Clarie Collins Harvey, who owned a Jackson funeral home, "You must be a part of this for both of us since I am employed by a state institution." Still he feared for her safety and told her years later that when she was in Mississippi, he worried every nighttime phone call was news that she had been shot.[52] It is safe to conclude that both men and women faced serious repercussions for working in the movement, but fewer women were killed.

Social class offered little protection to middle-class black women. While physical threats deterred many from taking action, fear of losing jobs and status had the most far-reaching impact. A *Clarion-Ledger* editorial warned black residents, "It might well be remembered by those who do lend an ear to the noise-makers that the job they hold could disappear on notice of participation in racial strife."[53] Thus, racists recorded license plate numbers at rallies, voter registration offices, and COFO headquarters. Historian Wilma Clopton, daughter of Mississippi's NCNW president Jessie Mosley, argues that the role of middle-class black women in the movement was (and still is) undervalued, and this misconception drove a wedge between the classes at the time. Middle-class black women worked in subtle ways that enabled them to "set foot in areas where most people would not venture ... interfacing with people. They offered their homes, they offered their time."[54] Certainly those who were financially independent had an advantage because they did not have to worry about losing their jobs, but they were not immune to intimidation. Thelma and I. S. Sanders had a bomb explode in their driveway, destroying their car, and blowing out the windows in the guest bedroom where several WIMS team members had slept weeks earlier. Fortunately, the family escaped physically unharmed.[55]

For the most part, boycotts and "selective buying" campaigns proved to be effective ways for anyone, particularly whites, to aid the movement without being on the front lines.[56] In March 1964, a group called the United Front sent letters to 31,000 white homes in Jackson informing them about a boycott by blacks of the city's prime business district on Capitol Street.[57] Later in the summer, one in five stores had closed. Participants used mail order houses, traveled to Memphis to shop, or did without.[58] Boycotts were not fool proof, however. The superintendent of schools effectively halted a boycott by predominantly black teachers after he compared past and present charge purchases in stores to see who took part.[59]

The Citizens' Council banked on fear to encourage whites to follow its line of thinking. As early as the mid-1950s, for example, it warned that if schools desegregated in Mississippi, they would face the same alleged fate as integrated schools elsewhere—white flight, falling test scores, lower curriculum standards, truancy, delinquency, over-crowding, and changing sexual attitudes (results of which were said to include black girls under age six contracting gonorrhea, white girls being fondled, rapes, assaults, and illegitimate births).[60] By 1958, the Jackson chapter, led by newspaper editor William J. Simmons, had created a file documenting the racial views of almost every white citizen in town, generating a "climate of fear that straight-jacketed the white community."[61] In 1963, Mississippi continued in a "state of hysteria," according to life-long Neshoba County resident Florence Mars. The state elected men who promised to stop the "advancing tide of integration."[62] After passage of the Civil Rights Act of 1964, the *Clarion-Ledger* reported that the Jackson Citizens' Council had called upon white residents to oppose the "so-called 'Civil Rights' act by refusing to eat, swim, or sleep under integrated conditions." After noting that the business community must decide which race it would choose to serve, the council threatened, "The few who have broken faith with the community will soon learn that principles are to be valued far above temporary financial gain or a pat on the head from a Washington politician."[63]

If Mississippians became the victims of abuse or intimidation, they had one organization to which they could turn for help—the Mississippi Advisory Committee to the United Sates Commission on Civil Rights, created in December 1959. Although Representative John Bell Williams (D-MS) called it a "gestapo" for the U.S. attorney general and urged Mississippians to refuse to take part, the committee formed, amid threats, with Jane Schutt as one of its original members.[64] The committee issued a report to the U.S. Commission in April 1963, in which Schutt, then the chairperson, stated, "The existing conditions under which our Negro citizens live are in the main intolerable, with a continuing deprivation of rights and an ever present threat of police brutality and economic reprisal directed against any citizen who attempts to break the established patterns of segregation. . . . The government of our state . . . brazenly espoused racist mythology as official policy, . . . encouraged the people of Mississippi to disregard laws and judicial decisions . . . and to place state loyalty above national loyalty."[65] The report cited specific examples of the state's failure to prevent abuse and provide equal protection under the law, as well as passage of legislation that created roadblocks to voting and testifying before the committee. Intimidation surely kept many from reporting abuse to the committee, nevertheless, the reports it did receive alerted the federal government to the need for its intervention.

SNCC activist Prathia Hall said of fear, "It would be insanely dishonest to claim that we were unafraid. Fear was an intelligent response. . . . The challenge was to see fear as a signal to exercise caution while refusing to allow fear to paralyze you."[66] That paralysis was what differentiated the activist from the average citizen trying to feel his or her way through the difficult times.

By creating a physical separation between the races and propagating fear, government and non-government organizations effectively cut off communication and understanding across race in Mississippi, and pitted neighbor against neighbor even within the races. This mistrust is not surprising considering the misinformation about the movement and the races was coming from the news media, the head of the FBI, community leaders, and ministers. Whites feared whites, blacks feared other blacks, and they were mutually afraid of each other.[67] Dorothy Height argued that rather than segregation being the result of prejudice, prejudice resulted from the estrangement caused by segregation. Because blacks and whites could not communicate with one another, they lacked knowledge of each other; and human nature made them fearful. Opening lines of communication enabled people to "find each other," to work together, and to focus on common goals.[68]

When whites dared to speak about racial matters, they were cautious in choosing when, where, and with whom. Even though race dominated every aspect of life in Mississippi, if it came up in conversation at a white social engagement, the event was ruined.[69] The wife of a business owner explained that southern whites had to be careful discussing civil rights in public, because a person had no way of knowing who was friendly or hostile to the cause, and what consequences might follow.[70] Southern white women were afraid to rely on telephones or mail, both of which could be compromised, and shied away from association with civil rights sympathizers.[71] Well-meaning moderates felt reluctant to make contact across race. Mississippian Danelle Vockroth explained to the WIMS team that whites had tremendous fear of African Americans, who likewise feared whites. Because neither group had social contact with the other, the fears worsened and the wall between them rose higher.[72]

Local black women expressed frustration at not being able to establish communication with Mississippi white women, some of whom they believed to be sympathetic to blacks.[73] These barriers translated to a lack of respect that devastated many African Americans. "Their eyes are simply dead," Ilza Williams, a black WIMS team member reported. "I can see why people who live there for ten or fifteen years, when they do come to the North, it's very hard for them to make the transition because you have more or less been treated as nothing. There's nothing so deadening or so chilling as to have a man look at you and not see anything."[74]

Reflecting on the status of race relations in the 1960s, Patt Derian wrote to Polly Cowan that whether it was called the "cotton curtain," the "high stone wall," or the "Magnolia Jungle," the resulting schism and lack of communication made it necessary to maneuver through myriad "dark places, dead ends, secret rendezvous, sunny glades, and the like."[75] This closed society was the reality of day-to-day life for the Mississippians the WIMS teams planned to meet.

Of the many influences shaping Mississippians' opinions on segregation and civil rights, religion was one of the most, if not the most, significant factor. Religious institutions and religious leaders, from the North and the South, played integral roles in upholding segregation *and* in attempting to tear it down. Historian Randy Sparks points out that before the Civil War, evangelicals became defenders of the social and racial hierarchies that rested on slavery's traditions.[76] Like the states, national Protestant denominations, including Baptists, Methodists, and Presbyterians, officially divided by region over slaveholding.[77] Methodists formally reunited as the Methodist Church in 1939 (the only denomination to do so before the 1980s), but not all of Mississippi's Methodists followed the national church. Churches not only reflected what was happening in society but also drove it.

The vast majority of Mississippians took pride in identifying as devout Christians who adhered to Christian principles and belonged to local churches. Evangelical Protestantism dominated, with Southern Baptists claiming sixty percent of the state's Christians. The Methodist Church, a mainline denomination, ranked second.[78] Evangelicals called for a literal interpretation of the Bible and "hellfire-and-brimstone" preaching of fundamentalism.[79] Religion scholar Samuel S. Hill Jr. found that they had little doubt as to the "ultimate truthfulness of the Christian claim" and entertained no alternative interpretations. Many Christians also subscribed to a belief that "love is the ultimate power . . . and the norm for human behavior."[80] Civil rights activists in the South often found, however, that the profession of this love was merely lip service that failed to open church doors to blacks.[81] While Jackson's Trinity Episcopal Church admitted mixed groups for meetings in the summer of 1963, Methodist Bishop Edward Prendergast instructed the Methodist churches as late as June 1965 not to admit blacks to their services.[82] Further, priests, rabbis, and ministers who spoke out for change often found their collars offered no protection. Radical white supremacists threatened them, beat them, and, if the racists sat on their church boards, removed them from the pulpit.

Even though some parishioners showed great courage in their actions, the individual and national churches often remained silent. MFDP organizer Aaron Henry called it a "thundering silence of God's Church" and asked why the "entertainment world, the sports world, and many times even the underworld" did more to promote brotherhood than Mississippi's religious institutions.[83] Perhaps the answer had something to do with the blurring of religious and cultural lines that had occurred by the 1960s.[84]

Although some still used scripture to justify racial hierarchies, churches and lay leaders began defending Jim Crow on the basis of tradition and states' rights. Forced to choose between religion and cultural traditions, the majority of white southerners chose the latter.[85] The board of Decell Memorial Methodist Church claimed in an official statement, "It is not unchristian that we prefer to remain an all-white congregation such as we have always been. It is our hope and our purpose that shall never be otherwise."[86] Schutt, active in multiple religious groups, heard people say of desegregation, "I just physically cannot do some of these things. It's just something I never anticipated."[87] Asking white Mississippians to turn their backs on two hundred years of southern racial protocol—even for the church—was for many of them asking too much.

The Citizens' Council often stood behind church-led resistance to civil rights, with white Baptists its most vocal supporters. Groups formed to support the Citizens' Council's position in moderate churches as well, including the Mississippi Presbyterian Laymen's Association, the Association of Christian Conservatives, and the Mississippi Association of Methodist Ministers and Laymen.[88] Charles Mantinband, rabbi at Temple B'nai Israel in Hattiesburg, Mississippi, from 1951 to 1963, wrote that the Citizens' Council cruelly and relentlessly put pressure on "misguided" journalists and clerics who refused to conform to its segregationist viewpoint. He added, "Freedom of speech or assembly is not the council's scripture. Truth, honor, justice, fair play—these fly out the window once the council goes into action."[89]

In a 1962 sermon, Jackson Episcopal priest Alex Dickson Jr. warned that the "official dogma of massive resistance" to desegregation called for reprisals against those who dissented and threatened to destroy the very liberties it claimed to preserve.[90] By 1964, when WIMS came to meet with local women who represented all of the faiths and religious organizations discussed in this book, the lack of freedom had become palpable in churches and synagogues across the state.

Both segregationists and integrationists used biblical scripture to support their positions. White theologians and lay people who subscribed to racist beliefs claimed that God had sanctioned a hierarchy of whites and blacks, men and women, and masters and slaves. The reasoning followed that if God created and ordained this inequity, then a reason must exist for it, and therefore it should not be questioned.[91] Many cited Old Testament scripture in which God warned the Israelites that disaster would befall them if they intermarried with members of the seven conquered nations that God had delivered to them.[92] As one man wrote to the *Mississippi Methodist Advocate,* published by the Mississippi Conference of the Methodist Church, God created "every race and color and intended for man to stay that way."[93] This fear of miscegenation became a focus of segregationists, who saw it as the end result of integration.

Civil rights proponents also invoked scripture to support their position, relying on the New Testament, which justified the freedom struggle by calling on the faithful to rise up "against spiritual wickedness in high places."[94] Religious activists quoted Galatians to show that the hierarchies mentioned in the Old Testament were dissolved: "There is neither Jew nor Greek, there is neither bond nor free; there is neither male nor female," because believers became one in Christ.[95] However, many argued that the call to love one's fellow man found in 1 John 3:1-11 remained the most important tenet.[96] Janet Purvis explained that churches' interpreting the Bible to support segregation, particularly in barring blacks from worship, provided the impetus for progressive-thinking congregants to seek out others who supported civil rights.[97]

Mississippi's two most outspoken rabbis argued that segregationists misinterpreted the Old Testament passages used to oppose integration. Rabbi Mantinband contended that Judaism was committed to the principle of equality of all men and that segregation was the "supreme sin" of the time.[98] The Old Testament scriptures cited by segregationists, he held, were originally intended to maintain religious purity but had become a "prop for the support of racial purity." Black and white Christians worshiped the same God, belonged to the same denominations, used the same Bible, and sang from the same hymnals, making racial distinctions irrelevant.[99] Rabbi Perry Nussbaum of Temple Beth Israel in Jackson wrote to Sam Ashmore, editor of the *Mississippi Methodist Advocate,* "I preach Judaism—the Fatherhood of God, the Brotherhood of Man whatever his racial, religious, national and social origins and current status," adding that Jesus and the prophets "would cry out in dismay at the hypocrisies" and the dichotomy between professed beliefs and behaviors regarding human relations.[100] Although much of the discussion revolved around white Protestants' interpretation of scripture, Nussbaum asserted that the debate was not "Christian," preferring instead to use the terms "Judeo-Christian" or "religious."[101] Jesus, he said, quoted from the Jewish Bible when he commanded, "Love your neighbor!"[102]

Nowhere did the religious rift become more visible than in the Methodist Church, where it played out in the *Mississippi Methodist Advocate* and from

the pulpit of white Mississippi churches that defied the national church's instructions to desegregate their services.[103] The debate, which pitted members
against members and ministers against their church boards and other ministers, raged following the *Advocate's* January 2, 1963, publication of "Born of
Conviction," a statement signed by twenty-eight young, native-son, Methodist
ministers in the Mississippi Conference. Initially drafted as a response to opponents of integration at the University of Mississippi, the final version also
called for freedom at the pulpit for ministers to express their beliefs without
censure; affirmed the teaching of the 1960 Methodist Discipline that Christ
condemned discrimination on the basis of race, color, or creed; opposed the
closing of Mississippi public schools following court directives to integrate;
and rejected communism, pointing out that being Methodists and Christians
put the signatories in "permanent opposition" to that ideology.[104] One minister, James B. Nicholson, explained, "For the past eight years we have known of
a well-organized movement spreading a doctrine of hate. We knew this, yet
we did nothing to offset this movement. We have let this group discredit our
national government, the United Nations, the courts, the Church, and some
of our most basic ideals. We sat idly by while this movement gained control
of our press and state government.... We have let prejudice shut out the Gospel and in many areas of our lives we have turned to the gods of segregation
and white supremacy to sustain us."[105]

The negative response to "Born of Conviction" appeared swiftly and
forcefully from Methodists and churches across Mississippi. Bishop Marvin
Franklin issued a statement reminding the Mississippi Conference, "Integration is not forced upon any part of our church," urging churches to focus on
"evangelism, education, missions, and other areas."[106] The Guinn Methodist
Board announced, "Our minister was reflecting only *his* opinion. We love
our pastor, but we do not agree with some of his opinions. We desire our
churches and schools segregated."[107] Laymen from the Methodist churches in
Kemper County said that the religious and social heritage handed down over
generations had stood the "test of time" and the laymen would not be forced
to alter their thinking, adding that "man's view . . . may not be changed by
resolution, supreme court, the army, nor the World Council of Churches."[108]
Here, they fell back on blaming the national government and, by referencing
the World Council of Churches, communism.

Several ministers who signed "Born of Conviction" found they no longer had churches. Two were ousted almost immediately, and a third followed
shortly thereafter under threats of violence. Their bishop denied that the ministers' appointments were changed for signing the document, but twenty left

Mississippi, with eighteen of them departing by June 1964.[109] Many moved to western states and all of them took drastic cuts in pay.[110]

Though less numerous, letters of support for the maverick ministers and the *Advocate's* editorials arrived from individuals, organizations, and churches in New York, California, Kentucky, Louisiana, and Tennessee. One from the National Council of Churches (NCC) pointed out the irony of needing courage to repeat the official teachings of the Church and of ministers having to risk their jobs and safety to do so.[111] A letter from Lawrence Rabb, a trustee of the Board of Hospitals and Homes of the Mississippi Conference Methodist Church, stated, "These ministers have held up for our Mississippi people the Christian ethic as a method of solving our problems in the matter of race as opposed to the spirit of hate which has been proclaimed so widely by public speakers and in a large portion of the Mississippi press." Rabb called on people to stand up against the fear tactics that stifled open discussion.[112]

A majority of white Mississippi Methodists disagreed that the "Born of Conviction" statement was necessary, but the reaction to its publication said otherwise. The backlash of racist rhetoric from church representatives, the firing of the ministers, and the threats of violence against them and their supporters demonstrate that the majority of white Mississippi churches had strayed from their Christian principles, and that they needed to take a more forceful stand in support of civil rights and human dignity. That time had yet to come, however.

Just six months after "Born of Conviction" appeared, the dispute over desegregation rocked Galloway Memorial Methodist Church, Jackson's oldest and largest white Methodist congregation, which had approximately 4,000 members. Originally First Methodist Church, it formed in 1836 as Jackson's first house of worship.[113] In the late nineteenth century, Charles B. Galloway served as First Methodist's minister and then as Mississippi's bishop until his death in 1909. He held liberal opinions on racial equality and the role of women. Like the WIMS organizers, Galloway believed women in social reform movements held the key to change in the South, stating, "The peculiar condition of the South calls upon her women to resuscitate her faded life and rebuild her fallen greatness. . . . The mission of southern womanhood . . . is the social, moral, and as a consequence, political regeneration of the South." Galloway opposed memorializing the Confederacy, attacked the new state constitution for instating segregation and black disenfranchisement, and opposed lynching; he also argued in favor of educational opportunities for blacks.[114] Despite these views, he remained revered by Mississippi Methodists, who later renamed the church in his honor.

Although the church carried Galloway's name, by the 1960s his beliefs about racial equality were forgotten there. When ushers turned away blacks at the door on June 9, 1963, Reverend William B. Selah, who had served as pastor at Galloway for almost eighteen years, closed his sermon by abruptly resigning.[115] The black worshipers went instead to a nearby Catholic church, where they were quietly admitted without incident.[116] Reverend W. J. Cunningham, who fondly remembered attending Galloway while a student at Jackson's Millsaps College, took over the pulpit.[117] But times had changed more than he realized, and the Citizens' Council held sway over the church's board. "The Council's philosophy [was] dominant," recalled Cunningham. The Citizens' Council, backed by the "awesome might of the State Sovereignty Commission," played a key role in restricting the church. The board exceeded its authority by passing resolutions that tied the minister's hands and restricted blacks from worship services as part of "time honored tradition," in contradiction to the national church's policy.[118]

Although Galloway's minister changed, attitudes did not, and race remained a central theme as congregants asked, "Are black people coming into this church?"[119] The conflict rested strictly on the issue of race. The majority of those attempting to integrate Galloway were established members and leaders in the Methodist Church. In October 1963, a college science teacher and Galloway member invited two black students and two out-of-state white Methodist clergymen to visit his Sunday school class. Police arrested all of them. Theologian Charles Marsh speculated that this was probably the first incidence in the civil rights movement "or perhaps the history of Christendom" of police arresting someone for attending his own church.[120] Blacks and whites came from across the country to desegregate Galloway services, and their arrests continued into the winter months of 1964, despite the Methodist Church's stance against jailing them.[121] Multiple times Cunningham attempted to have the charges dropped, but his efforts failed because the police held the visitors on city charges rather than church complaints.[122]

On Easter Sunday 1964, Galloway ushers stood at the sanctuary door and turned away Bishop James K. Matthews, a white man serving the Boston area, and Bishop Charles F. Golden, a black man from the Nashville area serving the Central Jurisdiction. The ushers, who called themselves "the Color Guard," did this even though Cunningham had specifically instructed them to admit the bishops.[123] Reactions reverberated across the community, the state, and the country to this act of religious intolerance; and few incidents so vividly illustrate the barriers to change within the white community or how segregationists exploited the church to further their agenda.

The ongoing conflict over race "severed the church membership," and "people began to leave in droves"—some because they did not want to worship with blacks and others because they thought the church should open its doors to all. The Galloway women made the first open split when they broke from the Women's Society of Christian Service (WSCS), affiliated with the national church, and formed their own auxiliary. Between 1963 and 1976, Galloway lost half of its membership to other churches and denominations, primarily along generational lines, with older members holding onto the old ways.[124]

Methodists did not stand alone in their opposition to integrated churches. One of the other long-standing Protestant Jackson churches, First Baptist Church, counted media powerbrokers T. M. Hederman Sr. and T. M. Hederman Jr. among its board members, and segregationist Governor Ross Barnett among its congregants.[125] Patt Derian recalled one church member telling her that the proudest moment in his own life was "when he stood on the steps of First Baptist in Jackson and turned black people away from the door."[126] On the other hand, Janet Purvis said it became increasingly difficult for her family, who attended Woodland Hills Baptist Church in Jackson, to stay there after the church decided to bar blacks.[127] It was difficult to know whether to leave in frustration or stay to work for change from within, and the climate presented no easy answers.[128] Even the more liberal Unitarian church lost three of its thirty families when a black man joined the congregation.[129] No house of worship remained immune to criticism or exodus, whether it had an open door policy or not.

Mississippi Catholics took a more progressive approach than Protestants. Following the example of the national church, a few Mississippi Catholic parishes became the first congregations to integrate in the state, as early as 1956.[130] Although Natchez-Jackson Diocese Bishop Richard Gerow was perceived as timid in the 1950s, Medgar Evers's assassination in 1963 changed how he viewed his role in protecting the state's 70,000 Catholics. Gerow knew the Evers family, including two of the children who attended Christ the King school, and he issued a statement blaming the white community for the killing.[131] When the Civil Rights Act of 1964 passed, he called on Mississippi Catholics to accept the law and reject the "spirit of rebellion by standing for justice, love, and peace."[132] Along with Father Bernard Law, editor of *The Mississippi Register* diocesan paper, and Episcopal Rector Duncan Gray, Gerow challenged segregation and encouraged Governor Johnson to appoint a commission on human relations.[133] Individual priests played significant roles in the movement and at times interpreted rules in creative ways to facilitate their participation. For example, after receiving instructions that his church could not be used for meetings, the priest at St. Mary's Roman Catholic Church in Vicksburg volunteered the use of his living quarters, which he interpreted as his own space and not part of the church itself.[134]

Mississippi's Jews often found themselves in awkward positions because of their small numbers and their marginalized status—their being not quite accepted into white Mississippi life. When Rabbi Nussbaum came to Jackson's Temple Beth Israel in 1954, the city had about 500 Jews, less than one percent of the local population but half of the Jewish population in the state. By 1965, the temple membership had grown by about forty families. Most Mississippi Jews were merchants and worked to assimilate for their economic survival, although they were not part of the "real power structure," as Rabbi Nussbaum noted.[135] After several temple bombings across the South in the late 1950s, a dilemma arose for southern Jews, who wanted to maintain the community's goodwill but who also sold goods to black customers.[136] They often supported the civil rights effort but feared being perceived by non-Jewish whites as different.

Jews experienced discrimination in ways linked to their class and religion. Although white-skinned, they were not considered white until the mid-twentieth century, when suburbanites, particularly in the South, sought to bar blacks from housing.[137] This shift enabled Jews to pass within the dominant culture, but they were not completely accepted, as evidenced by the threats they received and the anti-Semitic literature produced by white supremacist groups before and during the civil rights era. Likewise, because Jews' socioeconomic status ranked above that of most minorities, blacks and other nonwhite racial and ethnic groups did not accept Jews as minorities, even though they had experienced similar forms of discrimination, such as quota systems. Jews, therefore, experienced a doubly marginal status, not completely fitting in either the majority or minority culture.[138]

Jewish religious leaders found it difficult to enlist support for civil rights or integration among their Mississippi congregations.[139] From 1951 to 1962, Rabbi Charles Mantinband served at B'nai Israel in Hattiesburg, a town of 35,000 people with fifty Jewish families and half of its downtown businesses owned by Jews. Mantinband felt that "every time a press story associates a national Jewish body . . . with the cause of the black man, the Jew in the South is apprehensive and trembles." Even though Jews acknowledged that their religion was "committed to the principle of equality of all men under God," they preferred that references to Jews not appear in print in that context.[140] Lillian Burnstein, a Jackson Jewish woman who worked with WIMS—although reluctantly at first—said Jewish women would think, "Let's not start any trouble. . . . You've got it good, you're living here, you're comfortable, your house is okay, and your business is okay. Shut your mouth and stay still."[141]

Rabbi Nussbaum came to understand that in Jackson, Judaism did not rate on a par with Protestantism and Catholicism as one of the "three great American historical religions, which underlie the foundation of our country." Mississippians likewise failed to treat rabbis and synagogues with the reverence shown to Christian churches and clergy.[142] Racist groups like the Ku Klux Klan (KKK) and the Americans for the Preservation of the White Race (APWR) added Jews to the list of groups responsible for bringing about the civil rights movement—Jews were the leaders, the communists.[143] This belief came from segregationists' preconceived prejudices and the disproportionately large number of Jews who took part in the movement and who came to Mississippi for Freedom Summer.[144]

Threatened just for being Jewish, southern Jews with the Holocaust fresh in their minds had no desire to stir up further trouble by working for civil rights. They faced harassment, termination of contracts, boycotts of their businesses, physical threats, and social ostracism.[145] The outspoken rabbis received numerous threats, and their actions caused concern in the Jewish community. In some instances, rabbis were discharged like their Christian counterparts, though the reason given was usually a supposed inability to get along with people.[146] When Mantinband's replacement, Rabbi Ben Ami, was dismissed for that reason in 1964, the synagogue closed.[147]

As with other religious denominations, the difference between northern and southern Jews in this period was striking. The majority of southern Jews wanted to differentiate themselves from Jews in the North. Just like segregationist white Christians, they frequently viewed those who spoke out on civil rights or worked in the movement as outside agitators. Historian Debra Schultz found that "for most southern Jews, their primary struggle was over the right, opportunity, and sense of security to practice Judaism and to publicly identify as Jewish."[148] They saw the northern Jewish civil rights activists as a bad reflection on themselves and a danger to their security and lifestyle, particularly given their own small numbers.[149] Many northern Jews felt a commitment to Judaism's prophetic beliefs in social justice and therefore did not understand why southern Jews had not taken an active role in civil rights to uphold their faith's ideals.

Women's interfaith organizations offered the most effective avenue for uniting people across racial lines in the South. The Federal Council of the Churches of Christ in America (FCCC) started the interracial movement in

1919 to eliminate racial tension and improve the social conditions of minorities; but few southern churches took part.[150] In 1950, the organization became the National Council of the Churches of Christ in the USA (NCC), made up of twenty-nine denominations, eight interdenominational agencies, thirty-two million members, and 150,000 churches. It became the nation's largest ecumenical organization, with blacks making up one quarter of the membership.[151] From the founding of the FCCC until the 1960s, women's groups played an important role in changing attitudes, even if slowly. The YWCA, National Association of Colored Women (NACW), the Church Women's Committee of the FCCC's Department of Race Relations, the NCNW, CWU, and black women's missionary societies led the women's interracial movement and supported civil rights.[152]

CWU, which became a WIMS sponsor, began in 1941 as an interdenominational, interracial, predominantly white organization working for world peace. Historian Janine Marie Denomme contends that these women also began to recognize the "incongruence between their articulation of Christian faith, which proclaimed all human beings children of God, and the state of inequality and injustice among African Americans."[153] By 1950, the organization comprised ten million women in seventy Protestant denominations and 1,700 state and local affiliates, representing a wide spectrum of ethnicity, race, age, class, and religious tradition.[154]

CWU launched Assignment: RACE in October 1961 at a meeting in Miami, Florida—its first meeting held in the South, because it refused to meet in cities where Jim Crow laws prohibited public integrated meetings.[155] At that gathering, Jane Schutt, Helen Alford, Ann Ashmore, and others pledged to create an open fellowship in Jackson, a promise that led to their founding the Interfaith Prayer Fellowship, one of the city's earliest efforts to organize interracially.[156] When CWU became more involved with interracial work, some members in the South rejected those efforts and withdrew. As a result, the organization lost chapters.[157]

The YWCA, another WIMS sponsor, used strategies similar to those of CWU, focusing on interracial relationships, education, persuasion, and political lobbying for civil rights.[158] In 1944, Dorothy Height became a member of the YWCA's national board staff, where she played an important role in pushing for integration and racial equality.[159] Two years later, the YWCA passed the Interracial Charter that stated, "Wherever there is injustice on the basis of race, whether in the community, in the nation or the world, our protest must be clear and our labor for its removal vigorous and steady. And what we urge on others we are constrained to practice ourselves."[160] Despite the charter,

YWCAs in cities across the South remained segregated in the mid-1960s. Nevertheless, many of the WIMS team members and the Jackson women with whom they worked either belonged to the YWCA or were employed by the organization, including Height, who became director of the YWCA Center for Racial Justice in 1965.

Black women had taken part in every social movement from abolition to civil rights, working both inside and outside their churches. Black women belonged to a variety of denominations, with the majority being Baptists.[161] Methodist minister and professor of Christian ethics Rosetta Ross argues that "Black women's civil rights activism [was] their female enactment of Black religious values that reflected internal concern for the Black community's survival and . . . society's formal and conventional sources of inequity." They testified to their belief in "divine intervention in ordinary circumstances." Black women theologians found four dominant themes in the responsibilities of black women activists: to pass on the virtues of Christianity; to partner with God; to tend to the needs of the least, usually African Americans; and to work toward building and sustaining communities.[162] These themes played out in all aspects of the civil rights movement, from literacy and citizenship classes to voter registration and Freedom Schools.

Examples of how activists tied their civil rights work to Christianity can be seen in the work of Septima Clark and Ella Baker. A CWU member, Clark was influenced by the social gospel movement and her mother's activism in challenging discrimination, both of which connected religious piety with racial uplift. Clark served the community in Christian service by teaching literacy and citizenship classes, which she viewed as similar to Jesus's ministering to the least and caring for the needs of the masses.[163] Similarly influenced by her own mother's religious activism, Ella Baker worked for the Southern Christian Leadership Conference under the direction of Martin Luther King Jr., and encouraged the formation of SNCC by the movement's youth. She believed that God expected people to do good works, and that if civil rights activists operated cooperatively with the abilities God gave them, then they could positively affect their lives and the lives of others.[164] Committed to nonviolent direct action, SNCC cited religion as a rationale for activism in its statement of purpose, particularly the Judeo-Christian teaching of "justice permeated by love."[165]

The parents of SNCC's Prathia Hall raised her to understand that "faith and freedom were woven together in the fabric of life," and that "service to people was service to Christ." Therefore, when people committed to working in the movement, they made a religious statement that was as profound as praying.[166] Christianity, many African Americans believed, demanded that Christians reject segregation and form one community of blacks and whites—the beloved community.[167]

Activist and MFDP founder Fannie Lou Hamer agreed that religion and the politics of civil rights inherently intertwined. She claimed she had "seen more Christianity" with SNCC than she had ever seen in the church. The SNCC volunteers willingly worked with those who had never been treated as human beings by racist whites, and some of the civil rights workers had died supporting human justice. Although some people criticized churches—including black churches—for taking conservative stands, churches became bedrocks for black Christian activism. Hamer, for example, was critical of southern religion, but she understood that it sustained African Americans in a profound way.[168] She found that many churches were overly concerned with people who had already achieved something in life; and that whites would support change, but still did not want to worship with blacks.[169] She knew that the students who volunteered in Mississippi were not devout Christians for the most part, and she told them that whether they believed it or not, faithful black Mississippians saw them as the answer to prayers, not unlike the Good Samaritan.[170]

Black churches and worshipers often paid the price for stepping out of their "place." Many black ministers were part-time preachers dependent on white employers for their livelihood. Nevertheless, by 1963, some black churches and ministers had organized the Citizens Committee for Human Rights to join the rising number of protesters.[171] The increased activity, however, endangered their churches. For over sixty weeks, the churches experienced at least one bombing per week before the attacks began to decline.[172]

Violence against individuals and churches had begun to increase with the push for voter registration led by SNCC in 1961, and escalated further with the formation of the Council of Federated Organizations (COFO) in 1962.[173] In response to these infringements upon civil and human rights, Bob Moses began planning the Freedom Summer project for 1964, which would bring northern college students to the South to register voters and establish Freedom Schools and community centers. The program aimed to teach children and adults alike basic academics as well as their rights, and to develop grassroots leadership that could "sustain itself" after the college students returned home.[174] A math teacher from New York with a master's degree in philosophy from Harvard, Moses had worked with SNCC in Mississippi for three years and believed only outside intervention that put Mississippi in the national spotlight could bring about a significant change in voter registration.

Questions arose about the wisdom of recruiting six to seven hundred white students, many of whom came from prestigious schools and middle- or upper-class families. Utilizing the students to conduct the citizenship training and establish Freedom Schools promised new educational opportunities denied to blacks in Mississippi, but questions about local reactions and the students' safety also demanded consideration.[175]

COFO "fully expected" white resistance to the project to potentially turn violent, even murderous, as historian Steven Lawson points out. While killing blacks often went unpunished, "The architects of Freedom Summer recognized that similar violence against some of America's best and brightest white youths would attract intense national attention." Historian Charles Payne calls the plan "a deal with the devil and premised on the idea that white lives matter and Black lives do not." COFO used the white students as "a point of leverage" and believed that they might offer protection by preventing tragedies. Especially after the murder of Louis Allen, Moses believed those in the Mississippi movement were "sitting ducks . . . people who were just going to be wiped out." Adding white students became a matter of practicality—COFO needed help, and Moses felt certain that if put to a vote, local African American adults would favor the students' inclusion.[176] Tougaloo chaplain Ed King recalled, "There was no question in the mind of anyone I know in the leadership of the project but what that [sic] volunteers would be killed. . . . We would not ask anybody to do anything we were not going to do, and we assumed that most of the leadership of the movement would be dead by the end of the summer."[177]

The civil rights legislation proposed by President Kennedy and pushed forward by President Lyndon Johnson, rather than offer protection against the violence, seemed to intensify it. In early 1964, the White Knights, a "commando-style" offshoot of the Ku Klux Klan, formed in Mississippi and attracted nearly ten thousand members because many whites had come to view the Citizens' Council as "too tame." The White Knights sought to direct "white working-class rage" against the alliance between the government and blacks. The group burned over two hundred crosses in sixty-four counties on one night in April 1964, and it terrorized individuals by shooting into homes and bombing churches and businesses. Even when law enforcement knew the identity of the perpetrators, most of these acts went unpunished, as had been the pattern in the past.[178]

Newspapers fueled their readers' fears by associating Freedom Summer with communism. A few months before the students' arrival, the *Clarion-Ledger* reminded readers that FBI director J. Edgar Hoover frequently found

"Red infiltration" on university campuses, and that "communists look upon students as potential sympathizers, supporters, and contributors to the Party's cause." Therefore, it was logical to assume that the "communists may have some sort of active role in the so-called Mississippi Summer project."[179] In a June editorial, the newspaper reported that the purpose of the "invasion of Mississippi by misguided youths from the North and East is the occupation of our state by federal authority." It indicated that Freedom Summer organizers "not only expect mayhem but also see as one purpose of the operation . . . the compelling of federal intervention in force, by marshal or troops, to quell the violence."[180]

The majority of white Mississippians did not welcome the students coming to the state. Their presence challenged centuries of customs and ways of thinking for millions of white southerners, shattering long-held myths that race relations remained good and blacks in the South felt content with their lot in life.[181] The *Clarion-Ledger* called the young activists "communists" and "outside agitators."[182] Citizens' Council member William Simmons confirmed this perception about the students who "invaded" the state, saying, "They fanned out across the state, made a great to-do of breaking up our customs, of flaunting social practices that had been respected by people here over the years. . . . Many had on hippie uniforms and conducted themselves in hippie ways. . . . The arrogance that they showed in wanting to reform a whole state in the way they thought it should be created resentment."[183] This local sentiment prevailed even though—or perhaps because—most of the students were white, affluent, and attended esteemed universities, though mostly outside the South.[184]

COFO and SNCC recruited students and planned training sessions at Western College for Women in Oxford, Ohio. The training focused on Mississippi's history, safety measures such as checking cars for sabotage, means of defense against assault, and how to behave in the South. Meanwhile, Mississippi prepared for the invasion. The state legislature passed over twenty laws limiting rights to public assembly and free speech, broadening the jurisdiction of law enforcement and increasing penalties for crimes related to demonstrating.[185] Authorities warned black ministers that they should not make their churches available as Freedom Schools, nor should their members house the student-teachers.[186]

Local law enforcement began a series of paramilitary-style operations. In Jackson, Mayor Allen Thompson hired 200 additional policemen, purchased 250 shotguns, and procured an armored vehicle—a retrofitted ice cream truck known as "Thompson's Tank"—that carried ten policemen and had shotguns protruding from gun ports. The *New York Times* quoted Thompson as saying unabashedly that he considered "any demonstration or assembly by Negroes, peaceful or not, 'unlawful demonstration.'"[187] The Mississippi Sovereignty Commission sent investigators to visit each of the eighty-two county sheriffs and inform them of thirty-four laws that could be used against civil rights agitators.[188] In addition, the commission sent an undercover informant to the COFO training in Ohio.[189] The commission had the aura of a secret police, and many feared having their names added to its list of supposed communists.

By the mid-1960s, laws regarding race, both de facto and de jure, affected everything about Mississippi daily life—what people could or could not do or say; where they worked, shopped, or worshipped; whether or not they could vote or be educated; and, in some cases, whether they lived or died. The debate over civil rights was not merely about white southerners sitting next to blacks on a bus or in a restaurant; it represented the prospect of a complete overhaul of the southern way of life, and that presented far more frightening possibilities. The fear of a truly integrated society—and the loss of power that it and black votes implied—stood at the heart of the dispute.

As Freedom Summer and passage of new civil rights legislation became imminent, black and white Jackson women asked the NCNW to intercede, to calm the emotionally charged atmosphere. Through Wednesdays in Mississippi, the NCNW hoped to work for integration and black voting rights, not by demonstrating or forcing the issue as others planned, but by quietly winning local women to the cause one, two, and three at a time, by opening lines of communication between them. These southern women, estranged by the constraints of society and culture, held the key to a brighter future.

CHAPTER TWO

A Charter of Concern for the Tumultuous South

"We have to be aware that there was a great tempest of violence and hatred and unleashed hostility that just created a climate in the country where people of good will wanted to do something to express their feelings."

—DOROTHY HEIGHT[1]

WITHIN DAYS OF MEDGAR EVERS'S ASSASSINATION, STEPHEN CURRIER, A white philanthropist and president of the Taconic Foundation, sent telegrams inviting one hundred individuals he hoped shared his sense of urgency regarding civil rights to a breakfast meeting at the Carlyle Hotel in New York City on June 19, 1963. The ninety people who attended heard moving speeches by the heads of the nation's leading African American organizations, including Martin Luther King Jr. of the SCLC, Whitney Young of the National Urban League, A. Philip Randolph of the Brotherhood of Sleeping Car Porters, Roy Wilkins and Jack Greenberg of the NAACP, James Farmer of CORE, C. Eric Lincoln of the Black Muslim movement, and Dorothy Height, president of the NCNW and the only woman, representing the only women's organization. Within an hour they had raised nearly $1 million in donations.[2]

One of the attendees was Polly Cowan, a tall, svelte, elegantly dressed, white Jewish woman with silver hair. A longtime advocate for social justice and a member of the Citizens' Committee for Children of New York, Cowan later wrote that she never forgot her first impression of Dorothy Height, who looked majestic in a print dress and white hat and spoke "directly to the issue," stressing the urgent need for action. "She somehow reminded me of Eleanor Roosevelt who could state the tough issues in a ladylike way. And make you believe it."[3]

Stirred by the presentations, Cowan began volunteering at the Taconic Foundation. When away from New York, she wrote position papers on the civil rights struggle and sent them back to the foundation. The foundation's executive director distributed the papers to the civil rights leaders who spoke at the Carlyle meeting and later asked them if they could use volunteers. All the men declined. Height, however, said yes—provided she could work with the woman who was writing those position papers. Although Height and Cowan came to the movement from divergent backgrounds, as two like-minded women they forged a working relationship and friendship that lasted until Cowan's death in November 1976.[4]

Height's organization, the NCNW, was founded by Mary McLeod Bethune in 1935 to address the issues that affected the lives of black women. Bethune had served as the director of the Division of Negro Affairs of the National Youth Administration under President Franklin D. Roosevelt; had founded and acted as president of the Daytona Educational and Industrial Institute, which later became Bethune-Cookman University; and was a leader in both the National League of Republican Women and the International Council of Women of the Darker Races of the World. Historian Deborah Gray White theorizes that these activities "set the ideological foundation" on which Bethune based the NCNW. Bethune believed that it was because black women failed to present a united front that the government often overlooked them, and she founded the NCNW as an umbrella organization for black women's groups, to enable them to make progress in ways that were not possible when working separately. The organization sought "(1) To unite national organizations into a National Council of Negro Women; (2) To educate, encourage and effect the participation of Negro women in civic, political, economic and educational activities and institutions; (3) To serve as a clearing house for the dissemination of activities concerning women; (4) To plan, initiate and carry out projects which develop, benefit and integrate the Negro and the nation."[5]

Deborah Gray White concludes that "of all the national black women's organizations to emerge during this period, the Council was the most influential and, as it turned out, the longest lived."[6] Just two years after the NCNW's founding, Bethune recruited Height to volunteer with the organization.

Dorothy Irene Height was born in Richmond, Virginia, on March 24, 1912, to a middle-class family. At age four, she moved to Rankin, Pennsylvania, a suburb of Pittsburgh populated largely by European immigrants. Though she attended integrated schools, they did not insulate her from the discrimination that would threaten and derail her future plans. When she was a pre-teen, the YWCA asked her to pose in an interracial group for a Girl Reserves poster for its Pittsburgh facilities; but later, when Height and a group of other African American girls appeared at the downtown Chatham Street YWCA to swim, the director turned them away. As a senior at Rankin High School, Height entered a national Elks Club oratory contest for a college scholarship.

Declared the state winner, she went to the tri-state area competition, only to find upon arrival that an official had replaced her with a white male student claiming to be the Pennsylvania winner. Height went to a nearby drugstore and called the Elks's commissioner of education, who interceded on her behalf. After a lengthy discussion, it was decided that both students would compete. Height went on to win that and the national competition, earning her the four-year scholarship.[7]

Height first applied to Barnard College in New York City, and the school accepted her; however, prior to her interview the school had already admitted its full quota of black students—two. Administrators informed Height that she would have to wait another year. On the advice of her older brother, William Briggs, she rushed downtown to the Washington Square campus of New York University (NYU), where she arrived one hour before the close of business on the last day of registration. After looking at Height's credentials, the dean admitted her without further deliberation. With the Elks scholarship, Height obtained in her four years at NYU both an undergraduate and master's degree in educational psychology.[8]

On November 7, 1937, just a few weeks after Height became the assistant executive director of the Harlem YWCA's Emma Ransom House, her supervisor asked her to escort Eleanor Roosevelt to an NCNW meeting with Mary McLeod Bethune. That fortuitous meeting began Height's long association with the council, which continued until her death in 2010. Taking Height under her wing, Bethune laid the foundations of Height's methods in all her future work. "She helped me feel that the philosophical and spiritual dimensions of our work mattered as much as its material impact," Height recalled. This philosophy, along with Height's devout Christian faith, determined the direction she took when she became president of the NCNW in 1958. Having observed the working relationship between Bethune and Eleanor Roosevelt, Height saw the value in working interracially and followed suit. She believed that success in the civil rights battle would come not from the efforts of blacks alone, but also from the cooperation and support of whites.[9]

With this approach, it is not surprising that Height found a ready ally in Pauline "Polly" Spiegel Cowan. Cowan was born on April 10, 1913, in Kenilworth, Illinois, a white, wealthy, exclusive North Shore suburb of Chicago. Her German Jewish family had immigrated to the Midwest in the mid-nineteenth century and opened a furniture store, which her father and older brother converted to the mail-order catalog giant Spiegel's. At some point prior to Cowan's birth, her family's Kenilworth community prohibited the further sale of homes to Jewish families. Despite her family's standing as

prominent merchants and even their becoming Christian Scientists, Cowan
often found herself excluded from parties, dances, and other social events.
Even though her family did not practice the faith, they were part of the Chicago Jewish community, and Cowan was raised with the principles of "'Prophetic Judaism.'... The teachings of Isaiah: 'Learn to do good; seek justice,
rescue the oppressed, defend the orphan, plead for the widow.'" She said that
her life experience "just added up to always having my antenna out for what
was happening and where I could be of service."[10]

Cowan graduated from Sarah Lawrence College in New York and married
Louis G. "Lou" Cowan in 1939. The couple went on to have four children.
Cognizant of events in Europe in the 1930s and 1940s, the pair tried to locate relatives in Germany with whom they had lost touch; and when they
could not find them, they worked to assist Jewish refugees. Lou became a
prominent producer of radio and television and a CBS executive, and Polly
Cowan followed suit, becoming a producer in her own right. In the late 1950s,
circumstances forced her to quit her job to avoid a conflict of interest with
her husband's work. She then joined the Citizens' Committee for Children
of New York, an organization seeking to improve childcare services, led by
Trude Lash, a friend of Eleanor Roosevelt. In early 1963, Cowan took part
with friends Ellen and R. Peter Straus, owners of WMCA radio, in chair-
ing Call for Action, a program that reached out to New York's poor families
and encouraged them to report their problems—often related to substandard
housing conditions—and assigned volunteers who could assist in rectifying
them.[11]

With this history of working for others and her personal experiences with
quota systems and the exclusion of Jews from housing and social circles,
Cowan saw a kindred spirit in Height. Cowan's daughter, historian Holly
Cowan Shulman, explains that in working with Height and the NCNW, her
mother "found her spiritual home." The two women "worked together seam-
lessly, talking by phone at least once a day, plotting their course, sharing their
dreams." Their relationship quickly came to epitomize the kind of interracial
relationships they would seek to create by opening lines of communication
between black and white women in the South.[12]

When Cowan joined Height at the NCNW, the two immediately organized
a meeting of women, to be held the day following the March on Washington,
and to be called, "After the March—What?" Height was frustrated by the failure of the male leadership to include women in the March program, despite
repeated requests. Bayard Rustin, executive director of the March, told Height
that the program did include women by virtue of their membership in the

organizations the male speakers represented. Dissatisfied with that thinking and seeing it as a slight to women overall, Height believed a gathering of
women was crucial.[13]

Height proceeded even though March organizers had asked that no other
gatherings be held at that time. Through the NCNW, she hoped to broaden
the civil rights discourse—and action—beyond racial discrimination to include other issues important to women, such as housing, childcare, education, and employment. At the interracial meeting, women gathered to express
their own dismay at being shut out of the March program and to discuss
which civil rights issues, in addition to race, needed the national leaders' attention. Additionally, young southern women told participants about their
experiences with southern law enforcement. Height and Cowan closed by
offering the NCNW's help to everyone present but to the southern women in
particular should they need assistance in the future.[14]

About a month later, Susan Goodwillie joined the NCNW as director of
special projects. She had graduated from Stanford University the previous
year with degrees in French and Honors Humanities. She chaired the South
West African Committee, which aided South West African refugee students,
and went to Daloa, Ivory Coast, with Operation Crossroads Africa for a summer program after graduation.[15] Goodwillie recalled, "I fell in love with Africa." When she read about the March on Washington in *Time* magazine, she
"looked at this country through African eyes" and wanted to be part of the
solution.[16] She returned to Washington, D.C. and sought a job related to the
civil rights movement, but repeatedly found herself turned down for being
the "wrong color." After reading that President Kennedy had appointed Shirley Smith, a white woman in her thirties, to head the National Women's Committee for Civil Rights, Goodwillie convinced Smith to hire her to fill an open
position in the Women's Committee until a woman of color could be found.
Before long, Smith pointed out to Height that the NCNW staff was all black,
even though the organization championed interracial work. Recognizing the
inconsistency, Height agreed to interview Goodwillie and subsequently hired
her—a move Goodwillie called a "courageous thing."[17]

Almost immediately, Goodwillie felt she was "on the front lines" when she
received an urgent call asking for the NCNW's assistance from James Forman, executive secretary of SNCC, and Prathia Hall, a SNCC worker who
had attended the "After the March—What?" meeting.[18] Hall was working
with the "Freedom to Vote" project in Selma, Alabama, when three hundred
young people, ranging in age from as young as eight to sixteen, were jailed
for encouraging voter registration. Hall believed that if the NCNW women

came to Selma, they could draw attention to the abusive conditions in which the youth were held. Their cells were so crowded they could neither sit nor lie down. The food was cut with sawdust, the coffee contained salt instead of sugar, and only limited water was provided. They had no blankets and no privacy in the toilet facilities. Further, the girls were threatened with sexual assault. Since no single facility could incarcerate so many detainees, they were spread out to other locations, and parents became frantic, not knowing where police were holding their children.[19]

Height decided that an interracial team from the NCNW should travel to Selma to evaluate the conditions and determine what could be done. The team consisted of two white women, Cowan and Shirley Smith, and two black women, Height and Dr. Dorothy Ferebee, past president of the NCNW, a physician, and director of health services at Howard University.[20] Cowan later reflected, "We didn't relish going to Alabama. . . . We were sensible enough to be a little frightened. Sometimes fear propels you to action; and if those kids were taking it every day, couldn't we be a bit uncomfortable for forty-eight hours?"[21]

As traveling in interracial groups in the South remained culturally unacceptable and dangerous in 1963, the team planned to travel in segregated cars, but the car ordered for the black women never arrived. The four decided to risk riding together in the white women's rental car to Selma's black First Baptist Church. Ferebee joked that she and Height would ride in the back pretending to be Smith and Cowan's cooks to insure they would not be touched.[22] Cowan struggled with this—both as a truth of discrimination and as an injustice. She wrote of her frustration at the pretense's being necessary. "These two Negro women were individuals in leadership positions. They had dignity, scholarship, and wisdom. By comparison, Shirley and I were unexceptional. I felt degraded as a person of no-color: that people of no-color should put down people of color. Not that I think that to be a cook is anything but to be a person of skill. But each of us should be able to own up to her own skill, not pretend to someone else's for safety's sake."[23]

Smith and Cowan intended to drop off Height and Ferebee at the church. When they arrived, however, they could not resist the temptation to hear the stories of the young people, whom officials had released; the white women decided to stay. That night, October 4, 1963, all four women attended a rally at the church, where Forman invited the two black women to sit on a platform and speak. He asked the white women to speak as well, and Cowan, sensing from Forman's manner that he was daring her, accepted. Shirley Smith declined. She felt it inappropriate to speak on behalf of the co-chairs of the

National Women's Committee for Civil Rights without their permission. In addition, she had previously been arrested in Jackson, Mississippi, as a Freedom Rider and did not wish to return to jail.[24]

Attendees included white reporters and members of Alabama law enforcement, but this did not deter the Selma civil rights leaders from holding the mass meeting with approximately 750 people in attendance. The rally took place less than three weeks after the 16th Street Baptist Church bombing in Birmingham, which, it is easy to imagine, weighed heavily on the minds of the attendees. After taking up a collection, singing freedom songs, and a few short speeches, James Forman introduced Height and Ferebee as important northern women concerned about injustice in the South, and as role models to show the young people they did not "have to be pickin' no cotton fields all the time and scrubbing [Sheriff] Jim Clark's floor."[25]

Height and Ferebee offered words of encouragement and talked about women's role in the movement. Height's speech praised the efforts of the ralliers and called on them to continue working for voter registration and integration. Recalling Bethune's message that to be effective, blacks must work together, she assured the audience that their black brothers and sisters joined them in this effort.[26] Harkening back to Bethune's legacy of empowering women, Ferebee pointed out the expanded role young women and girls were playing in the civil rights movement, stating, "There was a time when women were not expected to do any of these things; when they were not expected to participate in any work of the community, in any work of society or anything that contributed to human betterment. But we know quite differently now that the young women are standing shoulder to shoulder with the men."[27] Continuing in this feminist vein, she added, "We know that the whole range of potential abilities that belong to men also belong to the women." She closed by thanking the attendees for their courage, and for prodding the older generation, herself included, into action.[28]

Rising to Forman's challenge to speak, Cowan briefly offered greetings from the Citizens' Committee for Children of New York, and both New York City and New York State. She informed the attendees that more and more news reached the North about the events transpiring in the South, and that the northern public received the messages about the needs of southern blacks.[29]

Comedian and activist Dick Gregory, whose pregnant wife had been arrested in Selma earlier in the week, gave the keynote address, in which he strongly criticized, and mocked, Alabama's governor George Wallace, its law enforcement, and its white racism for creating and maintaining the black population's status as second-class citizens. At one point, he pointed to Height and Ferebee saying that the two women had more education than Selma's entire police department.[30]

In his closing remarks, Forman reminded parents to encourage children who had spent time in jail to meet with the delegation from the NCNW to discuss their experiences while in custody. Sensitive to the unique plight of girls and young women, Forman acknowledged that they might not want men present to overhear what they had to say, but he assured them that they could tell their stories to the NCNW team and that the women would understand.[31] Height, Ferebee, Cowan, and Smith interviewed approximately sixty-five young people and a few mothers, who confirmed SNCC's reports of overcrowding and brutality, and that parents had been threatened with arrest for inquiring about their children. The girls, all estimated to be between twelve and sixteen years of age, indicated that the warden had frightened them by saying, "If you don't behave, the men prisoners will be let into your cells." They remained dressed at night and slept in a huddle to protect each other.[32]

When it came time for the NCNW team to leave the rally, young men from SNCC escorted them out of the church and told them, "Keep your heads down, walk straight, don't look to your left or right." Cowan confessed, "I had to look." Forty to fifty state troopers wearing helmets and carrying clubs, carbines, and cattle prods surrounded the church. Smith said that she felt threatened as she walked a few feet from a man with a cattle prod, which reminded her of a story she had heard about the Selma mayor displaying a similar one and saying, "You can make a nigger jump three feet with one of these." As Cowan walked between the two lines of troopers, she could not believe her eyes; the scene was frightening.[33]

As outsiders to the South, the NCNW team became associated with those trying to register to vote, and those aiding them, who were labeled criminals and often brought up on charges. Police attempted to arrest Prathia Hall the night of the rally but could not locate her; they took her into custody the following Monday morning for contributing to the delinquency of a minor. Height found on her return to New York that Selma law enforcement had issued a warrant for her and Ferebee's arrest on the same charge just hours after they left town.[34]

Cowan and Smith met the day after the rally with two "anguished" white women from Selma named Rosa Joyce and Katherine "Katty" Cothran. Joyce, a Selma native and the daughter of Alabama congressman Sam Hobbs and his wife Sarah, graduated from Randolph Macon Woman's College and did graduate work at Columbia University. During World War II, Joyce went to work for the War Production Board and later joined the Women Accepted for Volunteer Emergency Service (WAVES), taking part in its first officer training class as a member of the U.S. Navy. While in the WAVES she met and married Wisconsin native John H. Joyce, a pilot and flight instructor. At the war's end, the couple moved first to Wisconsin, and then to Birmingham, before settling their family in Selma in 1955. Joyce volunteered for the Girl Scouts, the local Literacy Coalition, her children's schools, and First Presbyterian Church.[35] Cothran, born in Montgomery, Alabama, was the daughter of Elizabeth and James Osgood, the latter of whom served as minister of the Church Street Methodist Church in Selma. She married businessman and farmer G. Frank Cothran Jr. in 1933. Katherine Cothran worked in broadcasting at a local radio station and taught Bible in the Selma schools before becoming the director of Christian education at First Presbyterian Church.[36]

Both Joyce and Cothran expressed concern at the state of affairs in Selma. Smith reported they found it particularly troubling that their church had recently rescinded its three-year-old "open seating policy." The change had followed a newspaper report that four black teenage girls had attended a service there and that the girls' efforts at integrating the church had been cheered later at a mass meeting of black civil rights advocates. In response, "rabid segregationists" called for the seating-policy change even though it made their pastor reluctant to preach there.[37]

The two Selma women found the accusations of abuse by law enforcement troubling. Joyce had met with the Selma mayor to ask what she could do to help the community. She told Cowan and Smith that the mayor had replied, "Go home and lock your door until it's over. Nothing is going to change around here." Despite their sympathies, Joyce and Cothran questioned whether or not communists inspired the black voter registration campaign and if some person or group had paid the children to go to jail as the news media reported. Cowan and Smith believed that Joyce and Cothran's doubts "blocked their feelings of concern for the young people."[38]

As Cowan and Smith left the meeting, they nevertheless felt they had made progress, because the two Selma women agreed to discuss their misgivings further with Dorothy Tilly of the Fellowship of the Concerned, an organization of southern white churchwomen intent on changing racist attitudes in the region; and with Amelia Boynton, an African American leader in the Alabama movement. Joyce and Cothran insisted that the meeting be held in a black home because they could not have African Americans come to their homes. Cothran agreed to pick up Tilly at the airport the following Monday and visit with her even though Joyce planned to be out of town.[39]

In the meantime, an account of Cowan's speaking at the rally appeared in the local newspaper. Neither Joyce nor Cothran were aware that Smith and Cowan had attended the rally, and reading the surprising news caused Cothran to refuse to meet Tilly as planned. Speaking by phone, Cothran told Tilly, who was waiting at the airport, that the newspaper account proved Smith and Cowan had come under false pretenses. "We have been betrayed. These women, Mrs. Polly and Shirley, told us they came because they were interested in our community. But they have been with *those* people."[40]

While Cowan's simple greeting to those at the rally contained nothing in and of itself that should have caused the women to feel betrayed, in the context of Selma in the early 1960s, the newspaper report included an air of accusation, and the layout suggested an intent to stigmatize Cowan. The initial part of the article, which appeared on the front page of the newspaper and carried over to the next, focused on Gregory's coming to Selma in response to his wife's arrest. On the second page, the article states only four whites (other than law enforcement and reporters) attended the rally. Two of those were Father Maurice Ouellet and Father Charles E. McNiece from Selma's St. Elizabeth's Mission, which was established by the Vermont-based Society of St. Edmund in 1938. Ouellet was credited with organizing civil rights marches of Selma school children in 1963, which might have included some of the children at the rally. The other two whites mentioned were Polly Cowan of the Citizens' Committee for Children of New York, and another unidentified white woman thought to be a former Freedom Rider (Shirley Smith).[41]

The news designating Cowan one of four whites in an audience of 750, and the only one to speak, likely caused racists reading the article to label her a "nigger lover." By identifying her as representing an organization from New York, the article branded her a northern outsider meddling in affairs that were not her business. The placement of the paragraph about Cowan, sandwiched between two passages reporting on Gregory's inflammatory remarks criticizing white southern society, gave the impression of something more calculating on her part than the simple greetings were intended to be. Calling herself naive, Cowan reflected on the decision to speak at the rally and its consequences: "Never act in reaction. I learned that." She had responded impulsively to Forman's challenge, and that impetuousness had hurt their overall mission.[42]

Although there is no way of knowing with certainty, it is worth considering the possibility that had Cowan and Smith told Joyce and Cothran that they had attended the rally and what they had observed there, the misunderstanding might have been avoided. That is not to say that Cothran would have met with Tilly; but if Cothran had not been surprised with that information by reading it in the newspaper, she might have felt less hostility, and less like Cowan and Smith had misrepresented themselves. At the least, the incident illustrates one of the many ways in which miscommunication caused estrangement in the South. With tensions running high over civil rights, anyone who gave the slightest impression of underhandedness was doomed to failure, no matter who or how well intentioned they were.

The trip to Selma was not a complete failure, however. Height and Ferebee served as an inspiration to many in the rally's audience who had never seen black women in leadership positions. As an interracial group of friends and coworkers, the four women demonstrated that the vision of an integrated society was attainable. For their own part, not only had the four women witnessed the abuse and determined an area of need, but they also learned from the experience. Height discussed how the lesson framed their future actions: "Having generated heat where we had hoped to bring light, we learned that if we wanted to be helpful, we had to be sensitive to the perspectives of people on both sides of the issue. We would have to go into tension-filled communities quietly, anonymously, and—even when our most deeply cherished principles were violated in the process—with respect for local custom."[43] Painful as their mistake had been, the lesson proved useful and served as a key to their future success with Wednesdays in Mississippi.

During the closing months of 1963, Height and Cowan remained intent on finding a way for the NCNW to reach out to the South and bridge the widening racial divide. Still working full-time for the YWCA, Height reported the details of their Selma experience to the national YWCA board and solicited input from the NCCW, NCJW, and CWU. Cowan, also pondering NCNW's future direction, realized that the team's "middle-class appearance was [their] main protection" while in Selma and that to "organize a group of wealthy and powerful women" might provide the opening the NCNW needed to become actively involved in the southern movement. The national leaders of these five women's organizations decided to hold an off-the-record meeting in Atlanta, Georgia, in March 1964, to bring together their leadership from the hottest trouble spots in the South: Albany and Atlanta, Georgia; Montgomery and Selma, Alabama; Charleston, South Carolina; Danville, Virginia; and Jackson, Mississippi. The leaders stated their purpose as "to arrive at a charter of concern for the protection of women and girls in an era of social change." In an effort to encourage participation, rather than label the agenda "civil rights," they planned a program to focus on police brutality and substandard jails, including the supervision of prisoners by male personnel, medical and health services, sanitation, safety, religious worship, and legal rights—all of which were appropriate concerns for mothers and women. Additionally, they invited victims of abuse from police to share their stories.[44]

Integrated public meetings, lacking both legal protection and social acceptance, rarely occurred in the South in 1963. Margaret Mealey of the NCCW observed that poor and wealthy women crossed paths across race on occasion, but seldom did white and black middle-class women.[45] The vast majority of the meeting's attendees had never before participated in such an interracial gathering. It was also a first for the American Hotel, which hosted the event. The NCNW had made sure in advance that the hotel's management would allow an interracial meeting, not wanting the attendees to be arrested on arrival.[46]

Race was not the sole consideration in assembling the group. Height felt strongly that the group of women should be interfaith. She based this on her own religious convictions, her work with the YWCA, and on strategic considerations. She remembered attending the 1937 World Conference of Churches in England, which she described as "a truly ecumenical experience," where she came to an understanding of interfaith cooperation. "The YWCA is Christian but open; to be ecumenical means to be what you are. . . . I don't have to be what you are, and you don't have to be what I am, for us to work together." Further, she explained that ecumenism was important strategically because liberal white churchwomen were the ones most likely to assist with civil rights efforts, and by joining together with black and white women of various faiths who shared common concerns, they would increase their chances of success.[47]

In the spirit of inclusion, and to avoid publicity and protect the participants, the planners decided to call the gathering the Women's Inter-organizational Committee (WIC), at the suggestion of Helen Rachlin, a member of the NCJW. The YWCA's Ethyl Christiansen called the name "truthful and harmless."[48] Mildred Fitzhenry Jones of the national YWCA assured the attendees that no newsmen would attend and that the women themselves would do the only reporting when they met with their organizations. Despite these precautions and assurances, the women in attendance remained on edge and fearful of reprisal should their participation be discovered at home. When someone tried to take a picture, one woman screamed, "I'll never be able to go back to Montgomery if you take pictures," and, "I'll be washed up." She did not stand alone in her fears.[49]

Dorothy Tilly, who had been rebuked in Selma, gave the keynote address. Tilly had worked her way up through the ranks of the Women's Society of Christian Service in the North Georgia Conference of the Methodist Church, and succeeded Jessie Daniel Ames as the Southern Regional Council's director of women's work. In the 1940s, she founded the Fellowship of the Concerned to push for justice for the disadvantaged, particularly African Americans and the poor. Historian Edith Holbrook Riehm explains that Tilly believed that encouraging white southern women to teach their children and husbands tolerance would go a long way toward ending racial prejudice. One activity of the Fellowship of the Concerned, "a loosely organized coalition of progressive-minded southern churchwomen," involved well-dressed white women attending the trials of those they suspected might not get a fair hearing. By their presence, the women hoped to "shame local authorities and juries" into delivering justice, rather than succumbing to outside pressure; and the women's efforts made a difference.[50] In anticipation of a favorable ruling in *Brown v. Board of Education*, Tilly wrote to her constituents in 1953, asking them to become "interpreters and shock absorbers" of the decision.[51] She reiterated the appeal at the WIC meeting as it applied to the civil rights movement and the need for women to "smooth the path." She encouraged attendees to work together through their organizations using community study groups to inspire social action. She summed up her philosophy by saying, "Women's power is neither financial nor political. Women are the shock absorbers. That has always been our role."[52]

During the WIC conference, women listened to accounts of discrimination and police brutality and offered suggestions for direct action at home. As the meeting progressed, the organizers felt a "sense of strength" gathering within the group. While cautious, the women seemed empowered by the experience. Cowan recalled, "When you saw women from Montgomery, Negro women who were most outstanding women, talking to white women, who were also outstanding women, and they had never been able to meet in Montgomery, you really began to feel the power of women and that somehow we should keep going."[53]

The Jackson, Mississippi, delegation included a prominent African American woman, Clarie Collins Harvey. She was the only child of Malachi and Mary Collins, owners of Frazier and Collins Funeral Home in Jackson. In 1943, Clarie Collins married Martin Luther Harvey, who became a dean of Southern University. In 1950 she joined her mother in managing the family business, which changed its name to Collins Funeral Home. Harvey became chief executive officer upon her mother's death and expanded the business

with innovations in funeral services and the addition of an insurance company. She had a master's degree in personnel administration from Columbia
University and completed post-graduate work at New York University School
of Business Administration and Union Theological Seminary, in addition to
earning numerous certifications in mortuary science.[54]

Described as an elegant, articulate woman, Harvey was well respected in
both the black and white Jackson communities as a successful businesswoman and humanitarian. In 1961, Harvey founded WomanPower Unlimited to
support the Freedom Riders on trial in Jackson. The organization grew to
an interracial network of over three hundred women who supported voter
registration, school desegregation, and other civil rights projects. Historian
John Dittmer theorizes that the group's being "independent of any male-
dominated civil rights group" enabled it to act quickly, "free from bureau-
cratic inefficiency and territorial infighting." Harvey also served in leadership
for numerous local, national, and international organizations and boards.[55]

Height presided over a luncheon on the final day of the WIC meeting.
She asked the women to sit together by city and consider what role the five
national organizations sponsoring the WIC meeting could play in helping
their communities. In response to Height's invitation, Harvey stood up and
gestured to the four white women seated at her table, saying, "Here we are.
. . . We have never met before, we have never sat together before, and we have
decided today that we will never be separated again. We have too much work
to do! Yes, there is value to each of us in being part of a national organization,
because you can help us. You can be like a long-handled spoon, reaching
down and stirring us up, bringing us together in ways that we could never do
by ourselves."[56] The women from Jackson discovered that they all were working with groups in their community, but none of them had known the others
were there. They vowed to collaborate in the future.

Harvey further expressed her concerns about violence in reaction to the
Freedom Summer project. Although Jackson remained a "bastion of segregation," she had not lost hope, and believed it would help if northern women
visited the community to act as a calming influence—a "ministry of presence." She envisioned Mississippi as "a vast oilfield" of latent goodwill. She
said, "We must go through the bedrock to reach it, but when we do, the good
will spring up." She thought that giving people a chance to talk would "help
people get some of their venom out," which could usher in change.[57]

As the meeting drew to a close, a woman from Charleston reminded the
group, "As we go back, we know things are very dark, but we must remember
that we are the Women's Inter-organizational Committee. . . . That says W-I-C,

and that's what each of us needs to be—like the wick on a candle, a light in the darkness." She added, "If we continue to work together we will make a difference."[58]

The atmosphere had changed markedly from three days earlier when the women arrived. Pearl Willen, president of the NCJW, praised the Atlanta WIC meeting for introducing women of similar interests to each other so that they might work together in the future. She added, "For me, it was one of the most interesting and emotional experiences that I have had."[59] NCNW staffer Susan Goodwillie felt that the women went home from the Atlanta meeting with a "sense of courage and solidarity that dispelled some of the fear," and a sense of hope.[60]

Height and Cowan recognized the need to reach out to the South, and they had been asked for help by the southern women; however, the two women also realized that their first attempt in Selma had failed because they had operated in ways that offended southern mores. This raised the question: how could the NCNW become that long-handled spoon the Jackson women were looking for without repeating its previous mistakes?

CHAPTER THREE

Plotting Their Course

*"The hope of the South is in the women. They have to be the interpreters
and the shock absorbers of the social change."*

—DOROTHY TILLY[1]

EVEN THOUGH THE SOUTHERN WOMEN RESPONDED POSITIVELY TO THE
WIC meeting, the words of Kathryn Cothran—"We have been betrayed"—
still echoed in the minds of Dorothy Height and Polly Cowan. Throughout
the planning and execution of Wednesdays in Mississippi, the Selma experience, more than any other factor, determined the approach taken by the
NCNW. It served as an example of how *not* to proceed with regard to interracial interaction in the South. At the same time, it *set* an example for how
women could use their gender, class, and age to shield themselves and their
civil rights activism from those wishing to thwart their efforts. Height and
Cowan applied these lessons in every facet of planning the WIMS project.

They strongly believed that to bring Mississippi women together across racial lines, the NCNW had to be invited to help. The organization could not
say, "We're coming down whether you like it or not."[2] Clarie Collins Harvey
provided that invitation at the Atlanta meeting when she asked the NCNW to
come to Jackson that summer as a "ministry of presence." Cowan, reflecting
on what she and Height had learned from the Selma trip, proposed bringing
women from the "Cadillac crowd"—women of stature—both black and white,
of various faiths and interests, who appeared beyond reproach, like proper
helpmates engaged in social housekeeping. Their prominence would act as a
"quieting influence" against violence and protect them even as they appeared
out of place in many of the Mississippi locations they expected to visit.[3]

Progressive-era women's activism provided a model for many of the wom-
en who would take part in WIMS. Focused on social reform work, their activism reflected their education and class privilege, which often put them in
contact with policy-makers. The women then used these associations to lobby for causes in which they believed. Several of the Wednesdays women, born

in the 1910s and 1920s, grew up in this Progressive tradition.[4] They came of age in the 1930s and 1940s when women activists adopted Progressive strategies to build networks and nurture interpersonal relationships. Younger team members had mothers who set similar examples.[5]

The WIMS strategy involved a smart and thoughtful twisting of class as it functioned in the 1960s. Height and Cowan planned to use class as a cover for activists—the WIMS teams—bringing real social change to the South rather than following a social housekeeping agenda. The team they took to Selma served as their prototype. The women coming into Mississippi would use their skills as observers and report to their communities on what they had seen; they would bring resources to the Freedom Schools and community centers and, thus, appear to be doing work appropriate for women and mothers; they would build bridges between the black and white women of Jackson. Expecting the participants to be busy women with limited time available— professionals, community leaders, and officers in local, state, and national organizations—Cowan suggested they fly into Jackson on Tuesday, fan out across the state to visit the Freedom Summer projects and meet with Mississippi women on Wednesday, and depart on Thursday—hence the name, Wednesdays in Mississippi.

The WIMS records do not indicate why Cowan chose Wednesdays specifically, but weekend days were never an option. Most likely, she preferred weekdays because the southern women were under greater scrutiny from husbands, families, and churches on weekends, making it difficult, if not impossible, to meet freely with the visitors.

The northern women's commitment to civil rights and their willingness to work for it while simultaneously projecting an image of southern propriety and moderation proved paramount to the project's design and, ultimately, to its success. Cowan wrote, "The raison d'etre for these women being in troubled spots should be the same as Mrs. Tilly's Fellowship of the Concerned: because they care, they want to know the truth, they want to help."[6] Height recalled that Cowan insisted, "We don't want them to go as sightseers. They have to be willing to do something that furthers the movement."[7] While this held true, timing was everything; the women's personal advocacy would have to wait until after they returned home, in order to avoid jeopardizing the project. The organizers made it clear that the women were not in Mississippi "as activists, but as listeners and interpreters of the struggle."[8]

Opening lines of communication across race was WIMS's primary goal, but Height and Cowan also felt concerned about the safety of the Freedom Summer participants. The two women understood that it frightened

Mississippians to think that a thousand SNCC workers planned to come in that summer. Height and Cowan wanted to refute misconceptions about the students' "invading" the state and reassure the southern women that the young people were really dedicated individuals. They hoped this would calm reactionary fears and reduce resistance to progress on civil rights issues. Cowan's two sons had volunteered to go to Mississippi, as did the children and relatives of other women WIMS recruited. The organizers reasoned that the northern women who were mothers of COFO students would be able to verify that the students were not advancing communism or endangering anyone; rather, they were offering an opportunity for education and extending the rights of citizenship to those who lacked them. In this way, WIMS could dispel the rumors being circulated about the COFO volunteers, and contribute to the NCNW's original mission of opening lines of communication. Further, some team members' children, both nonparticipants and participants in COFO, attended the same universities as the children of the southern women the WIMS teams hoped to meet. This gave the northern and southern women a piece of common ground on which to build a connection.[9]

Aware of the nuances of interracial relationships in the South, Height believed the NCNW needed to verify that the Jackson women still welcomed the NCNW's help and to begin building local networks. In May 1964, Polly Cowan and Shirley Smith traveled to Jackson to assess the situation. Height cautioned them that when contacting white women, Cowan and Smith needed to give the southerners a "clue" that they, too, were white. Height suggested that they mention that they were staying at the Hotel Heidelberg. Since the Civil Rights Act of 1964 had not yet passed, the Jackson women knew that the hotel did not receive black guests. This allowed Cowan and Smith to say, "I am white. You can meet with me," without saying it directly. This worked well until Cowan forgot to use the clue when arranging to attend an interfaith prayer meeting. She introduced herself as someone who had met the Jackson white woman at the interracial WIC meeting. The woman she spoke to, evidently fearing Cowan wanted her to integrate the prayer meeting, "gasped, and quickly explained her current group was inter-*faith*." Cowan sorted out the misunderstanding and received the desired invitation, learning another valuable lesson about communication and how to operate in the South to accomplish one's goals.[10]

During the May visit, Cowan and Smith met with eight white and three black women representing a cross section of Jackson's middle class. The black women were Clarie Collins Harvey, the business owner and founder of WomanPower Unlimited who had voiced the initial request for help; Thelma

Sanders, a dress shop owner; and Lillie Belle Jones, the executive director of the Jackson Branch YWCA. The white women attending were Jane M. Schutt, president of Jackson CWU and former chair of the Mississippi Advisory Committee to the U.S. Commission on Civil Rights; Mrs. T. P. Cote, the president of the Jackson NCCW; Ann Hewitt, a board member of the YWCA; Barbara Barnes, the executive director of the Jackson Central YWCA; Mary Haynes, the executive director of the Mississippi District YWCA; Florence Gooch, a board member of the YWCA; Lillian Burnstein, an attendee at the WIC meeting representing the NCJW, although no chapter existed in Jackson; and Beatrice Gotthelf, another delegate to the WIC meeting.[11]

At a meeting with Burnstein, Gotthelf, and Gooch held at the Hotel Heidelberg, the discussion centered on two themes: the activities of southern racists, and fear. While the Mississippi women did not think anyone from the North could be considered an invited guest, they felt that if women of stature visited with a specific purpose, and under the auspices of an educational foundation like the NCNW, then some of the southern women could quietly assist them. Indicating the heightened level of fear that Burnstein, Gotthelf, and Gooch felt, Cowan reported, "They spoke of martyrdom and said they didn't think anything would be helped by their becoming martyrs."[12] Even though the thoughts about martyrdom already held a place in their consciousness in May, the three women did not withdraw their support following news in June that three COFO volunteers had disappeared just two weeks before the first WIMS team arrived. Perhaps they viewed themselves as immune to that kind of violence since they were not openly working for civil rights. Perhaps the events caused them to feel a heightened need to take action against injustice, or they were drawn to continue because two of the young men, like themselves, were Jewish. Regardless of the reason, they did not withdraw, despite their fears.

Since anyone from the outside appeared suspect, some of the Jackson women, black and white, doubted the chances of the plan's success. Deeply affected by Medgar Evers's murder, Barbara Barnes felt concerned for the safety of both the students coming down and her YWCA students. Agreeing with the Jewish women, she thought that if the Wednesdays women had relationships with certain organizations, the plan might work. She saw the value in having members of the national YWCA board discussing what they had seen in the student projects with Jackson women, particularly with the women on her board who continued to resist the national YWCA policy against segregated facilities. Barnes told Cowan that she hoped she would live to see "the end of the Revolution," because when people could have "real friends in both races," then the South would be a nice place to live.[13]

The responses from the southern women Cowan and Smith met ranged from, "If Jesus Christ himself came in here nobody would listen," to, "Please try it, try anything." But no one said, "Don't come."[14]

Despite their limited numbers, these southern women provided a critical link to Mississippi communities, which the northern women could not initially have made on their own, to arrange for housing, transportation, and invitations to meetings. Additionally, they introduced the staff to contacts in and outside of Jackson to assist in arranging the trip itineraries. This cooperation enabled the northern staff and team members to come in as "marginal outsiders." They came from the North, but they did not fit the stereotype of the students and radicals who were criticized for their appearance and alleged communist leanings. Instead, prominent local women respected on both sides of the racial divide welcomed the Wednesdays women. Although there was a fine line between being marginal outsiders and being part of the northern invasion, being on the right side of that line played an important part in WIMS's ability to operate in Jackson as proper ladies.

Having gained support from local women, Height and Cowan rewrote WIMS's statement of purpose multiple times before deciding on a final version that defined the project's focus and goals. Height quipped, "I don't think any president ever had more drafts of a speech than we had of how this thing was to proceed." The statement read, "It is important that many private citizens of stature and influence make it known that they support the aspirations of the citizens of Mississippi for full citizenship, that they deplore violence and that they will place themselves in tension-filled situations as a point of contact and communication to try to initiate both understanding and reconciliation."[15] The specific goals of the project were "to establish lines of communication among women of goodwill across regional and racial lines, to observe the COFO student projects and discuss them with local Mississippi women, and to lend a 'ministry of presence' as witnesses to encourage compassion and reconciliation."[16]

As the project grew, Height felt that it represented exactly the type of program Mary McLeod Bethune had envisioned for the NCNW, one that brought together an interracial group from various women's organizations to further the cause of civil rights and improve the lives of African American women.[17] Height also liked that it had the potential to unite family members—mothers of the student volunteers with their children—and to build a bridge with the Mississippi women by putting the faces of real people on the COFO students, countering the demonizing portrayal of them in white-owned southern media. Humanizing COFO students would dispel the rumors that communist-inspired radicals were behind the Freedom Summer activities, and also aid the NCNW's mission of opening lines of communication.[18]

In keeping with sending women from the Cadillac crowd, Height and Cowan sought team members who had something to offer through their education, their resources, or their positions—either in their own right or through their husbands' connections. Height contended that women with a high degree of confidence in their personal strengths could better assess the situation in the South because they would not be distracted by any insecurity over their personal contributions to the WIMS mission. NCNW staff member Susan Goodwillie also explained, "The last thing we wanted was a bunch of northern finger-wavers . . . who really had no understanding themselves, of what [WIMS] was all about or what the struggle in the South was all about."[19] The women could not be sensitive interpreters of what they observed or offer meaningful evaluations without a dedication to principles of equality and experience working and socializing across racial lines.

The financial independence of the WIMS team members served as an important class marker, setting them apart from seemingly radical Freedom Summer organizations. Student volunteers came as part of organizations like COFO or SNCC, often staying in the homes of poor African Americans or in Freedom Houses with minimal resources. By contrast, most WIMS team members paid their own travel expenses, including meals and hotels, although in some cases, churches or organizations to which the women belonged sponsored their trips. The NCNW depended on donations for the majority of the funding. The largest of these contributions came from the Krim-Benjamin Foundation, the Louis and Pauline Cowan Foundation, and the Stern Foundation, all connections made by team members, as well as the Presbyterian Commission on Religion and Race. Several Wednesdays women made personal contributions.[20]

The NCNW estimated the total costs for 1964 at $9,200 for staff salaries, housing, transportation, meals, telephones, office supplies, transcription, and other miscellaneous expenses. The organizers kept costs to a minimum by working out of Cowan's home with a small staff, a few volunteers, and several phone lines. This arrangement enabled them to operate without constantly worrying about money.[21]

The WIMS women planned to fly together into Jackson in teams of five to eight and follow the proposed three-day itinerary, visiting the Freedom Schools, community centers, and voter registration drives, and meeting with local women to report their findings at the projects and open lines of communication. Every moment would be spent observing and discerning the reality of life in Mississippi for both blacks and whites, and pinpointing where the Wednesdays women might find common ground between the two groups to begin building bridges of understanding.

Always cognizant of their Selma experience, Height and Cowan remained determined not to jeopardize the project by alienating anyone and planned to operate within the bounds of southern social norms for gender, race, age, and class. To administer the program locally, they needed a base of operations in Mississippi and a small, biracial staff to work there.

They chose Goodwillie to be the white staffer. Height and Cowan believed that her work with the NCNW and the Women's Committee for Civil Rights gave her a sense of how to operate in both the black and white communities; but her age, at only twenty-two, raised concerns for her safety as an outsider in a hostile environment. To avoid going alone, Goodwillie recruited her college roommate, Diane Vivell, to work with her as a volunteer. Vivell was a Woodrow Wilson Law Fellow in her first year at Stanford Law School. Born in Los Angeles, she identified herself as "a red-hot Episcopalian," but more than that, she said, she was a Christian with a strong commitment to ecumenism.[22] This provided a complement to WIMS's interfaith focus and the image it hoped to cultivate for the young women while they lived in Jackson.

Adding to their air of respectability, Goodwillie and Vivell planned to live at the Magnolia Towers, a Jackson apartment building located at 809 North State Street and owned by members of the Citizens' Council. Ann Hewitt, who lived in the building, made the arrangements and identified Goodwillie and Vivell as her family members. While the NCNW paid the bills, their local supporters laundered the checks so the money could not be traced to the organization. Expecting that in a small city like Jackson questions would arise about why the women were in town, Goodwillie and Vivell went "undercover," armed with a letter of introduction from Cowan's husband stating that the publishing company he owned, Chilmark Press, had retained them to write a southern cookbook. They adorned their coffee table with copies of *Gourmet* magazine to complete the charade.[23] Despite these efforts, the owners of the apartment were skeptical of Goodwillie and Vivell, who did not sound southern, and suspected them of being call girls.[24]

For the black staffer, Height selected Pittsburgh native Doris Wilson, who had lived in the South and had experience working with interracial women's groups for the YWCA. Born in 1920 and raised with the expectation that she would attend college, Wilson had a bachelor's degree in education from

Tuskegee Institute, a master's in Christian education from Union Theological Seminary, and a master's in social administration from Western Reserve
University. She had worked with the Girls' Friendly Society of the Episcopal
Church and the national Student YWCA. The student movement, which organized in 1888 and began recruiting blacks in 1909, was considered the more
racially progressive division of the YWCA organization. It held integrated
conferences outside of southern states as early as the inter-war period, which
gave many African American and white students from the South their first
experiences interacting with each other as peers.[25] Wilson often worked with
women in teams, had contacts in Mississippi, and knew the environment—a
perfect match for the WIMS project. Having just graduated from Western,
Wilson had the summer free before starting a job with the Chicago YWCA.
Despite the risks involved, she had no hesitations about saying yes when
Height asked her to join the project.[26]

Wilson was named the senior staff member in recognition of her maturity
and experience. Goodwillie said that she and Wilson "liked each other from
the beginning." Goodwillie knew that Wilson was older, but was stunned
years later to discover that Wilson was older by a margin of twenty-one years.
Most likely, those years that Wilson spent working for the YWCA and obtaining her master's degrees contributed to an air of authority and confidence
that Goodwillie sensed in her—and for which Goodwillie felt grateful given
Mississippi's instability.[27]

Although scrutiny from the local community did not rise to the same level
for Wilson as it did for the white staffers, her path still had its bumps. Similar
to the white women, women in the black community were nervous. Upon
arrival in Mississippi, Wilson stayed with Ernestine Lipscomb, a friend who
was a librarian at Jackson State College. Lipscomb's mother, who lived with
her, became frightened by constant television reports of the Citizens' Council's activities, which forced Wilson to find new accommodations.[28] With help
from Jean Fairfax of the American Friends Service Committee (AFSC) and
Mississippians for Public Education (MPE), Wilson moved to the home of
Lucilla Price, a Jackson social worker. Price, too, felt apprehension and refused to leave a light on outside at night for fear she would be shot coming in
from her garage like Medgar Evers. Nevertheless, Price agreed to let Wilson
stay with her in the hope that WIMS could ease racial tensions.[29]

Height and Cowan felt a deep sense of responsibility for the staff's and
the team members' safety and, therefore, spent extensive time planning every
detail. Unlike the planners of Freedom Summer, who took calculated risks,
knowing that it might be necessary to sacrifice white lives to draw attention

to the cause, the WIMS organizers had no intention of risking anyone's safe-ty—black or white—if they could avoid it.³⁰ They made arrangements for se-curity through the Department of Justice and people in the local communi-ties. Height and Cowan were neither so brave that they would act foolishly in dangerous situations, nor so naive as to think propriety alone would shield them.³¹ The first "official communiqué" from Smith to Goodwillie and Vivell stressed the importance of their coming to New York as early as possible to prepare. Goodwillie planned to arrive on June 1, just three weeks before their departure for Mississippi, and Vivell would follow later in the month.³²

In case trouble should arise, WIMS took the precaution of notifying fed-eral and state officials each week of their impending visits. Those notified included President Lyndon B. Johnson, Attorney General Robert Kennedy, Mississippi governor Paul Johnson Jr., and the head of the Civil Rights Divi-sion of the Department of Justice, John Doar, who remained in close contact throughout the summer. Following a meeting with three Department of Jus-tice representatives on June 10, Smith reported to Cowan, Height, and the Jackson staff that the men expressed "unqualified enthusiasm" for WIMS and believed it would be a "valuable addition" to the summer projects, adding a "missing dimension that [would] help hold down violence." The three men divided on the wisdom of notifying the Mississippi governor's office about the trips. Doar and the Mississippi desk officer, Bob Owen, argued in favor of notification, and civil rights attorney St. John Barrett advised against it. Height and Cowan opted to notify Governor Johnson.³³

Doar, Owen, and Barrett had few concerns about the project. Owen saw the women as a potential source of information on police and private brutal-ity, and requested that they report any other "*facts*" that the women found worth noting. The men suggested Hattiesburg as a "good first trip" and gave instructions that WIMS should work closely with the National Council of Churches (NCC). Although Doar, Owen, and Barrett offered pointers on vig-ilance, Smith noted that they voiced no concern for the staff's or the teams' safety. That soon changed.³⁴

The WIMS staff prepared extensively for their trip because they were not only responsible for their own safety but also needed to protect the visiting teams. Following the Justice Department's advice, Smith and Cowan met with representatives of the NCC to discuss the staff's needs and the unique nature of their role in Freedom Summer. Wilson, Goodwillie, and Vivell attended the COFO training for Freedom Summer volunteers sponsored by the NCC, held at Western College for Women in Oxford, Ohio, June 14–20, 1964. The train-ing offered instruction in the political and social climate of Mississippi, the volunteers' legal rights, Mississippians' rights, and nonviolent civil disobedience.[35] The WIMS staff also met in the living room of Cowan's Park Avenue apartment to role-play how they should dress and how to answer questions they might encounter. To be beyond reproach in Mississippi, they would wear white gloves and go to church "three times on Sunday." Goodwillie said, "If we were going to get through to white women we had to be totally acceptable to white Mississippi upper-class standards." They would maintain decorum at all times, even divorcing themselves from outward contact with friends participating in Freedom Summer during their time in Jackson.[36]

The plans for WIMS continued despite tragic news from Mississippi that confirmed the thinking of Freedom Summer organizers that white lives mattered more than black ones. Mississippi immediately became the center of national attention when two white COFO volunteers, Michael "Mickey" Schwerner and Andrew Goodman, and one black volunteer, James Chaney, disappeared. The day after they arrived in the state following the COFO training, the three men left Meridian, Mississippi, to investigate the burning of a church. The Neshoba County sheriff's department arrested and later released them, but the men never returned to the Meridian COFO office. Even as rumors swirled that the disappearance was a hoax perpetrated by civil rights activists, federal law enforcement and news media poured into the state for the investigation, in contrast to their relative silence when blacks alone were murdered. Wilson, Goodwillie, and Vivell were in Ohio when they heard the news. Goodwillie said, "It was awful, awful testimony to the reality that we were about to enter." The disappearance showed that nobody was safe, and racist Mississippians would take drastic measures to maintain the status quo.[37]

News of the disappearance caused some team members to withdraw from the project; for others, it strengthened their resolve. Weeks before, Cowan had planned a meeting in New York for team members and their spouses to hear reports from the staff members, who would describe the COFO training and encourage participation.[38] Now the tone had changed, and the risks seemed greater than they had just days earlier. Despite reassurances from the WIMS organizers, some husbands forced their wives to drop out, others questioned Cowan about provisions for the women's safety, and still others were supportive or left the decision to their wives. For example, Josie Johnson was thirty-four years old at the time, with three children, ages ten, eight, and six. Although as a child in Houston, Texas, Johnson had joined her father, Judson Robinson, in soliciting signatures to end the poll tax, and later had done some "silly things" as an activist in her adopted home of Minneapolis-St. Paul,

Minnesota, and other places, she had never worked in Mississippi. Johnson said that although her husband usually supported her activism, this situation led the couple to contemplate how he would care for their children if she failed to return. In the end, they decided that everything would work out and agreed she should make the trip.[39] Team member Sylvia Weinberg's husband opposed her going because of the dangers. She enlisted the help of her rabbi and a friend's husband to convince him to let her decide whether or not to go, pointing out, "You have to live dangerously sometimes for your own purposes."[40]

The area coordinator for Washington, D.C., withdrew out of fear after hearing tales of abuse against civil rights activists by white supremacists in Mississippi. She attempted to dissuade the WIMS staff from going to Mississippi, but they knew from the COFO training that such stories were intended to weed out those "who couldn't take it." Cowan recalled that Wilson stayed calm, and that Height reassured Goodwillie and Vivell, who remained committed to the project, though concerned. Fortunately, the area coordinator's withdrawal had no effect on the participation of the other Washington women.[41]

The disappearance of the civil rights workers also caused the Department of Justice to reevaluate its earlier lack of concern for the teams' safety, and Doar expressed apprehension until team members proved they could go in and work "quietly." Cowan said, "He thought we were going to be foolish and . . . he was busy enough worrying about the boys and girls who were there. . . . [Having] to worry about a group of daffy women was something he really didn't want to do but . . . he began to respect us."[42] Every week WIMS provided the department a list for each team trip, labeled Team 1 through Team 7, giving the team members' names and the city outside Jackson they planned to visit. Before the first team's departure, the Department of Justice sent a message to the Mississippi state police advising them of the coming trip. On July 6 highway patrol officers received a notice stating, "These women are coming here by invitation from the Department of Justice."[43] The notification had its risks because it alerted Mississippi law enforcement—some of whom used their positions to abuse civil rights advocates—that outside visitors were coming; however, it also let them know that the highest national and state officials had an eye on them.

The WIMS staff referred to the Jackson women who assisted them as their "angels," and this group proved invaluable at making the crucial connections with other southern women. Ann Hewitt was a key contact in the white community. From finding the staff apartment, to laundering the rent checks, providing cars, and more, Hewitt "navigated the treacherous shoals of Mississippi society" for the staff and introduced them to most of the people they worked with across the state, as Goodwillie explained.[44] Even though Hewitt worked for social justice most of her life and was active in the Presbyterian Church and CWU, she was less visible as an activist than women like Jane Schutt who served publicly. Goodwillie believed that the secret to Hewitt's success rested upon her invisible activism, and called her "formidable" in a quiet, southern way.[45] During the first WIMS visit, Hewitt sat knitting, reminding team member Marian Logan of Madame Defarge, a character in Charles Dickens's *A Tale of Two Cities*, who hid her plans for revenge during the French Revolution in the patterns of her knitting. Logan mused that Hewitt probably hid her own plans for the Jackson civil rights revolution in the blue sweater she crafted.[46] Hewitt admitted that being a widow of independent means enabled her to take action because no one could threaten her husband's job or her source of income.[47]

Jane Schutt assisted the staff in understanding the state of affairs in Mississippi and in arranging meetings with Jackson women. Initially, Goodwillie felt fearful that Schutt's "breezy manner" might blow the staff's cover. Yet, when they met, Goodwillie said of her, "[She is] both an oak and a reed for she has been steel-strong and unbending and yet she has been struck with challenge and hate and fear and reprisal and misunderstanding in such a steady, . . . insidious hostile way that no normal human being could stand under it."[48] Schutt attributed her ability to withstand the onslaught to her experiences in the Episcopal Church and the ecumenical movement. She worked for desegregation because she had faith that God had made the human race of one blood and instructed his followers to "make no peace with oppression."[49] She reported that it was not until she joined the Mississippi Advisory Committee for the U.S. Civil Rights Commission that she "learned the true state of affairs regarding everyday trials" that blacks in the state suffered through.[50] Although many local women shunned socializing with Schutt, she received numerous letters, including one from Team 6 hostess Miriam Ezelle, thanking her for bringing Christian values to the Advisory Committee's work in solving Mississippi's problems.[51]

Lillian Burnstein might best be described as a reluctant angel. She turned down the first requests to host the northern women, but came to meet with multiple WIMS teams. Cowan reported that she continually said to the northern women, "Give us a program. Tell us what we should do." The northern women refrained, however, knowing the Jackson women would not accept a "northern" program.[52] As the summer progressed, Burnstein's involvement increased, albeit grudgingly at times. Team 1's Jean Benjamin reported that she appeared well-intentioned and willing to help if her "active participation" could be hidden.[53]

Clarie Collins Harvey made key contacts with other black women, and she hosted several of the teams in interracial groups at her home. Team member Peggy Roach recalled arriving at the Collins Funeral Home, owned by Harvey, as if her team were attending a wake; but then, Harvey escorted them to her living quarters, where the team had a chance to talk candidly with local women in a secure environment.[54] Justine Randers-Pehrson commented that Mississippi's segregationist white women had completely misjudged the black women. She reflected, "How difficult it would be . . . to line up anyone who could match these handsome women in terms of sophistication, intelligence and style (not just clothes—style of mind, style of speech, and general approach to the world). . . . How calmly they refer to the last trip to Paris, the mission to Congo, the conference in Seattle, the jail in Birmingham. . . . I can't help wondering just how the white Mississippi ladies would stack up socially if they ever had to compete."[55]

Other black and white women offered aid to WIMS with what Goodwillie called an "earthy, soulful pragmatism."[56] Barbara Barnes and Lillie Belle Jones, directors of the central (white) and branch (black) YWCA respectively, opened their doors for meetings. Thelma Sanders, the African American owner of a dress shop and a close friend of Harvey's, welcomed many team members to her home.[57] Other black women who hosted teams included Doris Green, Rubye Lyells, Marie Miller, Mrs. J. L. Reddix, Mrs. N. T. Sampson, Ruth Shirley, Nellie Williams, and Aurelia Young. White women hostesses included Ann Ashmore, Miriam Ezelle, Eleanor Fontaine, Florence Gooch, Mrs. Power Hearn Sr., Arene Nussbaum, Jay Shands, and Danelle Vockroth.[58]

The white women were a "piteously small, brave little band," Benjamin commented; and, "They did not seem to hold out much hope for enlarging their forces."[59] Beyond their few angels, Goodwillie estimated that only about twelve to fourteen white women in Jackson indicated they had even a remote interest in helping the civil rights movement—an incredibly small number for a town of over 180,000 residents.[60] Goodwillie stressed, "Without the Mississippi angels . . . we couldn't have done this; it [WIMS] would not have been possible. They cleared the way, they opened the doors."[61]

An early opportunity for the angels to offer assistance arose when the WIMS organizers were seeking a suitable place for the biracial staff to meet, since they could not gather publicly. Wilson certainly could not come to the Magnolia Towers, and the two white women could not risk taking a taxi or bus to Wilson's residence. After much discussion, Lillie Belle Jones finally agreed to let the staff meet in the back room of the black YWCA at 501 N. Farish Street, provided they were careful and kept meetings brief.[62] Goodwillie recalled the plan they devised to get there after looking at a map: "We figured out that the Sun-n-Sand Motel, which is where we housed most of the white team members, was sort of on the edge of the black community. So we'd take a white taxi to the Sun-n-Sand Motel, walk through the lobby, past the swimming pool, . . . through the crepe myrtle hedge at the back of the motel property, . . . and [then] walk the six blocks to the Y. . . . We were safe in the black community. . . . They knew we were pals, and it's the only time we felt safe."[63] The elaborate nature of this route illustrates the level of paranoia in Jackson at that time, which prevented freedom of movement and created obstacles to interracial communication or open discussion of civil rights advocacy.

Shortly after the staff's arrival in Jackson, Barbara Barnes explained to the white WIMS staff why their presence presented challenges, and cautioned them about their conduct. Barnes walked a delicate line between the national YWCA's movement to integrate and the sentiments of some of her board members who had ties to the Citizens' Council. While she indicated that members of the local YWCA board would happily meet with visiting YWCA members, she warned, "The minute they [the WIMS teams] visit a project, they are part of it as far as our people are concerned." Even though Barnes identified set patterns of activity as a disadvantage, she stressed the importance of the staff's going to church regularly, because "the best people" did.[64]

Barnes also pointed out that when meeting with Mississippians, the WIMS teams should stress that they had come to learn, a motive local women would appreciate. In this way, the WIMS visits offered a chance for the white southerners to be heard and understood rather than criticized. Barnes told Goodwillie and Vivell, "In other sections of the country there is not personal concern for anybody as there is here in the South—that is why it is so hard sometimes. . . . when we think of all this pressure on us for integration— we don't just think about public accommodations. We think of total social integration."[65] While achieving a truly integrated society was the movement's ultimate goal, racist organizations used assimilation, which they contended would lead to miscegenation, as a tool to fan the flames of fear. The WIMS teams sought to counter that fear.

Obtaining transportation presented challenges for outsiders coming to Mississippi that summer. Hewitt coordinated vehicles for the white staff, at times having her daughter drive them, other times loaning them her personal car or renting cars, for which the NCNW reimbursed her.[66] Rental cars posed a problem by identifying the driver immediately as an out-of-towner, and thus a civil rights worker—"a dangerous person."[67] For her part, Wilson found an African American man to drive her and the black team members to their destinations. He knew the lay of the land and the places that they could travel safely.[68]

After arriving in Mississippi, the three-woman staff planned to visit the surrounding towns to contact key leaders and identify the communities each team would visit. The staff originally considered visiting Hattiesburg, Vicksburg, Canton, Meridian, Greenville, Greenwood, Laurel, and Natchez. In actuality, the teams visited Meridian, Ruleville, Vicksburg, Hattiesburg, and Canton, with the latter two cities receiving visits from two teams each.[69]

As the various components of the plan came together, Height and Cowan began to select women for the visiting teams—arguably the single most important consideration in opening dialogue with southern women. Both well-connected, Height and Cowan called on women they knew, women who served in organizations to which they belonged, women who had children participating in Freedom Summer, and women referred to them by others. Women just "tended to find women." To facilitate this process, the organizers designated a community coordinator from each departure city to assist in the selection. For example, Cowan's friend Laya Wiesner became the Boston community coordinator. Wiesner served as a national board member and chair of human resources for the League of Women Voters (LWV) in Massachusetts, and she was the wife of the dean of the School of Science at Massachusetts Institute of Technology. Wiesner and Mrs. Mark Howe, cofounder of Voice of Women-New England, an affiliate of Women Strike for Peace, hosted a get-together at Howe's home for fifty women, five or six of whom expressed an interest in taking part.[70] Height invited Josie Johnson to join the project. Both women belonged to Delta Sigma Theta sorority, and Johnson served as president of the Minneapolis–Saint Paul NCNW. In addition, Height invited Mary Kyle, an editor of the *Twin City Observer,* a black newspaper.[71] The women recruited for WIMS often shared common interests and similar points of view. They had the interpersonal skills and connections to aid southern women.

Every woman completed a registration form once the community coordinator had selected her for the team. The form asked for contact information and details such as religious and organizational affiliations, education level, husband's name and business, and any connections the team member had to people in Mississippi. The form also asked the women to identify their race.

A few left this blank, but most listed either "Negro" or "white." Two women identified themselves as both white and Jewish for race, in addition to indicating Jewish for religion. Marian Logan, special projects coordinator for the New York City SCLC, gave the most appropriate answer to race when she wrote, "Human!" and then in parentheses, "Negro, if you insist!"[72]

A woman's interest did not guarantee her acceptance, because Height and Cowan insisted on selectivity to avoid problems caused by women who had their own agendas. Cowan cautioned the coordinators, "Be sure every team member is known to you personally or to someone whom you know."[73] She recalled that one woman said, "If I see something that I don't like going on, I'm going to go to jail." Cowan told the woman to go to Mississippi with another organization, because that kind of publicity would stop WIMS's activities.[74] Only two of the submitted registration forms hinted at previous "radical" civil rights activities hidden amongst memberships in religious and civic organizations. Lucy Montgomery, who served on the Women's Board of the University of Chicago, had attended the COFO training as a staff resource person, and Wilhelmina "Billie" Hetzel, wife of the U.S. Employment Services director, belonged to SNCC.[75]

Height and Cowan wanted a diverse group of team members who could relate to the equally diverse women they found in Mississippi, and who could be paired with southern women with similar organizational or religious affiliations to create common ground. As a result, another instruction for composing the teams was to make each one "a cross-section of women's organizations, religious affiliation, and professions," with no less than two African American women per team. At the time, the organizers expected members of the Maryknoll Sisters of St. Dominic in New York to participate, and, therefore, Cowan encouraged the team coordinators to each recruit one or two nuns.[76]

The organizers assembled seven teams, totaling forty-eight northern women. Thirty-two were white and sixteen black; thirty-two were Protestant, eight Jewish, six Catholic, and two undesignated. Forty had college degrees, including ten with master's degrees and five with doctorates. They came from Illinois, Maryland, Massachusetts, Minnesota, New Jersey, New York, Pennsylvania, and Washington, D.C.; one woman from California joined the Washington team. Sixty percent were working women, many of whom served on community boards and government commissions. They belonged to at least twenty separate organizations, including the NCNW, the YWCA, the NCCW, the NCJW, CWU, the LWV, and the AAUW. The latter two became official participants following the WIC meeting. One quarter of the women held positions of responsibility in these organizations, with four serving as national presidents. Participants' husbands included doctors, academicians, the former governor of New Jersey, the president of United Artists, the director of the Twentieth Century Fund, the head of the Associated Negro Press, the executive vice president of the Federation of Jewish Philanthropies, and an administrator for the Metropolitan Museum of New York.[77]

The team members joined WIMS for many reasons. Some belonged to organizations in the North that took an active role in the fight for civil rights. Josie Johnson sat on national boards for the NAACP, the NCNW, and the LWV that had her lobbying for fair housing, school desegregation, and human relations training for police officers, fire fighters, and teachers.[78] Similarly, Ruth Batson served as chair of the Education Committee for Boston's NAACP. Active in the Democratic Party, she received a personal request from then vice president Lyndon Johnson to join the President's Committee on Equal Employment. When she heard about WIMS, Batson said, "I felt that this was an opportunity not only to be of help, but also to strengthen my own convictions and determination to end 2nd class citizenship."[79]

Some women followed the examples of their mothers and fathers, black and white, who had worked to create a better world for African Americans. Johnson's parents taught her to work to change the laws rather than to hate. Working as activists was "like eating. It was what was expected of you."[80] Claudia Heckscher and Sylvia Weinberg both cited the Holocaust and their fathers' activism on behalf of Jews as inspirations.[81] Priscilla Hunt credited the influence of both her parents for her activism. Her mother had taken part in sit-ins and insisted that Hunt volunteer with youth at the Phillis Wheatley Club; her father served as president of Oberlin College, one of the earliest schools to grant degrees to blacks and women employing the same curriculum used with white men.[82] Similarly, Maxine Nathanson was spurred by the example of her father, a dentist who treated black patients.[83] Jean Davis said her inspiration came from her father's instruction to "use your head."[84]

For others, particularly the younger team members in their thirties, it was the times that drew them to the movement. The country had elected John F. Kennedy as president in 1960, and people had the feeling, Goodwillie recalled, that they "could do anything." Geraldine Kohlenberg remembered being influenced by the 1960s ethos—the confrontational push to make change happen and the breaking down of "stuffy barriers" through nonviolent means.[85]

Many team members wanted to lend support to family or friends volunteering in Mississippi. Polly Cowan, Alice Ryerson, Henrietta Moore, and

Jean Davis all had children who had volunteered for Freedom Summer. Miriam Davis and Mary Cushing Niles had family members in the southern state, and Kohlenberg went because Ryerson, her best friend, asked her to go.[86] Hetzel knew some of the students from American University and feared for their safety.[87] Similarly, Weinberg had met COFO volunteers through her activities with the Human Relations Committee in the Chicago area.[88]

Some were called by their religious beliefs to join the civil rights movement. Peggy Roach grew up in a devout Catholic family where she was taught to respect others and to view discrimination as sinful. As an adult working with the NCCW, she was influenced by the Second Vatican Council's Pastoral Constitution on the Church in the Modern World, which states, "The joys and the hopes, the griefs and anxieties of all humankind must be the joys and hopes, the griefs and anxieties of the people of God." That, Roach said, "puts you right there in the middle of things."[89] The daughter of a minister, Miriam Davis believed her faith required her to act. "There was never an instance in the stories in the New Testament where Jesus was not open to everyone, all of the sinners. . . . He forgave them and he didn't hold grudges."[90] Having attended the Quaker college Bryn Mawr, both Kohlenberg and Ryerson were influenced by its spiritual teachings. Kohlenberg felt "an impulse to help people who were deprived or suffering in one way or the other" and believed that her support for civil rights "came emotionally out of the same place."[91] Although religion was not Johnson's main reason for taking part, she was attracted to the ecumenical structure of the group.[92]

The activism of the Jewish women often had its roots in the "prophetic calls for universal justice," as historian Faith Rogow notes.[93] Going back to the Progressive Era and the formation of the NCJW, Jewish mothers had instilled in their children a social conscience applied in all aspects of their lives. Further, facing discrimination and quotas in everything from housing to college admissions, they understood the impact of Jim Crow.[94]

In the end, each team of four to eight women had at least two African American women and usually included a Jewish woman, a Catholic woman (though only one nun took part), a Protestant woman, a member of the LWV or AAUW, and one or two women from other organizations. Many had multiple affiliations through which to make connections.

Accommodations for the team members were arranged according to race. Black Jackson women welcomed the northern blacks into their homes. By contrast, white team members stayed at one of two Jackson hotels, the Sun-n-Sand Motor Hotel or the Hotel Heidelberg. The staff followed John Doar's advice never to house anybody outside of Jackson, where he evidently thought the federal government's ability to offer assistance would be limited.[95] This practice continued until the last two teams arrived, and the northern white women received invitations to stay in southern white homes.

To keep their teams informed, the community coordinators disseminated information sent from the New York office via numbered memoranda, while the NCNW conducted orientation sessions and provided briefing materials to prepare the women for their trips.[96] The briefing kits included basic facts on Mississippi and the towns they would visit, background information on local civil rights projects, readings on southern segregationists' attitudes, a pamphlet entitled "Behind the Cotton Curtain," and the text of a speech by University of Mississippi professor James W. Silver, which he later turned into the book *Mississippi: The Closed Society.*[97] Additionally, the Jackson staff prepared a sheet of questions that team members might be asked, so that the women could prepare their responses rather than be caught off guard. The organizers requested that each woman keep a notebook of her observations so she could send a report to the NCNW on her return. Cowan planned to use these reports to prepare an overall "Trip Report" for the Department of Justice and the President's Lawyers' Committee at the project's end. The team members could use their notes to write journal articles for the organizations to which they belonged. Height and Cowan believed that these articles would prove more valuable than newspaper reports because journals circulated nationally. Although the NCNW planned to send out a press release through United Press International (UPI) at the project's end, doing so did not guarantee the story would appear nationwide.[98]

Misinformation about Mississippi and the Freedom Summer projects presented challenges for the WIMS teams. They had to determine, as best they could in a short time, the truth about life in Mississippi while being careful not to perpetuate any misconceptions themselves. In a July memo, Cowan cautioned the women that they would hear many rumors in Mississippi that they should verify before reporting as fact. "In the same way there may be rumors about us which we can dispel by our integrity," she added, referring to their strategy to differentiate themselves from other Freedom Summer activists. To dispel the belief of white southerners that subversive organizations paid northerners—including the Wednesdays women—to come to the region, Cowan reminded the women to assure anyone who asked that they were not part of SNCC or COFO, and that they had not been paid to come or sent by any group. They could say this truthfully since many paid their own way. Any hint that the women had received payment to come or were associated with one of the Freedom Summer organizations would raise red flags to wary white southerners about the visitors' intentions.[99]

Height and Cowan insisted on a strict rule against publicity out of fear that reports appearing before the last team came out of Mississippi could endanger the teams and the staff. They wanted the story released on the NCNW's terms. No doubt, this policy also grew out of their failure in Selma following the newspaper report of Cowan's speaking at the rally. At the team orientation, the leaders requested that the Wednesdays women inform only their immediate families of their plans, in order to prevent news leaking to outsiders.[100] Just days before the first team's departure, and after Barbara Barnes had issued her warning about varying the pattern of activities, Cowan cautioned the community coordinators to refer to "weekly visits" rather than mentioning Wednesdays specifically, so as to prevent calling attention to activities on that day each week. If questioned by the press, Cowan instructed the women to provide a statement about their goal to act as a "ministry of presence," to assist in meeting human needs and relieving suffering, and to act as "sensitive interpreters . . . through personal observation and conversation," with the thought that women could accomplish more by demonstrating concern than challenging people to change their way of life. Cameras were forbidden. Further, team members were instructed not to participate in civil rights demonstrations or marches while in Mississippi, which would call attention to their presence.[101] This final instruction contributed to their image as proper ladies whose presence was nonthreatening.

The organizers believed that traveling in segregated groups on the teams' arrival in Jackson was critical to WIMS's success, even though it seemed to contradict the goals of the civil rights movement they sought to advance. Mississippi Delta resident and activist Unita Blackwell explained, "A white person riding in the car with black people had to crouch down on the floor when a car passed so no one would see him or her. Merely seeing blacks and whites together in any kind of equal situation was enough to send law enforcement officials and some in the general public into a frenzy."[102] Fannie Lou Hamer, a founder of the Mississippi Freedom Democratic Party (MFDP) who became a symbol of the civil rights movement, agreed. She had expressed concern over the COFO students "commingling" across race, especially men and women, in opposition to southern customs. She felt it compromised the safety of blacks in her hometown of Ruleville because black men were blamed if any trouble arose, and she believed that it jeopardized the outcome of the movement as a whole.[103] Because the white Wednesdays women were not staying with black families or traveling with black men, the white WIMS team members did not risk the criticism of inappropriate sexual contact with black men that the white female students faced. Nevertheless, the WIMS organizers recognized and respected the concerns expressed by Mississippi women like Blackwell and Hamer.

Segregating was problematic for some participants but, ultimately, essential to the image they sought to present as observers. The teams would fly together from their departure point and, when they deplaned in Jackson, separate by race, not speaking or acknowledging the others' existence. The staff would follow the same procedure, acting like strangers. Wilson would meet the black women, Goodwillie and Vivell would greet the white women, and the groups would depart in separate cars. Some women balked at this plan. Ruth Batson, a black member of Team 2 and commissioner of the Massachusetts Commission Against Discrimination, almost canceled her trip because she believed they should lead by example, and this policy represented exactly the kind of behavior they hoped to stop. "It seemed to me that we should give witness to our beliefs and not accede to the degrading customs of an evil system," she said. Fortunately, she also had confidence that the WIMS planners had a reason for this decision; she continued on, albeit unhappily. When Batson's team arrived, she discussed her concerns with Wilson, who explained the southern customs, what WIMS hoped to accomplish in Mississippi, and the teams' roles. Wilson's explanation convinced Batson that adhering to the segregated system did not betray her principles.[104]

White women also found the policy troubling. Maxine Nathanson, a white member of Team 4 from Minneapolis, missed the orientation session and was therefore unaware that the organizers had instructed her fellow travelers that they could leave Minneapolis as an integrated team, but once they arrived in Chicago, Illinois, they had to sit in separate groups.[105] Nathanson wrote in her report that the team had developed a friendly rapport before leaving the Minnesota airport, but when they arrived in Chicago, she got "a very strange sensation" when the black women said they would sit together for the rest of the trip. They chatted across the aisle until reaching St. Louis, Missouri, but less so from there to Memphis, Tennessee, where the white women briefly deplaned. Once Nathanson and her companion returned, the black women stopped speaking to them altogether. Unaware of the reason behind this behavior at the time, she later described her feelings: "I could see that this was the pattern that was to be from this point on. Any of the gaiety that existed up to that point disappeared, and I could feel the grave seriousness that surrounded our trip. It seemed to be greater in our Negro friends, and by their attitude, I became almost frightened by what may lie ahead. . . . I was angry at what I was experiencing even though I knew that it would be only for a day."[106]

Though WIMS's actions might appear circumscribed, in reality WIMS operated in this manner because the situation in Mississippi remained dangerous. Additionally, they did not want to repeat the Selma failure. Height explained that, painful as these separations were for the Wednesdays women accustomed to socializing and working with women interracially, "We helped to get them to understand the importance of living within the pattern. . . . There was no way we could bring about change if we went down there and tried to upset it." The fact that WIMS employed subtle tactics in no way mitigated their efforts to bring about change.[107]

As the pieces of the Wednesdays in Mississippi plan came together, the organizers deliberately examined each facet to be sure it promoted their overall goals and avoided their earlier missteps. The organizers ensured that the teams engaged in activities considered appropriate for women and mothers, and that they projected the image of the Cadillac crowd. The plan called for the staff and teams to hold fast to their principles while remaining flexible in executing the project so they could respond to events as they transpired. They had reached the moment of truth—the time had come to go to Jackson. As Goodwillie and Vivell took their seats on the plane, Goodwillie remembered Alan Paton's words in *Cry, the Beloved Country,* which Shirley Smith had used to close her farewell letter to them: "Go Well, Stay Well."[108]

CHAPTER FOUR

Into the Lion's Den

"No one really sings much in Mississippi—unless his face is black
and he is crying for freedom. People don't really laugh very often
either . . . unless it is late at night and doors are tightly closed
and window blinds are drawn."

—SUSAN GOODWILLIE[1]

THE WEDNESDAYS WOMEN—PROPERLY ATTIRED IN DRESSES AND WHITE
gloves, handbags on their arms—departed for Jackson, Mississippi, confident
that their gentility and quiet approach would open doors that other activists had found closed. Once they got in those doors, however, they needed
firsthand knowledge of the civil rights struggle in Mississippi to converse
with the women they met there who could not, or refused to, visit the projects themselves. Hence, the teams began their trips by observing the Freedom Summer projects to gain an awareness of the student volunteers and
their civil rights activities. Both black and white Wednesdays women found
this information useful in meeting with their Jackson counterparts, but the
knowledge base was critical for the white team members, who faced greater
resistance to change. Jackson's middle-class white women would have immediately dismissed the Wednesdays women's comments if they had not been
able to gently say, "I have seen this with my own eyes." Without this kind
of dialogue, the WIMS teams had no hope of dispelling the local women's
misconceptions about the reality of life for Mississippi blacks, the student
volunteers, and Freedom Summer.

Although the itinerary details varied depending on each team's outreach
community and the events occurring in Jackson that week, a typical schedule
involved the black women leaving the airport for the homes of their hosts
and, after dinner, attending an NAACP rally. The white women checked into
their hotel and went to a meeting with the white staff. On Wednesday, all of
the women met in a designated community outside of Jackson to visit Freedom Schools and the local COFO office and community center, and to hear

reports on voter registration and public education. On returning to Jackson, the teams met with local women in segregated groups and attended the Interfaith Prayer Fellowship or a meeting of WomanPower Unlimited. On Thursday they returned home.[2] This pattern, followed by most of the teams, enabled them to conduct the fact-finding part of their mission prior to hearing local women's perceptions of the civil rights movement and the treatment of Mississippi blacks.

The first WIMS team, which included both Height and Cowan, arrived on July 7, 1964, just five days after President Lyndon Johnson signed the Civil Rights Act of 1964 into effect, prohibiting discrimination in public accommodations. Given that the trips' intent was to open lines of communication rather than test the new law, the WIMS women followed the original plan and separated by race at the airport. The teams only met interracially at the Freedom Summer projects and when an evening meeting could quietly be arranged, often at the home of Clarie Collins Harvey for dinner.[3]

The fact-finding mission encompassed two elements, each of which offered a unique perspective on Mississippi during the civil rights era. First, by visiting the Freedom Summer projects, the team members assessed the validity of allegations that the students were engaged in subversive activity, and determined whether the stories of abuse against blacks and civil rights workers appeared credible. If their observations warranted it, the Wednesdays women then offered their southern counterparts an alternative version of the facts to those reported in media outlets owned by members of the Citizens' Council. Second, as they traveled in Mississippi, the WIMS teams observed the treatment of outsiders and reported on travel conditions and security issues that arose. The particulars of their experiences traversing the state proved to be as telling about conditions of life in Mississippi as their observation of the Freedom Summer projects.

While presenting themselves as proper ladies who shared organizational affiliations with the southern women helped to create common ground, the fact-finding part of the trip created the necessary basis in fact for the WIMS teams to open dialogue. Only then could they learn about the Mississippians' attitudes, feelings, and fears regarding civil rights, and begin to open lines of communication across race, region, and religion.

The Freedom Summer project—creating schools, community centers, and voter registration drives across Mississippi—was conceived in response to the slow pace of change in Mississippi and the upsurge in activities by the KKK and the Citizens' Council as support for civil rights began to grow across the nation. In the project's prospectus, the organizers stated, "Political and social justice cannot be won without the massive aid of the country as a whole, backed by the power and authority of the federal government." With little hope that Mississippi's political leadership would "steer even a moderate course in the near future," Freedom Summer organizers recruited college, law, and medical students; teachers and professors; ministers, technicians, folk artists, and attorneys to take part. Efforts in previous summers had brought 100 to 150 workers to the state, but police intimidation made such small groups ineffective. A larger force could draw national attention and enable the project to engage in education along with voter registration.[4]

Since local media reports misrepresented Freedom Summer's purpose and participants, WIMS intended to go where local women could not go—from Freedom Schools to mass meetings—and to be fair reporters, bringing the true story to the Jackson women. These encounters enabled the WIMS teams to speak from firsthand experience. No less significantly, they motivated the WIMS participants to take action when they returned home.

Visits to the Freedom Schools became a central part of each team's trip. Just like Harvey's request for the NCNW to send women to Jackson, the schools offered another invitation of sorts to reach out to the South. Height explained, "When Bob Moses made his call for the Freedom Schools, it gave something that you always need when you're working for social change: you need a handle to take hold of." The Mississippi-based schools gave WIMS that handle.[5] The teams appeared to engage in non-adversarial women's work and, at the same time, afforded the NCNW an opportunity to facilitate educational progress.

The Freedom Summer prospectus described the schools' curriculum as being designed to "challenge the student's curiosity about the world, introduce him to his particularly 'Negro' cultural background, and teach him basic literacy skills in one integrated program."[6] Eager to learn, young and old alike attended in large numbers. While some schools held classes in churches, others met in abandoned buildings, converted barns, or open-air facilities. Younger students typically had a "hard study" in the morning, with a break in the afternoon when temperatures soared. Adults, usually in evening classes, learned their rights as citizens and discovered African American history, something which, as Freedom School teacher Arthur Reese told Team 1, opened a "whole new world" to the students and served as a source of pride.[7] Approximately 2,500 students, from preschool-age to adult, attended classes that summer at nearly fifty Freedom Schools.[8]

The ways in which team members interacted with students and teachers at the Freedom Schools served to educate all concerned. The team members learned from the children about life in Mississippi and the state of education there. The children learned new ways to look at the movement and civil rights from the Wednesdays women. Lastly, the women offered their expertise and support to the teachers and schools. In each case, the teams presented themselves as northern women and mothers concerned about children and education who had come to learn about the South and see how they might help.

Some of the stories about the children are heartbreaking. Goodwillie recalled a little girl who was proud of knowing that the reason black people were inferior to white people was that the brains of blacks only weighed ten pounds, compared to the brains of whites, which weighed thirty pounds. It never occurred to the girl to question this "fact," which she had learned at a public school. Multiple teams reported that the Freedom School teachers begged them to send science books that did not perpetuate this myth.[9]

Several Wednesdays women remarked on the surprising maturity and awareness of the children. Marian Logan recalled one boy telling her that he wanted to learn as much as he could at the Freedom School so that he would not be embarrassed as his parents were (and he for them) when they attempted to register to vote.[10] Team 7 member Ruth Minor, a consultant in guidance and curriculum for the public schools in Rosalie, New Jersey, told of one boy who impressed her. He said, "I have been in this fight a long time. I have been on picket lines. I have rung doorbells. I have walked these streets of Hattiesburg. I know what I'm fighting for." When he told her he was seven the first time he stood in a picket line, she asked his age. He replied, "As I told you before, I've been in this fight a long time. I'm ten."[11] Such comments from ones so young inspired the teams to become more active when they returned home and to build the movement's support outside the South.

Much of the curriculum was intentionally motivated by politics and incorporated life lessons related to the needs of the children. Geraldine Woods, president of Delta Sigma Theta (Deltas) service sorority and Team 3 member, explained how one teacher used the example of what happened to a person's heart if he or she was running from a Klansman to illustrate how blood carries oxygen through the body.[12] Height reported that the children at a Hattiesburg school were learning to write by composing letters to the mayor about injustices in their community that concerned them. The instructor's assessment of the children at that school matched the observations of WIMS team members at many schools in saying, "Their technical education has been limited, but their thought processes were by no means dulled. . . . They know so much more clearly what is happening to them than the northern

Negro student who is faced with a much more subtle, sophisticated system [of discrimination]."[13]

On several occasions, team members had the chance to offer their own lessons to the children. One young boy in Hattiesburg asked Logan, who was black, if she thought his school principal was right in telling the children not to fight amongst themselves but to fight the white race. Inspired by the sight of fellow white team member Jean Benjamin's blonde hair and two white Freedom School teachers, she replied, "No, son, I don't." She asked the boy if he liked her friend and the teachers. When he responded, "Yes," Logan realized that he did not consider them "white" in the same sense as the whites he labeled "the enemy."[14] She told him that he could not fight a race but, instead, needed to fight the system with which he did not agree and that stood against what he knew was right. Logan later exclaimed that the look of realization on the boy's face made the whole trip for her.[15] The lone black nun at Canton's Holy Child Jesus Church and School, Sister Thea, spoke to an audience at her alma mater, Viterbo College in Wisconsin, about southern racial attitudes, explaining how important it was to teach children who had grown up with prejudice "to take a man and evaluate [him] as an individual," as Logan had done, because by looking only at "the mass of white society" the children would become embittered.[16]

Just as the young boy did not see the teachers and WIMS team members as white, some whites working in the movement self-identified as black. The blending of the teachers and students as one race arose at a Canton Freedom School where a white teacher referred to the black students and herself as "us." Geraldine Kohlenberg, a teacher at the Shady Hill School in Cambridge, Massachusetts, observed that the white COFO volunteers had indeed "passed" in reverse, becoming "white Negroes." Although white supremacists used it as a derogatory term, Cowan called herself a white Negro at the debriefing for Team 1, claiming it as a badge of honor to identify with her black teammates. Marian Logan, however, responded, "No, you're not," reminding Cowan that no matter how much a white person—including one who was Jewish and faced discrimination with quota systems and social ostracism— might identify with the black freedom struggle, empathy only went so far. A white person could never completely understand the experience of being black, especially not in Mississippi.[17]

Each WIMS team offered unique contributions to the impromptu lessons for the children at the Freedom Schools, because individual team members had varied qualifications. Team 6 included the internationally known singer and actress Etta Moten Barnett, the first African American to perform at the

White House, for Franklin and Eleanor Roosevelt in 1933. Barnett spoke to the children about Africa and the "rich heritage of the American Negro." She taught them songs and demonstrated how to accompany the music with makeshift bongo drums. Finally, she led the group in singing "Getting to Know You," a popular song from Richard Rogers and Oscar Hammerstein's musical *The King and I.* Fellow team member and NCNW board member Arnetta Wallace said the song "seemed particularly significant in that it explained both the purpose of 'The Movement' and the reason for [WIMS's] presence there."[18] The women were, indeed, getting to know what life was like behind the cotton curtain.

When Team 2 member Sister Catherine John, the only nun to make the trip, was called upon to answer religious questions, she wisely served more as a facilitator than an authority. An eight-year-old girl at one Freedom School asked the nun, "Is God black or white?" In return, Sister asked the child her opinion; she responded, "I think He seems to be white because all the pictures we see of Him on calendars are white—but somehow that doesn't seem right for even God to be white?" Sister Catherine John asked her who she thought made those calendars, causing "a glimmer of understanding" to pass over the child's face. "White people," she replied. Goodwillie recalled, "Recognition of some complications began to creep into what might have been a fairly cut and dried theological inquiry." Another child suggested, "Maybe God doesn't have any color at all because if he did he would have to have a body, and if he had a body, he couldn't be every place at once." Sister Catherine nodded; they had found a satisfactory solution to the original question.[19]

In some instances, team members expressed concern about the teachers, who lacked training as educators and led discussions that could be interpreted as encouraging blacks to take violent action against whites in retaliation. Ilza Williams, a black woman and assistant principal of the Clara Barton School in New York, called it "utterly cruel" to raise questions to high-school-age boys that gave them a "glimpse of freedom" in the classroom without their being able to experience it in their daily lives. At the same time, Williams felt it was "tremendously exciting to have a white girl [teacher], sitting there, saying to these six foot tall Negro boys, with all that this implies, . . . 'What are you going to do when you have the power? . . . Give them a taste of their own?'" Although Williams believed encouraging youth to think was valuable, she felt uneasy about their speaking so frankly about their frustrations to whites—perhaps not to the teachers but certainly in the larger community.[20] Kohlenberg expressed her concerns similarly, calling it "almost unbearably moving, [but] also scary," and wondering if the teacher that she observed had the skills to leave the students with a "strong impression that just plain working together would be a better way." Regardless, Kohlenberg was glad that the Jackson white women her team had met the night before were not on hand to hear this discussion.[21]

Rather than criticizing, the team reports consistently commented on the COFO students' dedication and the importance of their work. As Trude Lash, executive director of the Citizens Committee for Children of New York and member of Team 5, pointed out, the COFO teachers were the first teachers many of these children ever had "who did not teach them fear, or to obey white people because they were white."[22] Of course, many of the student-teachers did not live in the South, and did not have the day-to-day pressure of finding ways to protect children from the retribution of white supremacists, as the children's regular black classroom teachers did.

Prior to each team's departure for Mississippi, Susan Goodwillie contacted the schools the women would visit and provided the teams with a wish list of supplies to bring with them. Although the school facilities varied widely, they all needed equipment, books, and supplies. The vast majority of the requests were for serious needs, but the volunteers were not without a sense of humor. When Goodwillie contacted the Ruleville COFO office, an Australian girl answered the phone and went to check with her colleagues. She came back on the line "with a bewildered sound in her voice and said, 'I really don't know what this means . . . but somebody wants 1 dozen bagels and ½ lb. of lox?!'" at which Goodwillie "howled."[23]

Many schools requested typewriters. Efforts to procure equipment were generally delayed until the teams returned home, but Team 2 had the unique opportunity to offer assistance almost immediately in Canton. Early in the day, they visited a class where students learned to type using cards with a keyboard drawn on them and took turns with one typewriter. Later, the Wednesdays women visited Holy Child Jesus Church and School, which was closed for the summer. Team member Sister Catherine John described the school as "an island" with little to no contact with the black community outside its walls, even though the school served 175 black children during the school year. While there, the team and nuns listened to a report on the Canton movement by organizers George Raymond and Annie Devine. After refreshments, the sisters offered to give the visitors a tour of the school, and the team was stunned when the sisters ushered them into a room full of idle typewriters.[24]

Kohlenberg urged George Raymond to seek the nuns' advice on the Freedom Schools, which he did, opening a discussion on how the Canton movement and the sisters of Holy Child Jesus might work together.[25] This meeting proved fruitful not only for the possibility of using the typewriters, but also in aiding the school's nuns. Since the church had no car, Raymond offered to drive the nuns into town or to Jackson for supplies when needed, and to assist Sister Thea, the lone black nun and a Canton native, who could only move around town with her family and not with the church's white sisters because of heightened racial tensions in the community. Alice Ryerson, a school psychologist in the Boston area, wrote of the whole experience, "We really felt like successful catalysts."[26] The team visit had bridged the separation between the two groups, both of which worked to educate black children in Canton.

The WIMS team members continued to work on behalf of the Freedom Schools when they returned home, where they sought donations and supplies. Cowan's husband contacted a friend in the grocery business to donate 750 pounds of food, or about seventy meals per person, to the Vicksburg COFO students.[27] Team 1 member Jean Benjamin, whose husband was president of United Artists, took advantage of her connections to raise funds for the schools in the Hattiesburg area, which served approximately 600 students ages eight to eighty-two, and which her hometown of Great Neck, New York, adopted. She explained her actions after the trip by saying, "My visit to Mississippi may influence a great many people in my community that felt that what goes on in Miss[issippi] really doesn't concern them. . . . They will look at this situation quite differently now. . . . The local Human Rights Committee has taken a list from me of the materials most needed. . . . We are also holding a large fund-raising party for SNCC on August 8th at our house with Harry Belafonte. . . . I very much doubt that I would have agreed to hold the above-mentioned affair before I went to Mississippi. As committed to the human rights' [sic] cause as I felt, I really needed to see those COFO student-workers at work to realize what a marvelous job they are doing."[28]

While not everyone could offer a fund-raiser with Harry Belafonte, all the contributions to the Freedom Schools were important. Besides the basic school supplies, they sought classics and African American history books, dress material for sewing classes, literacy kits for adults, remedial reading aids for children, musical instruments, typewriters, movie cameras, record players, magazine and newspaper subscriptions, foreign language textbooks, and primary books with pictures showing black and white children together.[29] Although the WIMS women ultimately hoped to encourage others to take an active role in civil rights, their experiences visiting the Freedom Schools illustrated that contributions of any type furthered the cause.

The Wednesdays women also gleaned ideas from the Freedom Schools that they could use in their own communities. They observed how children and teens actively participated, articulating ideas and engaging in role playing, at a workshop on nonviolence conducted by an interracial group of ministers. Hannah Levin, assistant professor of psychology at Rutgers University and a Team 7 member, commented on "the remarkable discussion of the young people on non-violence. To hear these children discussing issues that most adults I know don't even think about was quite exciting."[30] Likewise, her teammate Olive Noble, also an educator, suggested that the workshop's approach could be used in Harlem, Newark, Philadelphia, and other cities to emphasize a nonviolent approach to their problems.[31]

Batson best summed up how the teams felt about the COFO volunteers and the importance of the Freedom Schools: "I thank God for the young people, black and white, from all over the country who are working with the children in these schools . . . for their strength—for their courage—for their confidence in their ability to erase evil. . . . They personify hope."[32] This was critical given that hope remained key to maintaining the movement's momentum.

Freedom Summer organizers conceived the community centers as "long-range institutions . . . [to] provide a structure for a sweeping range of recreational and education programs." These included providing social services, job training, programs to supplement school curriculum, literacy and African American history classes, libraries, public health programs, recreational facilities, entertainment, discussion groups, and adult workshops on family relations, federal service programs, home improvement, and other needs.[33] Centers also served as a place where students who were out of school and the unemployed could safely gather and learn.[34]

Facilities ranged from a "broken down old shack" to rooms in a church (some of which restricted activities like dancing) to a storefront with windows boarded up from bombings. In some instances, the community centers served as both office and living quarters, which local people furnished. Ann McGlinchy, a retired history teacher and member of Team 1, noted that the local women took charge in fulfilling the students' needs—without the benefit of committees or subcommittees or agendas. For example, Jackson women furnished an apartment for several volunteers and arranged for a safe location to deliver food donated by people who wanted to help but did not want to be seen aiding the COFO students.[35]

Establishing libraries, central features of the community centers, proved challenging for the COFO workers, and the Wednesdays women saw why.

Geraldine Woods explained that too often, well-meaning souls sent books, such as texts on learning Hebrew, without consideration of the people's needs. Josie Johnson, with the Mayor's Commission on Human Rights in Minneapolis, reported that the center in Vicksburg had received "truckloads of books" for a facility located in a field with little shelter, let alone storage space.[36] These observations enabled the teams to identify the needs of centers they visited, and they relayed that information through the New York WIMS staff to organizations that focused on building library collections designed around the centers' educational purposes.

Serious difficulties arose from the harassment inflicted on the COFO volunteers, and nowhere was that more apparent than in Meridian, where Mickey Schwerner, James Chaney, and Andrew Goodman had worked. The volunteers at the community center explained to members of Team 3 (who visited about three weeks before officials found the men's bodies) that Schwerner had insisted on staff members' always reporting where they were going and calling on their arrival; his hand-written instructions still hung on the wall. The students told the team that a nearby storekeeper recorded the license plate numbers of cars that stopped at the COFO center; and as predicted, the women saw him pull out a notebook and write something down as they departed.[37] Other incidents included nails being thrown in front of the volunteers' tires and employees of an electrician's shop next door yelling at the students. The men from that shop came out to record Team 3's license number but kept quiet, leading Justine Randers-Pehrson to conclude, "Our high-heeled splendor held them in check." The most unnerving harassment, however, must have been the placards that read, "We will do to you what we did to Mickey."[38] The signs left no doubt that the missing were dead, and that those responsible for the crime (and some who were not directly responsible) felt no remorse, and might kill again.

The Meridian experience built a connection between the community center and the team members, as demonstrated by the report of Mary Cushing Niles, in which she took ownership of the center: "CORE has begun to raise $25,000 to establish the Schwerner Chaney Goodman Community Center in Meridian—our center—and Rita Schwerner [Mickey's wife] is going back as director."[39] As Height and Cowan had surmised before the trips began, seeing the projects firsthand impacted the women on a very personal level.

Following their visit with Team 6, sisters-in-law Jean and Miriam Davis traveled to Ruleville to visit Jean's daughter, Linda, a summer volunteer; and while there, they too experienced harassment. The two women arrived in Ruleville later than planned, a little after dark, making them nervous. They found themselves holding fast to their white gloves as a bit of security should they be stopped. As Jean, president of the Winnetka-Northfield Girl Scout Council, and Miriam, wife of a congregational minister, traveled up a dirt road, Linda and a friend startled them by emerging from the bushes on either side. If the sisters-in-law had not arrived in the next five minutes, the girls said, Linda and her friend would have called the FBI. Jean reported at her team's debriefing that within twenty minutes of their arrival at the house, police came by to check the license plate of their rental car; and when a red pickup truck passed by multiple times, they moved their conversation from the front door to an interior room for fear of making targets of themselves. Linda explained that men harassed them every night, and occasionally during the day, driving by the house repeatedly and ostentatiously displaying their guns. Jane and Miriam, heeding Doris Wilson's words that whites hated "nigger lovers" worse than anyone else, decided not to venture out while in Ruleville.[40]

Although the staff made advance arrangements for teams to visit the summer projects, word did not always reach everyone concerned. How unsuspecting COFO volunteers perceived the team members' outward appearance demonstrated their mistrust of unknown whites. When white team members arrived at the Hattiesburg COFO office wearing dresses and gloves, the workers who had not been told of the visit seemed to think the "local DAR" (Daughters of the American Revolution) might be descending upon them, ready to attack. After Goodwillie explained whom the women represented and their purpose in coming, the "reception rapidly turned into a cordial greeting."[41] Ryerson reported a similarly cool reception by a young woman volunteer she sat next to at the Jackson Supper Club in Canton. Once the girl found out Ryerson's daughter also worked with COFO, the young woman's "hostility disappeared."[42]

These connections proved important to the morale of the volunteers, fulfilling WIMS's goal of supporting the students. Wilson told Randers-Pehrson, "The COFO kids say yours are the first friendly white faces they have seen in Mississippi."[43] This sense of ostracism certainly took its toll on many of the young people, even though they knew that the summer would be difficult. When Ryerson asked her team's escort in Canton what she did on weekends, the girl replied, "We cry a lot."[44] This must have deeply distressed Ryerson when she thought about what her daughter Susan was experiencing. Team 3 member Peggy Roach, executive assistant to the NCCW, confirmed that the COFO students and the local people welcomed WIMS's interest.[45] A little kindness went a long way toward sustaining those in hostile territory far from home.

Because the WIMS teams engaged in women's work and demonstrated concern for the volunteers, they could observe and interact with the students in ways that federal agents could not. Therefore, the Department of Justice asked for WIMS's help in sorting out truth from fiction in the complaints it received about interracial dating among Canton COFO students, which incensed segregationists. Team 2 reported that the Canton students met at the Jackson Supper Club, which served lunch and acted as a nightclub, and was the only local establishment to welcome them. The COFO leaders insisted that volunteers check in and out so that everyone knew where everyone else was at all times, and that they return to their lodgings by 9:00 p.m. Men and women worked and socialized interracially; however, one volunteer explained that they did not date as much as spend time together, and female volunteers were "very careful about their own behavior."[46] Even though the WIMS teams and segregationists held different views of appropriate interracial contact, the Wednesdays women provided the Department of Justice with more accurate information about the students' interactions, contrasting with reports of public interracial sexual behavior.

The educational programs at the community centers played an integral role facilitating the voter registration drives. Systematic blocking of blacks from the polls in Mississippi had staggering results. In Madison County, for example, the MFDP registrar, Wilbur Robinson, reported that in 1963, 500 blacks out of an eligible 10,000 had officially registered; but most had their names mysteriously removed, and only 125 remained on the rolls. By contrast, just forty-two out of 5,500 whites failed to register. The registration form had thirty questions, including the most subjective one requiring an interpretation of the state constitution. "If you had a PhD, you couldn't register necessarily in Mississippi," Robinson told Team 2. At the first Freedom Day in Canton, 300 blacks came to register; but by midday, the registrar had deliberately called only three of them to take the voter registration test. After that, a judge ruled only twenty-five people at a time could appear at the courthouse to register.[47] Other forms of intimidation included newspapers publishing the names of newly registered voters for two weeks so that employers, bankers, and other businessmen could pressure them not to exercise their voting rights. Threatening to fire them, evicting them from their homes, recalling their loans, and withholding credit were a few of the methods used to exert pressure on potential voters.[48]

When COFO launched the Freedom Registration project in early February 1964, it set an ambitious goal: registering 400,000 blacks. That many registrants would give legitimacy to the challenge of the official state rolls and the fall election.[49] It would discredit segregationists' claims that blacks in Mississippi did not want to vote, were not capable of voting, and liked life as it was; it indicated, instead, their desire to take part in the process and to express their will at the ballot box—happy or not.[50] The MFDP allowed applicants "to just sign up" to join the party.[51] Further, since the MFDP leadership believed that the State of Mississippi had made it difficult if not impossible for most blacks to receive a proper education, the party did not make literacy a requirement for registration.[52] The MFDP had its own county registrars chosen by local citizens and followed the state convention system for choosing delegates.[53]

The COFO students faced harassment from local officials, but many residents believed their presence was essential to change. For example, Linda Davis planned to slip into Ruleville unnoticed but found that the mayor had circulated photos of her and other volunteers to local citizens. Meridian residents explained to Team 3 how typical Mississippi police action worked: COFO students went into a black barber shop to solicit signatures, and while there, someone reported their license plate number to police; later, police arrested the students at a private home for "breach of peace" because the shop owner had allegedly asked them to leave, and they did not "move fast enough."[54] Billie Hetzel reported that the people with whom Team 3 met concurred that no registration of blacks would have taken place had the students not come to assist them.[55] This was a common refrain heard by multiple teams.

Ruleville, the home of MFDP organizer and spokesperson Fannie Lou Hamer, offered Team 5 a special glimpse into the determination of blacks to gain the right to vote, as well as an opportunity to meet the woman who was turning Mississippi politics upside down. Hamer intended to attend the 1964 Democratic National Convention in Atlantic City, New Jersey, as an MFDP delegate to formally request the seating of its delegation instead of the regular Mississippi Democrats who denied African Americans the right to take part in the election process and failed to support the national party's candidates and platform. Team 5's Florynce Kennedy, a New York attorney, described Hamer as "just one of the little rural ladies—hardly indistinguishable in that crowd." At the same time, Kennedy felt that the team was watching history in the making as they listened to Hamer speak.[56] Francis Haight, president of International Social Service, recalled that Hamer "gave an emotional and heartrending account of humiliation, beatings, and hideous treatment in jail" in retaliation for her efforts to register voters. Rather than being discouraged, Hamer seemed to become braver and stronger as she continued to inspire others in the civil rights movement. Hamer, Haight said, "Gives the impression of boundless energy and aggression, a real fighter who said herself to me, 'They can do what they can but I'll never give in again.'"[57]

The WIMS teams served as a source of inspiration to MFDP members hoping to make a place for Mississippi blacks at the Democratic Convention. When Ruth Batson, an African American, was introduced as a "real live delegate from Massachusetts," the team saw Wilbur Robinson, Canton's head of voter registration, "visibly [light] up." Ryerson noted that his expression said, "Such things *can* happen."[58] Inspired by what she had seen and heard, Batson pledged to the Mississippians that she would do "all that [was] humanly possible" to see that party officials seated the MFDP delegation at the convention.[59]

The day after her return home from Mississippi, Batson began lobbying the Massachusetts delegation to join the other seven states already lending their support. She outlined the challenge to seating the MFDP and explained that the process required "popular and community support to ensure that the purely legal process [was] undergirded by an outside force, independent of the internal politics of the Congress." The goals included: 1) disseminating the real issues involved to the largest possible audience, 2) creating "home-town interest" that would influence congressmen to lend support, and 3) building closer relationships between the MFDP and northerners.[60] After political maneuvering during which a friend informed Batson of a plan to table her motion, Batson surprised the Massachusetts delegation, telling them she was aware of the plot and did not intend to back down—an intensity that came from witnessing conditions in Mississippi.[61] Batson spoke of her trip's impact on her actions and the reaction of her fellow Massachusetts delegates. "I said to them, 'Now I just got back from Mississippi'. . . because they're used to people talking about what happens in the South when you haven't been there. I said, 'I've talked to these people. . . . And you may be sick of hearing this issue, but they're sick of bearing it.'" She reminded them that the regular Mississippi Democrats did not vote for John F. Kennedy in 1960, an inexcusable act to Democrats from Massachusetts. Batson concluded that her firsthand account made "all the difference in the world" to these "hardnosed politicians."[62]

The effort to seat the MFDP delegation ultimately failed in 1964; however, the MFDP shed national attention on the systematic exclusion of blacks from the electoral process. The failed attempt contributed to the passage of the Voting Rights Act of 1965 and made it possible for Mississippi blacks and others to participate at the 1968 convention. Supporters like Batson aided that effort, as did other WIMS members who attended the convention, including Height, Logan, Benjamin and her husband, Helen Meyner, Lucy Montgomery, and Laya Wiesner.[63] In a true testament to how the experience also changed the northern women, Barbara Cunningham, a registered Republican prior to her trip to Mississippi, became active in the Democratic Party to lend her support to the MFDP.[64]

While in Mississippi, the black WIMS team members attended rallies as a matter of course, but the white women participated only when the staff considered it safe, beginning with Team 3. Civil rights organizers used mass meetings to communicate happenings in the movement, inspire action, and maintain the participation level necessary to keep the movement viable. Finding out the location of these meetings "was like a floating crap game." Goodwillie called a phone number and gave a password to find out where that week's rally would be held, usually at a black church. This procedure helped to keep at bay police and others who recorded the license plates of attendees.[65] The WIMS teams went to rallies that included reports and debates on the status of a local boycott, the upcoming integration of the first grade in Jackson public schools, as well as inspiring stories from the civil rights struggle, prayers, freedom songs, dramatic performances, and speeches by movement leaders.

Rally leaders introduced the team members at a few of the mass meetings. In recognition of Marian Logan's work for the movement, she received an ovation, which she found embarrassing. She felt she had done so little compared to what people in Mississippi were doing. She thanked the crowd for letting the team members attend and asked for the black Mississippi women's guidance in identifying ways the northern women could assist them.[66] At a rally attended by Team 6, Gloster Current of the New York NAACP called Etta Moten Barnett to the platform. Even though it was a hot August night, men rose and donned their coats as a show of respect.[67] A woman who spoke at the rally attended by Team 2 said that the northern women inspired the audience; however, over the course of the summer, the team members overwhelmingly agreed that it was they who were inspired by the southerners fighting for civil rights.[68]

At the rally attended by Team 5, rally leaders introduced the "visiting ladies." This appears to be the only time the team members were a distraction. Trude Lash recalled that the "first part of the meeting was rather stormy and showed clearly the tension and conflict between the old-time leadership of the movement and the younger militant group."[69] The debate centered on whether or not to suspend a boycott against Barq's beverage company before it acted on its promise to start hiring blacks. Someone in the audience questioned if they should argue in front of their visitors, but another person replied, "Discussion is the democratic way, and I'm certain they understand why we would be discussing this under these circumstances."[70]

Freedom songs played a critical role in buoying spirits and creating bonds among activists and Mississippians living the day-to-day struggle. "We Shall Overcome," considered the anthem of the movement, captured its "religious, interracial, and nonviolent emphasis," as historian Paul Harvey explains.[71] Barnett noted that the songs were the "secret of not only the kids in Mississippi, but the secret of . . . at least two hundred years of living, and being, and working, and striking in America. If it were not for the songs, the Negro couldn't have survived." Although the songs were not the only source of strength, they united people and served as a "safety valve" to relieve stress.[72] Identifying with "This Little Light of Mine," Hamer believed that the Lord helped her help her people, and she connected her religious beliefs to daily life through gospel music and prayer. Professor of Christian ethics Rosetta Ross argues that Hamer saw a distinct relationship between "getting the vote, freedom, and what 'the Lord required.'"[73]

The songs helped the WIMS women grasp the emotion of the freedom struggle, and especially how freedom was intertwined with this religious music. Miriam Davis contemplated the relationship between the songs of the civil rights era, "with their expression of release, solace, and determination," and the Negro spirituals. She found a "quality of militancy" in the freedom songs that the nineteenth-century spirituals lacked. The earlier songs seemed resigned to submission and called upon one to wait for reward in heaven. As she observed a white COFO volunteer singing freedom songs while holding hands with a young black person and an older black person, Davis concluded, "The COFO worker is likely to be an agnostic, a humanist, or an atheist. The young Negro *may* be an agnostic, a humanist, or an atheist, but his Mother most definitely is not." She went on to conclude, "All of these children of God (though they may have renounced their Father) are acting in pursuit of freedom for *all* of us, but motivated individually by as many different sets of ideas as there are individuals involved."[74]

In her report on the trip, Ruth Batson recorded the thoughts that ran through her mind as her team sang and clapped at a rally in a black church. She had not known what to expect when Sister Catherine John, who was white, joined the black team members there. Batson wrote, "I steal a look at Sister Catherine who is sitting beside me, and I smile at her slapping away and singing as if she had been doing this all of her life. The singing warms me, and I am moved to tears. I am mindful from time to time that men are outside guarding the church."[75] Here, Batson captured the essence of the experience. Freedom songs balanced hope with the reality of life in Mississippi.

Tensions ran high during the four-hour rally attended by both black and white members of Team 3 at the Masonic Temple on Lynch Street in Jackson on July 22, 1964; the rally featured civil rights leaders Martin Luther King Jr., Ralph Abernathy, John Lewis, Bayard Rustin, Bob Moses, and Charles Evers. Several team members worried that "one bomb could have wiped out the movement."[76] King had come to Mississippi to support desegregation and encourage support for the MFDP.[77] Although the Jackson *Clarion-Ledger* reported that King "vigorously denied . . . the so-called civil rights movement [had] any connection with the Communist party," it also reminded readers that "Bayard Rustin, director of the 1963 civil rights march on Washington who [had] been linked with communist activities, sat less than five feet from King."[78] The local press frequently employed this language, referring to the "so-called civil rights movement" and implying communist ties by association, to discredit the cause and its leadership in the eyes of white Mississippians.

King made an impression on the WIMS team that was not soon forgotten. Peggy Roach recalled he told the crowd, "You're not slaves. We are God's children. To be free, we must believe." As they joined hands to sing "We Shall Overcome," Roach said, "One couldn't help but feel the dream was nearer reality—even in Mississippi—deep in our hearts we did believe that we shall overcome someday."[79] Justine Randers-Pehrson commented, "It was almost too much to be borne. I didn't cry, I sang, but it had been a long and drastic day; and when you realized where you were, and how many [had] died— well, if it didn't get to you, I would say you might as well be dead yourself."[80] Such emotion played a critical role in generating support for the movement. It buoyed the spirits of those working for freedom in Mississippi and it solidified the resolve of outsiders like the WIMS teams to continue the fight at home.

For some civil rights activists, both black and white, dedication to the movement became like a religion in itself. Geraldine Kohlenberg said that the Freedom Summer volunteers she observed had adopted "a sort of primitive communistic Christianity, with The Cause as their god, nonviolence as their dogma, and [had] said in effect that as black equals white, so 'outsides' don't count, therefore distinctions of dress, race, or even sex are of no importance."[81] When Kohlenberg discussed her theory with a female theology student she met in Mississippi, the young woman became excited by the idea and indicated that the training experience in Oxford, Ohio, had been like "a conversion and baptism, after which none of them could ever be the same."[82] This devotion added a dimension to the civil rights movement that caused racists to react in alarm and united pro-movement activists. For most white Mississippians who did not identify with either the racists or the civil rights movement, it likely left them perplexed.[83]

The WIMS teams engaged Mississippi black women in churches and prayer meetings. Miriam Davis found many similarities between Mississippi's black church services and the fundamentalism of the small Methodist churches she attended as a child in southern Illinois. There she experienced a similar "emotional fervor" that was missing from sophisticated, mainstream, urban churches in the mid-1960s. Observing the congregants at black church services, Davis was "fascinated by the outpouring of their spirits. . . . No matter how dreadful their day-to-day lives were, there was unbelievable release when they came to church."[84] Helen Meyner of Team 7 believed these shared religious experiences across race were critical to the success of WIMS's mission. She recalled a secret meeting at the African Methodist Episcopal (AME) Pearl Street Church where blacks and whites joined hands and sang "We Shall Overcome," and another meeting with eight courageous white Jackson women "who love[d] their city and state but who hate[d] the atmosphere of harassment and fear. There was a stifling feeling of tension at first, but we began the meeting with prayer. . . . Suddenly [the] tension evaporated, and we could communicate—North and South, black and white—together."[85]

The vast majority of black women with whom the WIMS teams met subscribed to the blending of religious principles and civil rights. For example, Clarie Collins Harvey indicated that her impetus for creating WomanPower Unlimited to help the Freedom Riders came from Matthew 25, where Jesus says, "For I was hungry and you fed me. . . . I was in prison and you came to visit me."[86] This blending of religion and activism propelled the movement forward and offered the earliest contacts with the white community.

The small group of women in Jackson who worked across racial lines could be found in WomanPower Unlimited and the Interfaith Prayer Fellowship. WomanPower Unlimited originated in response to the Freedom Riders' needs as they awaited their court dates in the Jackson jail without extra clothes or blankets. Harvey explained that the organization's name referred to "the inner, divine power of women as all women work together for peace among the people of a given community, the nation, and the world. This power is unlimited because it is God's power."[87] It represented a friendship chain in a sense, built on prayers, finance, and influence. The leadership of the organization included Harvey, activist and NAACP secretary A. M. E. Logan, and dress shop owner Thelma Sanders.[88] Others who joined the interracial effort included Ann Ashmore, Pearl Draine, Miriam Ezell, Ann Hewitt, Rosa Holden, Lillie Belle Jones, Jessie Mosley, Jane Schutt, and Hazel Brannon Smith, at least six of whom later worked with WIMS.[89]

Team 1 members Jean Benjamin and Ann McGlinchy went to a Woman-Power Unlimited meeting attended by approximately forty women. The only other whites present were Jane Schutt, Ann Hewitt, and two COFO students. The group supported the local selective buying campaign, voter registration, and the COFO volunteers; its activities included furnishing the student volunteers' accommodations and treating them to a Fourth of July picnic with food discreetly provided by Lillian Burnstein and members of the Jewish community. WomanPower Unlimited also worked with Jean Fairfax of the AFSC to facilitate the fall desegregation of the first grade in Jackson schools.[90] WomanPower Unlimited demonstrated that the potential to change existed in Jackson; and as more women came forward to help, it bore witness to the fact that local support existed for the movement even if only in small numbers.

The Interfaith Prayer Fellowship grew out of two 1961 meetings attended by Jane Schutt, one with the Fellowship of the Concerned and the other with CWU's Assignment: RACE. M. G. Haughton, a black woman and wife of the pastor at Jackson's Pearl Street AME Church, joined Schutt at the first meeting. Although the two women felt that they could not hold multiracial dinner meetings in Jackson as women from other cities intended to do, they believed interracial groups could pray together. On their return to Jackson from the Fellowship of the Concerned meeting in Atlanta, they organized the Interfaith Prayer Fellowship, which met on the second and fourth Wednesdays of the month.[91]

Schutt and Haughton, along with Harvey and two ministers' wives named Geneva Taylor and Vanilla Johnson, structured the meetings around praying for the community and its leaders, and for guidance. Although people of all faiths and colors were welcome, black women far outnumbered the white women. They met in black churches such as the Pearl Street AME Church, Central United Methodist Church, and Pratt United Methodist Church because the only white church that allowed integrated meetings was the Unitarian Church on Ellis Street.[92]

The meeting attended by Team 6 most directly engaged the WIMS women and featured Quaker minister Fay Honey Knopp speaking on the beloved community, where blacks would have their freedom. Like WIMS, Knopp came to Mississippi on a fact-finding mission with a "great compulsion to bear Christian witness to the struggle for freedom . . . and desiring to establish lines of communication," as team member Arnetta Wallace reported.[93] Describing her mission, as a "ministry of presence" and a "ministry of listening," Knopp identified three things needed to achieve a beloved community: 1) communication within and across racial groups, 2) women who sympathized with the cause finding others who thought the way they did, and 3) differentiation of communists from civil rights workers, to counter claims that the movement was communist-inspired. Challenging the audience to be proactive, she said, "The beloved community begins with you."[94]

All of the women at the meeting broke into interracial "buzz groups" directed by Doris Wilson, who asked each group to suggest ways to establish and maintain communication across race, class, and other barriers. The team members found the meeting inspiring and appreciated the chance to meet with other "women of goodwill," who also sought "the answer" to the problems dividing the community and the country.[95] Miriam Davis concluded that the Interfaith Prayer Fellowship encouraged the local women to go beyond simply attending events at the predominantly black Tougaloo College, for example. The fellowship involved blacks and whites in one-on-one encounters interacting as equals—absent "the maternal relationship which [existed] between the white woman and her maid," which Davis noted was unfair to and hated by blacks.[96] Calling the relationship "maternal" was generous at best, but it reflected how many southern white women, and even some northern women, saw their role. By contrast, black women had a far greater awareness of the hierarchies involved and their status as inferiors in the eyes of white employers.

Clarie Collins Harvey credited the Interfaith Prayer Fellowship with laying the foundation for much of the early progress made in Jackson, including integrating the local CWU chapter. A bond of trust developed so that the women could communicate with one another when unrest developed and not be drawn in by rumors. Jane Schutt reported that once blacks and whites could worship together, she experienced "a real feeling of exhilaration and joy," and she believed other women shared this sense of "completeness."[97] Elaine Crystal, a Jewish woman who worked with MPE, saw the Interfaith Prayer Fellowship meetings as "the focus of peaceful integration and the focus of good religious and non-religious contact." She added that once they began to "live what [they] were saying," the Mississippi women grew within themselves and had a greater understanding of what was going on in the community.[98] This understanding was exactly what WIMS hoped to facilitate on a much larger scale.

Much of the debate over integration in 1964 played out in the battle over desegregating Mississippi public schools, which still had not changed their enrollment policies ten years after *Brown v. Board of Education*. In early July, U.S. District Court Judge Sidney Mize ordered three districts to desegregate immediately, but not all grades. Jackson planned to begin with the first grade and add additional grades in subsequent years. Many racists equated integrating schools with "race mixing," by which they meant miscegenation, and an end to everything that the South held dear, as an editorial by the *Meridian Star* indicated: "We can find no words to adequately express our shock—our revulsion at the abominable crime of race mixing. . . . Some of us may be tempted in the agony of our oppression to give up hope—to yield the struggle. Yet this we cannot—dare not—ever do. It is our sacred obligation to keep up the fight for our precious Southern way of life. We must never rest until this foul pollution of integration is forever banished from our soil."[99]

Politically progressive Jackson women formed Mississippians for Public Education to fight for the educational rights of students regardless of race. They sought to prevent the kind of unrest that had occurred in other southern cities, as well as the state's shutting down public schools altogether or funding private schools for white students. Two white Mississippians, Patt Derian and Winifred Falls, began to enlist support and lobby to keep the schools open after deciding that the situation had reached "a state of insanity." Derian and Falls had the help of Jean Fairfax, a black woman, and Constance Curry, a white woman, both of the AFSC and both experienced in human relations and civil rights work.[100]

Predominantly white women from old southern families joined MPE. Derian worked exclusively on education at the time because she "wanted to be attacked for the right thing," and believed closing the public schools held serious implications for the education of all races. Plus working for education remained appropriate for white women.[101] Elaine Crystal, who hosted a WIMS team member in 1965, invited herself to join the group because she disagreed with the racist views expressed by the *Clarion-Ledger*.[102]

Although this small pocket of women found a common cause, one could never exercise too much caution, and appearances had to be maintained. Eleanor Fontaine, hostess to Team 6 member Henrietta Moore, worked for MPE but would not appear at public functions because her husband worked for a member of the Citizens' Council.[103] Constance Curry recalled "the smothering fear" among whites and her own sense of isolation as a northerner working with the AFSC. Although MPE leaders introduced her as Winifred Falls's college roommate, at one meeting Curry had to hide in the closet because an attendee knew of her affiliation with the AFSC, an organization many segregationists labeled as leftist and accused of stirring up trouble. The MPE could not risk the success of its project to keep schools open or Curry's safety by having her identity exposed.[104]

MPE had a two-pronged approach: convincing whites to fight to keep public schools open, and encouraging blacks to register their first-grade children. It ran display advertisements in daily newspapers stating that its purpose was "to insure that the public schools of our communities and the state [were] not penalized or disrupted in any way."[105] MPE contended that children should be able to go to school in a peaceful environment, and that the peaceful environment was threatened by the newspapers' plans to publish the names of black families whose children registered to attend white schools.[106]

MPE faced many obstacles in convincing whites to fight to keep public schools open and to peacefully accept enrollment of black children in all-white schools, including the Citizens' Council's "Dial for Truth" campaign. Team members reported that after dialing 948-5511, the caller received a message stating, "This group [MPE] should be Mississippians for Integration, reflecting their real purpose. They pretend to be concerned about the quality of education, but they *know* that Mississippi spares no expense in the education of our children, that the state pays equally for each child. Can you put a price tag on our children? Everyone knows that under an integrated system, standards and discipline deteriorate. . . . Integrated education has had tragic results everywhere it has been tried."[107]

White ignorance created another obstacle. Patt Derian explained that poor white mothers often said that they did not mind sending their children to an integrated school, but that their husbands refused to allow it because the children would catch diseases from sharing toilet seats with black students.[108] This reflected the rhetoric of racist groups that warned of "mongrelization" of the races and of children contracting venereal diseases from the inevitable miscegenation that would result from blacks and whites interacting socially at school.[109]

Another facet of the debate centered on the state government's paying for white students to attend private schools. Although many segregationists found this idea appealing, it was not financially feasible, with MPE estimates exceeding $50 million per year if only half of the eligible students enrolled.

Other states that tried this found white children in inferior facilities with inexperienced teachers, poor discipline, and an absence of activities such as athletics. Was it worth jeopardizing a child's education to avoid having a few black students in the same classroom? Ann Hewitt found this predicament over parochial schools amusing as she imagined the Baptists "being faced with the agonizing decision of having to choose between sending their children to school with Negroes or Catholics," and choosing "Negroes as the lesser of two evils."[110]

To enlist the help of the black community, Winifred Falls explained at a meeting attended by Team 5 that MPE sought volunteers to canvass the homes of children entering first grade and to urge their parents to take advantage of open enrollment. Despite MPE's encouragement, black parents had reservations about their children's safety. When the meeting's leaders called for a show of hands of those with first graders, only one or two hands went up, even though many more had children in that age group.[111]

An MPE mass meeting attended by Team 7 demonstrated the conflicting emotions involved in deciding whether or not to integrate Jackson schools. John Pratt of the NCC's Commission on Religion and Race challenged the audience by asking them, "What right have you to *not* send your children to an all-white school when your people *and* my people . . . have been working and dying to bring this about?" Nevertheless, team member Priscilla Hunt felt it was "almost too much to ask" of people to take taxis to the school and register their children, and then to send the children—first graders—into a potentially hostile environment. It reminded her of Norman Rockwell's 1963 painting, "The Problem We All Live With," which showed a young black girl being escorted to school by federal marshals. "Oh my God, if I was that mother," Hunt exclaimed, empathizing with the conflict black parents felt.[112]

Demonstrating the lack of overt white support for integrated schools, Jane Schutt addressed the group, saying that she regretted she did not come as an official representative of any white group. In a quiet tone, she encouraged the audience not to fear acting and talked about how her faith gave her strength—much like Fannie Lou Hamer. Olive Noble said they could have heard a pin drop when Schutt told the crowd that she was not afraid to walk any street in Jackson, because she never walked alone; she walked with Christ. She received a "tremendous ovation."[113]

A month after school started, Eleanor Fontaine wrote to Henrietta Moore that the school desegregation had gone off better than expected. Fontaine estimated thirty-nine out of approximately 1,300 black children old enough to attend first grade had enrolled in Jackson—illustrating what small steps constituted progress in the eyes of Mississippi white women. Two sub-par private schools opened with approximately 200 white students, while a school run by the Citizens' Council never opened because it did not get enough students to make it economically feasible.[114]

Doris Wilson had explained to the WIMS team that MPE benefitted both whites and blacks—a point lost on the majority of white Mississippians, and one with which Height agreed. Both sides suffered under the existing system, which outwardly discriminated against blacks, but also handicapped the white community by keeping it isolated from the rest of society. MPE was not one race doing something for another; this was both groups doing something to the benefit of all.[115] Although the WIMS teams could not, nor did they attempt to, resolve the conflicts over public education during their visits, the women learned from what they observed and applied what they learned in their work for education programs in their own communities.

The WIMS team members also acted as observers when they attended the hearings of the Mississippi State Advisory Committee in July, and the U. S. Commission on Civil Rights in August. Weakened by compromises in Congress, the Civil Rights Act of 1957, enacted on September 9, did little to protect the rights of African Americans; however, under the auspices of the act, the federal government established the U.S. Commission on Civil Rights within the Department of Justice to explore these deficiencies. Individual states created committees, which held hearings on violations and reported back to the national organization.

At the hearings, tales of abuse perpetrated by civilians and law enforcement officers against blacks, most of whom were attempting to register to vote, shocked the northern women. Police arrested and beat people for taking part in demonstrations or civil rights meetings, including one woman who was jailed fifty-five times. A thirteen-year-old girl was beaten and held for five days before her parents knew she had been arrested. Blacks reported harassment that included whites' levying excessive fines, putting sand in gas tanks, stopping suppliers from delivering to stores, doubling rent or evicting tenants with one day's notice, firing employees, shooting livestock, and beating blacks who stepped out of their "place."[116] Some blacks were abused for simply asking their due, like a woman who insisted on getting her change when she purchased a bus ticket, and the clerk beat her on the head and hands with a lead pipe. This proved too much for Team 4 member Maxine Nathanson, board member of the NCJW, who had to leave the hearing because the testimony made her physically ill.[117]

During Kennedy's administration, the Mississippi State Advisory Committee, headed by Schutt at the time, asked the U.S. Commission on Civil Rights to hold public federal hearings in Mississippi. After repeatedly denying the request, the commission agreed to conduct a hearing in Jackson in mid-August 1964. In addition to testimony from individuals who had suffered abuse, the commission sought reports from the organizations taking part in Freedom Summer, including WIMS.[118]

Clarie Collins Harvey, who joined the Mississippi committee in early 1964, explained that the federal hearings caused many people, particularly southern whites and northerners of both races, to realize that the accusations of abusive treatment they had heard were not "just fabrications of the imagination of a deprived people." The general public could watch on television and hear a black man from Natchez, Mississippi, for example, tell the commission how, even though he was not in the movement, he was stripped of his clothes, flogged and beaten, had castor oil poured down his throat, and was shot at as he ran—all "just because he was colored" and many thought his blackness meant he was "contaminated," and might endanger society. Viewers saw that the man told "the stark truth," and they began to question whether what they had been told and believed about life in Mississippi was correct.[119]

Cowan testified on behalf of WIMS and the NCNW, stressing their role as women seeking to improve conditions for young people. "We are not just northerners visiting the South; we are parents, who must act upon our concern—now intensified by our own direct confrontation—that children everywhere in the United States must be able to grow up, to acquire education, and to build their lives without living constantly in the presence of fear."[120] The statement brought to bear the concerns of women and mothers in the broadest progressive traditions that crossed region, race, religion, age, and even time. Cowan framed their purpose for coming to Mississippi as an effort to make a better world for children—and this was indeed one of their purposes. The ultimate objective, however, involved a broader scale than the seemingly innocent image the WIMS teams projected.

As the Wednesdays women observed the various activities taking place as part of Freedom Summer, they expanded their knowledge of the civil rights struggle in preparation for their meetings with the southern women. But the impact of their experience went far beyond visiting schools, sitting in meetings, or attending rallies. The conditions the WIMS teams observed as they ventured out of Jackson comprised the second element of their fact-finding mission, and offer insight into their emotional responses to the trips and the passion they conveyed as they met with local women.

"If anyone wanted to stop us, they wouldn't have any trouble because there's no place for you to go. They just pull up beside you and cut in front of you," recalled Flaxie Pinkett, a member of Team 3 who owned a real estate company in Washington, D.C.[121] In 1964, Mississippi had only a few miles of divided highways, and with the exception of a short segment outside Jackson, the teams traveled on two-lane roads with narrow or no shoulders. Service stations and restaurants only sparsely dotted the countryside. Of the towns WIMS visited, Canton and Vicksburg were the closest to Jackson, thirty and forty miles away respectively. Hattiesburg and Meridian were each approximately eighty-mile drives. Ruleville lay just over a hundred miles to the northwest in the Mississippi Delta. Josie Johnson of Team 4 recalled her surprise at seeing the green landscape on the road to Vicksburg, because she thought of people being lynched and abused in Mississippi rather than the state being "God's earth." Driving through the swampy areas, however, she could not help wondering if Schwerner, Chaney, and Goodman had met their demise in similar surroundings. Adding to the disquiet, Geraldine Kohlenberg pointed out it was a "different era" and "not exactly easy to get help if you wanted it."[122] Plus, they had no guarantee that any "help" that did arrive would be on their side.

Going back and forth between the white and black communities on several occasions gave Kohlenberg the sensation of a "palpable wall down the middle of society," putting the WIMS women in the "eerie position" of crossing that wall multiple times in the course of a day. Many team members, black and white, felt safer in the black community than they did in the white. The "otherness of Mississippi was just stunning," Kohlenberg remarked, especially for the team members who had little previous experience with the southern way of life, values, or points of view.[123]

Events surrounding the teams' travel around Mississippi, their treatment in hotels and restaurants, and their encounters with law enforcement, segregationists, and integrationists all said something about the state of life there—good and bad. Just as with the Freedom Summer projects, white people in Jackson often lacked an accurate picture of how others, from black Mississippians to northern visitors, were treated in their state. The teams' firsthand experiences gave the Wednesdays women a diplomatic way to initiate those conversations.

It took courage for these women to step onto a plane in the North and Midwest and get off in Jackson. Yet, despite their resolve about taking part, their sense of doing the right thing, and the precautions in place, the emotions the WIMS women felt did not always mirror their expectations. Batson wrote that when her flight stopped in Birmingham, "I stare[d] out the window trying to see something different or strange that [would] identify this as the city where dogs were unleashed on American citizens, where fire hoses sent Negroes sprawling to the ground. I [tried] to *see* the bigotry and hatred, but I [saw] nothing but an airport, with ordinary people, some traveling, some working."[124]

Arriving at the airport had its own set of anxieties. Staffers Wilson, Goodwillie, and Vivell waited, not speaking to each other, to take the women to their destinations. One white team member remembered mentally questioning whether police officers in the air terminal had come to make note of civil rights sympathizers.[125] Kohlenberg felt like she was unwelcome in a hostile country. "I certainly didn't feel that I was about to be attacked, or that someone was going to throw a bomb, but I felt a great deal of tension; and it also felt like a very foreign place."[126] When the hostess for Team 4's African American members ran a few moments late picking them up, it fanned the fears of Josie Johnson, who had anticipated the KKK's being at the airport when she and teammate Mary Kyle arrived.[127]

The teams drove through the streets commenting on the number of churches and nicely landscaped homes where black and white families lived in close proximity to each other. They saw blocks of black homes with blocks of white homes perpendicular to them in a kind of checkerboard pattern, unlike the segregated neighborhoods in the North. Driving past Medgar Evers's house, one woman commented that it was like seeing a shrine.[128]

The white women received chilly receptions from the white staff at hotel front desks, but more welcoming overtures from the black bell staff. Randers-Pehrson described the Sun-n-Sand Motor Hotel's desk staff as "unsmiling and steely-eyed," with one person clearly saying "damned civil rights."[129] Some team members felt a sense of "paranoia," and Kohlenberg remembered Alice Ryerson being afraid, after seeing the desk clerks' unfriendly reception, that the staff would not forward calls she received from her daughter working with COFO.[130] Hotel staff remained hostile throughout the summer, even as the women departed. Team 5 member Marjorie Dammann, president of Jewish Family Service of New York, thought she heard the cashier saying "get out" under her breath because the clerk did nothing to hide her hostility at check-out.[131] It is unclear whether this behavior reflected the hotel staff's suspicions of everyone traveling to Jackson that summer, or whether they recognized the women's northern accents or registration addresses.

In contrast to the white desk staff, one black bellman seemed to be an ally, pointedly telling Team 2, "If there's anything you need, ask for Dale."

Kohlenberg said it gave them a reassuring feeling of having an underground network protecting them, but was also unsettling, as if they were spies infiltrating another country.[132] Interactions with black hotel employees had to be tempered with wisdom, however. At an NAACP rally, Peggy Roach held hands with a young black man next to her while the group sang freedom songs. The next day, she recognized him working at the hotel, but he refused to make eye contact. She realized that any friendliness toward him might jeopardize his job—or worse, his safety—for having inappropriate contact with a white woman.[133]

The white women who came with Team 6 and Team 7 stayed in white homes and, as a result, did not encounter the same negativity as the women staying at hotels. Priscilla Hunt pointed out that no one ever asked her what she was doing in Mississippi or treated her badly.[134] In this way, homestays provided a more intimate relationship with host families while insulating the team members, to a certain extent, from the animosity of those opposed to civil rights.

Even though the black team members stayed in private homes where they were welcome, they had anxious moments. Ruth Batson's hostess, Doris Green, left her in the house alone for an hour on Wednesday night. Batson heard a car race by several times and became terrified, crying like a child. Because a racing car could signal danger in Mississippi, she eventually stood in the hallway as the car went by three more times before she finally returned to bed. The clock read 5:00 a.m. before she fell asleep, long after her hostess returned.[135]

The Wednesdays women came with expectations of what they would see in Mississippi that did not necessarily match the reality. Had they gone to meet with local women carrying only their northern ideas and not their observations, it is highly unlikely that their meetings would have been productive. Likewise, the apprehension they felt enabled some of the team members to identify more readily with the reluctance of women of both races to work for change.

In advance of the trips and during the summer, the organizers and staff took many precautions to ensure the teams' safety, but not everything went as planned. Although no one was ever injured, the women certainly experienced fearful moments and a few close calls that began with the first team's visit.

On July 2, 1964, less than a week before Team 1 arrived, President Johnson signed the Civil Rights Act of 1964 into effect, making businesses in Jackson prime targets for testing the new law. On July 6, twelve black men from state, regional, and national NAACP offices checked in at the King Edward Hotel, Hotel Heidelberg, and Sun-n-Sand Motor Hotel—the latter two of which housed WIMS teams. The city provided police escorts to those going to the Heidelberg, and plain-clothes city detectives observed all three properties. A *New York Times* article reported that C. A. Tibbets, manager of the chain operating the Sun-n-Sand, stated, "We're just going to abide by the law."[136] The nearby Robert E. Lee Hotel shut its doors rather than integrate, even though municipal facilities integrated without incident and with apparent consent from the city government.[137]

On Tuesday night, July 7, when the cameras had stopped rolling and reporters had dispersed, it was a different story. Because Height had attended a YWCA meeting and missed dinner, Harvey suggested that she, Height, and Logan have dinner at the Sun-n-Sand because they were "receiving people." After they sat down, a manager asked if they were from Jackson. When Harvey said yes, he replied, then, the women should know better than to come in the restaurant. The server made it known that the three women were unwelcome, throwing down the bread basket and silverware. The trio became nervous and called Wilson to inform her of their whereabouts. As they prepared to leave, the black kitchen and bus staff formed a protective line to ensure their safety as they walked to the car. Later, at the team debriefing, Height reminded the attendees that the visions seen on television and the reports published in the *New York Times* about blacks integrating Jackson hotels on July 6 covered a "kind of dress rehearsal to make sure that all the proper people [had] all the proper treatment" so that the "proper reports" could be filed showing compliance with the law. However, the manager had made "his true feelings" known when he asked the three women, "Where did you get the nerve to come in here?" That experience more accurately reflected the reality for Mississippians who attempted to integrate certain business establishments.[138]

On returning to New York, Cowan, also a member of Team 1, wrote to the Jackson staff, addressing Wilson's fears that the black women could have been injured at the Sun-n-Sand, and that if that had happened, all subsequent trips would have been canceled. Citing her experience in Selma, where she had spoken at Jim Forman's insistence, Cowan cautioned the staff not to get "pushed" into activities that did not suit WIMS's purpose. Wilson had a "special responsibility," because "most of the pushing" would be aimed at the black women.[139] Cowan followed up with a memo to all teams stating that even though the newspapers reported good treatment of blacks integrating businesses, the women should never travel alone and must keep in touch with the staff.[140]

In August, Cowan wrote to Wilson that it was too early to lodge black team members at previously all-white hotels because doing so would generate the "wrong kind of publicity" and give the impression that WIMS's purpose was to "demonstrate and integrate instead of to support and report."[141] Contrary to her own advice, two weeks later and one week before the last team trip, Cowan, Height, and Smith traveled to Jackson to testify at the U.S. Commission on Civil Rights' hearings and stayed together at the Sun-n-Sand. A group of teens began harassing them, knocking on the door, chanting, and throwing beer cans. When Cowan's son Paul, a COFO volunteer, arrived, he saw that newspapers had been placed in front of the hotel room door, and he felt certain someone planned to set the papers on fire. The women packed their bags, paid their bill, and Paul drove them to the airport.[142] Evidently Cowan's first inclination—to wait to integrate hotels—had been wise.

Team 1 witnessed the potential for violence while visiting the Freedom School at Mt. Zion Baptist Church in Hattiesburg.[143] As Marian Logan stepped outside to call her husband, a car sped by, and someone threw an object out the window—a Molotov cocktail that "mercifully fizzled." Inside, one of the COFO volunteers walked over to the piano and played the "Hallelujah Chorus." Height recalled, "We joined him with our voices, clasping hands in a circle as each one sent up a private prayer of thanks that no one had been hurt. . . . We were a group of strangers united in a common crusade for which, each of us knew, all were prepared to die." Goodwillie remembered being afraid, but said, "this was nothing relative to what women, Mississippi women, had been through. . . . Imagine having to live your life like that."[144] A similar event occurred when the Vicksburg Freedom School was bombed the day after Team 4 departed from it. Just as the women had taken ownership of the community center in Meridian, Johnson said, "They bombed *our* school." The team felt guilty and speculated that it happened because of their visit.[145] Realistically, all the Freedom Summer projects risked being bombed at any time because they irritated racist extremists, whether a WIMS team had gone there or not.

Cowan later said that the WIMS organizers never emphasized to the teams "the kind of thing that might have caused hysteria." In fact, following her return from Mississippi, Cowan withheld information from Team 2 about the incidents experienced by Team 1. In a letter to the staff, she stated, "I did not tell them about the incidents at the Sun and Sand [sic] restaurant, or about the bombing event in Hattiesburg. Since neither had [ended in] disaster; why worry them?"[146] Although the teams had an awareness of the dangers and an effort was made to verse them in what to expect, by withholding the information from Team 2, Cowan was not as forthcoming as she implied earlier to them or their spouses who expressed concerns. Whether it would have made a difference in the individual team members' decision to participate, no one will ever know.

Withholding information did not typify Cowan's methods. On Team 3's return, she told the team members, "While we're responsible, we take [your safety]very seriously. Don't forget that the other trips have had some hazardous experiences." Speaking about the night they went to the King rally, she said, "I sat up until 3:00 [a.m.] in order to get in touch [with] Susie Goodwillie to be sure that you got back safely. I felt I could not rest." Yet, she informed them that they had no reason to be fearful when they went to Meridian, "because it was not dangerous. It was very carefully researched." She faulted herself for not making this clear to the team members before they left, given their concerns about Meridian's proximity to the location where the three civil rights workers had disappeared.[147] Cowan obviously felt conflicted on the issue of safety, and adapted her directions based on each team's feedback as the summer progressed.

Travel to and from the Freedom Summer projects presented its own set of challenges. The white staff generally used a different car from one team visit to the next. Hewitt occasionally loaned her car to Goodwillie and Vivell, and other times she arranged for rental cars. The driver Wilson hired to chauffeur the black women switched among the eighteen cars in his fleet (seven of which were of identical make and model) so that the same license plate numbers would not be recorded.[148] Even a well-respected Jackson native like Harvey used different cars, telling Ilza Williams, "We have to change because of the feeling of harassment."[149]

On multiple occasions, civilian and law enforcement vehicles followed the teams, all of which expressed a fear of law enforcement officials.[150] WIMS notified the president, the attorney general, the Department of Justice, and the governor of Mississippi of their intended plans by sending a list each week of the dates of the trip, the names of those traveling, their destinations, and where they would stay. When possible, the New York staff also included descriptions of the cars in which the women would travel.[151] These notices made it difficult for the teams and staff to know if officers followed them for their protection or harassment.

Several teams reported being followed by men with guns in pickup trucks. This occurred across the state and was a common means of intimidation against outsiders. Into the late twentieth century, the sight of a truck with a gun rack holding one or more rifles or shotguns was common in the South, particularly in rural areas. Blacks and outsiders like the northern team members, however, certainly saw this as a threat that was frightening in the climate of violence against civil rights activists—a fact that was not lost on those bent on intimidation.[152]

When the Wednesdays women could not determine if they were followed by friend or foe, the teams used their gender, age, and class to diffuse the situation. For example, Goodwillie and Vivell stopped to ask directions in Canton, where the team "picked up an escort"—a man in a straw hat, smoking a cigar, driving a broken-down pickup truck, who turned out to be the local deputy sheriff. Goodwillie described the nervousness of the team members and how they used their gentility to get the upper hand. "[We] did our best to comfort the ladies who all of a sudden started rambling on a bit less forcefully than they had earlier . . . 'of course I'm not nervous—he's still there?' and when we arrived . . . our rear escort pulled up ahead of us on the other side of the road so he could have a full front view. . . . The sheriff could hardly believe his eyes—we were somewhat analogous to the funny little car in the circus that pulls into the center of the ring and lets fifteen people out—we were only 7 out, we were hatted and gloved and proper Bostonians and when dear Sister Catherine stepped out into the morning sun, he almost dropped his cigar. Diane finished him off with a beaming smile and a ringing 'Good morning, Sir.' And he wandered off dazed and dumfounded."[153] Later, the man followed them as they left Canton. This reinforced the team's view of local whites as "hostiles" and the movement activists as their safety nets.[154]

African American team members were also followed. After departing from an NAACP rally, members of Team 3, traveling with branch YWCA director Lillie Belle Jones, noticed the police following them. Geraldine Woods was "delighted," thinking the officers had come to protect them—until Jones said, "Lock your doors." Flaxie Pinkett became nervous because she did not want to be stopped while in possession of the printed Freedom Summer material she had picked up earlier in the day. Eventually Jones did some maneuvering to lose the police. Team members speculated that when the officers saw Jones drop off one of the light-complexioned black women, they may have thought she was white and driven away.[155] As Team 4 met people in Vicksburg and Jackson, Josie Johnson realized that the terrible stories that she had heard about the dangers in Mississippi had proved true, and she concluded that, even as protected as her team was by the WIMS staff and the consideration given to their itinerary, in reality, they could become victims too.[156]

To identify outsiders, state law enforcement set "booby traps," such as stop signs turned the wrong direction—those who stopped must not belong, but those who did not stop were guilty of running stop signs; it was a no-win situation. Even knowing this, the WIMS staff occasionally stumbled. One evening while carrying a car full of women, Goodwillie was stopped by an officer as she turned the wrong way on a one-way street. As he reprimanded her, she said, "Something just clicked in my head. I said (in a southern accent), 'Officer, I'm just so sorry. Well, I didn't see that sign. You really ought to put better lights on those signs, officer.' This dripping magnolia stuff, and batted my eyelashes."[157] Of course, if he had known her true identity and why she was there, he most likely would have taken her, and possibly the team, to jail. At the least, she should have received a ticket, but instead got nothing. Goodwillie had learned enough about Mississippi law enforcement officers to use her gender, her race, and their own prejudices against them.

The debate over when and where it was acceptable for blacks and whites to travel in the same cars reemerged over the course of the summer, but tensions seemed to relax by mid-August. Black and white members of both Team 6 and Team 7 reported riding in cars together without fear.[158] Jackson women still exercised caution, however. Lucy Montgomery observed that when she and Jean Davis, both white, rode with Etta Moten Barnett and her hostess Thelma Sanders, both black, and two students, "One couldn't help but notice as you drew up to a red light and stopped that there was a great deal of notice taken, and it was also very obvious that our guides . . . were constantly on their guard, looking first one way and [then] the other."[159] Montgomery and Davis did not return home until almost midnight, and their hostess, Miriam Ezelle, greeted them at the door. She had become quite worried and planned to give them fifteen more minutes before she called the police. She told them, "If what I hear and read in the northern press is true, you could be in jail and I would never know!"[160] Montgomery and Davis felt bad for causing Ezelle concern, but the incident had illustrated the severe differences in one's ability to move around freely in the North versus South.

The rallies proved to be events where team members felt energized and, at the same time, nervous about their security because of the uncertainty involved—law enforcement officers might arrest them, racists might attack, and the sheer number of people in attendance made them unsafe. Beryl Morris, lieutenant at the Bedford Prison for Women in New York and member of

Team 2, had attended many NAACP meetings. In Jackson, though, she noticed the attendees dividing their attention between the rostrum and the back door, creating a "general atmosphere of people looking over their shoulder wondering what's going to happen." Morris added, "I felt the tension in the air," and she found it difficult to accept that feeling of unease, which differed dramatically from northern meetings.[161]

This discomfort was nothing compared to the tension during the July 23rd rally in Jackson with Martin Luther King Jr. and other key movement leaders on the dais. About 4,000 attended the event at the Masonic Temple. The only whites present were the WIMS team, forty COFO workers, and a few reporters. During Charles Evers's speech, "bedlam" broke out in the balcony in opposition to his remarks. At that moment, the doors slammed shut, which frightened Justine Randers-Pehrson. Even though it was a storm that had caused the doors to close, Harvey said to her, "There is something unhealthy here tonight. . . . Something is wrong, and I think we should leave at once." Recognizing safety in numbers, however, Harvey decided it was too dangerous at that moment for Randers-Pehrson, who was white, to leave with Harvey and her friend, both black; instead they decided to move to the back of the room and wait for the rally to end, when others would also be departing.[162]

The following week, Team 4's black members attended a voter registration rally at a black Baptist church in Jackson. Even though this meeting did not have the list of renowned speakers, a bomb threat prompted the black men to stand guard over those in attendance. Men carrying shotguns patrolled the perimeter of the church, and others guarded the front. Inside the WIMS women heard about the abuses faced by those trying to register to vote, but the realization that "a house of God would have to be protected like that" seemed to be as telling to the team members as the infringement on voting rights.[163]

Threats of violence and retaliation confirmed the need for the many precautions the WIMS organizers had taken. The teams came to Mississippi well prepared with knowledge about the South, their mission, the dangers, and how to conduct themselves, which Goodwillie believed was critical to their safety and success.[164]

As the summer progressed and the teams were debriefed, Cowan noticed that the later teams made observations about the Freedom Summer projects' impact on local people and about the roadblocks to communication in the communities they visited that earlier teams were unable to make; particularly Team 7, which had returned to Team 1's destination of Hattiesburg. Cowan believed that the variation stemmed in part from the later teams' not being burdened with the same fears as the earlier one, and that they experienced a greater openness because they stayed in private homes. She speculated on the reasons for this shift: the WIMS staff's increased experience in Mississippi, the added presence of FBI agents and news media investigating the three civil rights workers' murders, and WIMS's improved relationship with Department of Justice representatives fostered by Cowan's weekly reports to them. Goodwillie agreed that the staff was "savvier" and that white Mississippians had come to realize that "the state was not going to burn in flames and go to hell because of Freedom Summer." She added that the staff had built a rapport with more locals who had joined them in the cause, even if only discreetly. No doubt, all of these factors combined to ease the tensions with each successive team's travel.[165]

Goodwillie, Vivell, and Wilson faced the daunting tasks of making local contacts, finding suitable projects for the women to visit, arranging for the social gatherings, handling reservations and homestays, and escorting the teams while in Mississippi—all without meeting publicly (except with the teams at the Freedom Summer projects) or talking as frequently as they needed. They had a tremendous amount of ground to cover while avoiding the scrutiny of curious white southerners and Citizens' Council members, like the owners of the Magnolia Towers where the white staff lived. Goodwillie created an outlet for herself by keeping a diary on a roll of shelf paper fed through her portable typewriter. The staff functioned remarkably well, but understandably the stress got to them at times. Goodwillie wrote to a friend describing their "full and sad and wonderful days," which, she added, "Pick us up and knock us down every 24 hours and leave us breathless."[166]

The two white staffers respected Wilson and looked to her as their leader; but, at times, the three women clashed over when it would be safe to allow the teams to meet or travel interracially. Near the end of July, Goodwillie observed how hard the situation was for Wilson because the black team members had more limitations on what they could do. For example, they had no LWV or similar organization with which to meet. Wilson thought it was "unfair" to "her" women, and the white staff found this difficult to address. Two days later, Wilson and Vivell had a "head on collision" born of frustration more than personal differences. Wilson had concluded, that the white community could not be "saved" until it would meet with the black community. Vivell argued, and Goodwillie agreed, that WIMS had to take "baby steps" before taking any "giant step" that would offend the white community, and that WIMS could facilitate acceptance of an integrated society sooner by gently easing the transition. A budding lawyer, Vivell took a "very individual line of argument," and Wilson lost her temper. When Vivell stepped away, Goodwillie made peace between them by explaining that Vivell "felt just as trapped and frustrated by this ugly system" as Wilson, and that in reality, they were fighting the society, not each other.[167] Nevertheless, understanding the situation did not diminish Wilson's hurt feelings.[168]

Other times, the staff lifted each other up, and their shared secret helped them find the lighter side of life in their charade. Wilson and Goodwillie stood in the airport terminal acting like strangers and waiting for the members of Team 3 to deplane. They could see each other's reflections in the window as people began coming down the stairs and walking across the tarmac. "Then a lady with an unmistakable air got to the ground, stepped aside and waited for another lady of similar countenance," Goodwillie wrote that night. Wilson began to giggle. Goodwillie tried to ignore it, but it was "so wonderful and so silly" that she could not contain herself. As a man looked on disapprovingly, Goodwillie stepped aside as the "object of [their] amusement" approached the gate.[169] The white and black staff once again went their separate ways.

Goodwillie and Vivell found their own friendship tested to the limits during the summer. As college roommates, they had developed a strong bond, but they had never worked with one supervising the other. The NCNW employed Goodwillie, who took part in WIMS from its inception and ultimately had responsibility for the white visitors. Vivell joined WIMS as a volunteer, and she did not always feel fully qualified to take on the required tasks. This new dimension to their relationship, combined with Mississippi's oppressive atmosphere, boiled over at times. When they arrived, they found their apartment a "perfect haven" where they could be themselves with no false pretenses.[170] They balanced each other in their work. When Vivell could not make headway in convincing one of the local Jewish women to host Team 1, Goodwillie successfully made arrangements with the Catholic women.[171] At other times, their roles reversed. Some days they questioned if they made any headway. But on another day Goodwillie wrote, "There is joy and hope that come with the frustration and that sustains us—every now and then there is a glimmer of light, a chink in the wall and two spirits find each other, communicate, and begin to understand."[172] Multiple times, they worked through their differences, pledging to be more supportive of one another, and when the "venom" was out, returned to being "just plain old friends." When Goodwillie was asked how they accomplished that, she replied, "We learned to pray." They had to make it work, or the project would suffer.[173]

Ironically, the WIMS staff often kept abreast of incidents in Jackson from their northern contacts more than from local news. Goodwillie wrote in her diary on July 2, 1964, "We know (at least we think we know ... we are actually familiar with many fewer facts about what is happening than we ever were up yonder) that the many faceted strife of a difficult summer is teaming around us in the rest of the state, but we cannot feel it—it is like being in the eye of a hurricane."[174] The situation did not improve, and again, on August 16, she wrote, "Last night was pretty bad all over. ... 5 crosses were burned here and there were two shootings—and we first heard about it from Lou Cowan on Martha's Vineyard."[175]

Like others working in the civil rights movement, the staff coped with fear, although they tried not to focus on it. Mary Cushing Niles reported that Goodwillie and Vivell told her team, "When we first came, we decided that if we could remain free from fear, we could influence the system a little bit, but if we, too, became afraid [like Mississippians], we could accomplish nothing."[176] Wilson reflected that when one is in the midst of a situation, "you're about doing something."[177] The WIMS staff did not have time to be afraid. Plus, Goodwillie pointed out, the WIMS angels, black and white, set an example by "sticking their necks out, and being courageous." She added that she "psychically leaned" on the black women, who were role models with inspiring "soulful pragmatism."[178] If these women could live it day in day out, so could the staff.

Continually the teams praised all three staff members and their professionalism. Kohlenberg observed, "The staff in Jackson was marvelously well-organized—even when things (such as Mrs. Hewitt's car) broke down. We were not rushed—except emotionally! The three staff members were especially tactful in that although they supplied us freely with information, they did NOT, as would have been very easy, tell us what to notice, think, or observe."[179] Miriam Davis noted that Goodwillie and Vivell demonstrated an ability that "belied their years." When the women arrived in Jackson, the staff handed team members small brown envelopes with their itineraries, contacts' phone numbers, and other information they might need, their "security blankets" for the duration of their stay. "Our destination was Tougaloo College," Davis recalled. "I couldn't help being aware of Diane's frequent—almost continual—glances toward the road behind as she briefed us on the plans."[180] Similarly, Edith Savage of the Trenton, New Jersey, planning board offered praise for Wilson: "The warmth and reassurance given to us by Doris Wilson who served as our guide and source of information gave me a feeling of security."[181]

The emotions the team members felt ran the gamut. The debriefing tapes and oral histories conducted over the years reveal an intensity of emotion that cannot be conveyed in the written word. Comments from two team members, however, represent those expressed by many of the women. Reflecting on the overall experience, Kohlenberg recalled, "I have a visual memory of getting back from Canton and being exhausted but also tremendously hyper, sort of an altered state, partly fatigue and partly the intensity of the experience. . . . It's amazing to think how short the experience was because it felt like much longer—like a trip to the moon and back for instance."[182] At the debriefing for Team 1, Logan told those assembled, "I can't really tell you how I thought about Mississippi. Even now it's just much too complex. . . . It was one of the most rewarding experiences I've ever had. And sad, really sad, at times there were things [that] can just break your heart. It is just unbelievable."[183]

All of these experiences and events—whether at a Freedom School, a community center, a rally, a meeting, or just driving across the state—created a body of knowledge that team members would use in conversing with southern women about what they had seen when the two groups met for coffee. This direct knowledge was essential if the team members hoped to allay white southerners' fears about the COFO students, integration, and black voting rights. In this way, the Wednesdays women became the eyes and ears of the Mississippi white women who could not talk with civil rights activists or venture out to see for themselves what was happening at the Freedom Summer projects. Instead of reading accounts in newspapers owned by Citizens' Council members, Mississippi white women had a chance to hear about the projects face-to-face from respected women who had witnessed them personally. Middle-class Mississippi black women, who faced losing their place in the community for participating in the movement, benefited similarly from interacting with the team members.

As the teams visited projects or attended meetings, they projected an image of motherhood and stature, based on their gender, age, and class. They represented themselves as women who held concern for children in the highest regard and had come to learn about the South. This remained a key element of their strategy to set themselves apart from others working in the civil rights movement. They were "classy dames," and they intended to use that to their advantage.[184] WIMS counted on this to make a difference in the southern white women's perceptions about the team members, and in how Mississippians thought about civil rights. Would it work? The true test came when the teams met for coffee with groups of white women from Jackson.

CHAPTER FIVE

Meeting Woman-to-Woman

THE REAL WORK FOR CHANGE

*"Reflecting on it . . . we women had some power to make an impact.
Women in their subtle ways can change the world."*

—GERALDINE KOHLENBERG ZETZEL[1]

AT 10:00 A.M. ON A BEAUTIFUL SUNNY DAY, WEDNESDAYS IN MISSISSIPPI
team members mingled as guests arrived for coffee at the home of a prominent Jackson woman. The group was "white, all white." Nevertheless, one
woman walked in and immediately went around drawing the curtains on all
of the windows. Their surprised hostess asked, "Mary, what are you doing?"
She replied, "If anybody sees me here, if my husband sees me here, it'll be the
end of our marriage."[2]

The organizers and staff structured WIMS to conduct its real work for
change in the casual setting of similar coffees held in the homes of white
Jackson women. Although some local women remained wary, in this non-
threatening environment the white Wednesdays women could listen to the
Mississippians' perceptions of the civil rights movement and share what the
teams had seen during their trips. This kind of discussion opened lines of
communication across race and encouraged the southern white women to
take a more receptive attitude toward civil rights and interracial cooperation.
When asked in 1968 if WIMS operated on the theory that women, not men,
truly held the key to changing attitudes, Polly Cowan replied, "Absolutely. We
knew that the men would never move as fast as the women."[3]

WIMS exploited the team members' gender, age, and class to open doors
closed to more radical activists. This included creating the perception of doing women's work in the Progressive tradition, acting in ways appropriate for
mothers, and taking a quiet approach to activism. As the WIMS teams worked
to build bridges of understanding across race, region, and religion, they experienced both successes and setbacks. In the end, their non-confrontational

approach and their identities as respected women enabled the NCNW and WIMS to make inroads in the civil rights movement where other organizations and Freedom Summer activists could not.

To accomplish WIMS's goal of reporting what the teams had seen at the Freedom Projects and allaying Mississippians' fears about the civil rights movement, the staff first had to find Jackson women willing to meet with them—no easy task given that the southern white women expressed reluctance to meet the northern women, even in all-white groups. Dorothy Height believed each team should be made up of more white than black women to break down those barriers. She explained, "Black people were born into segregation . . . and a northern black person going into the South immediately was a part of the community. If white women went in larger numbers, they could be paired, they could help each other."[4] Because segregationist southern white women were, it was hoped, being persuaded to change their positions on civil rights, and because moderate southern whites often found themselves isolated, the white team members bore the greater burden in tearing down the barriers to interracial communication. Doris Wilson concurred, saying that she had the warmth of the community, but Susan Goodwillie, as an outsider, struggled to get white Mississippi women to have coffee with the white team members. Goodwillie attributed this to Mississippi's being "in a state of paralysis . . . [where] anybody from outside was feared."[5]

Goodwillie and Diane Vivell worked long hours daily to "make contacts and to nurture relationships" in order to find white hostesses for the coffees.[6] Before the first team arrived, Vivell contacted Lillian Burnstein, a leader in Jackson's Jewish community, to ask her to host a coffee. In "sharp tones," Burnstein said she had told Cowan that she thought the women coming down would cause trouble. Taken aback at this "first run-in with a scared moderate," Vivell collapsed, reluctant to make another call. Using a different approach, Goodwillie called Barbara Brinson of the local Catholic women's council, who was delighted to meet with the team at the staff's apartment and promised to bring Mrs. T. P. Cote, also a leader in the Catholic community.[7] Burnstein later accepted an invitation to attend.

Amidst the climate of fear toward outsiders, hostesses felt compelled to keep up appearances of propriety. Elaine Crystal, who hosted a team in 1965, explained, "There was a generalized fear by white women in Jackson of doing anything that was out of the ordinary, about hosting anyone that was from the North; that may not be socially acceptable or would not be part of their ordinary lifestyle."[8] Ann Hewitt explained to Goodwillie and Vivell that some moderates would be willing to entertain them if the staff dropped in with

Hewitt, for example, but they could not invite the staff to their homes—that was too "risky."[9] Patt Derian speculated that because the hostesses were true southerners, "a lot of scrubbing, painting, and cooking" went on to make a good impression. Derian added that at the last minute, the southern hostesses probably had second thoughts; but once they realized the visitors were friendly and of the same age and class, they engaged in conversation.[10] Wilson found it easier to schedule visits with local black women, although initially she had difficulties arranging for the homestays.[11]

Most significantly, Jackson white women did come to the coffees to meet the northern women. The Mississippians attended for a variety of reasons— because of curiosity or a desire to learn, because they agreed with the visitors, or because they disagreed. Why they came did not matter as much as getting them in the door, however; without that, the Wednesdays women had no hope of persuading anyone to open their hearts and their minds.

When white women agreed to meet with the WIMS teams, it was often a clandestine affair. Laya Weisner explained how Jackson women hosted a coffee for Team 2 under the pretense of an LWV meeting to avoid raising suspicions—one woman arranged for the meeting, a second telephoned the others to come, and a third woman offered her home for the gathering. Approximately a dozen women attended to talk with the northern women about their impressions of the COFO students and the summer projects. Geraldine Kohlenberg was "impressed really by how brave they were to come at all" since they certainly were not obligated to make that effort.[12] Cowan estimated at the Team 5 debriefing that like the woman who drew the drapes lest her husband discover she had attended the coffee, 150 women had expressed similar sentiments about their husbands' reactions.[13] For some of the wives the teams met, the husbands' threats of divorce appeared to reflect the husbands' racist attitudes; but for others, it had more to do with the fear of economic reprisals if the wives engaged in civil rights activities.

Throughout the summer, several themes repeatedly arose in the conversations with southern women. Some of the prominent concerns included who had the right to speak for Mississippians, what kind of parents let their children take part in Freedom Summer, criticisms of the COFO volunteers, the North's causing the South's problems, and the three missing civil rights workers. Both northern and southern women had to overcome certain preconceived notions to make headway. Regardless of the direction the conversations took, the WIMS teams listened and worked, with the help of their hostesses, to encourage the white women to view civil rights and the movement in new ways.

The teams quickly learned that the definitions of "liberal," "moderate," and "conservative" differed significantly in Mississippi from how the terms were used in the North. As communism increasingly became associated with civil rights, so did the term "liberal," which was derogatory.[14] Moderates were those who rejected elements of Jim Crow and accepted the Civil Rights Act of 1964 as the law of the land.[15] Josie Johnson reported how a woman Team 4 met at Tougaloo College explained it: "The definition of a conservative and a moderate is that the former still believes in separate and unequal, whereas the latter is beginning to think of separate but maybe equal." Johnson added the team also learned that "the general impression" was that blacks were not human."[16] Many black Mississippians found that the wheels of change barely moved and that many segregationists refused to acknowledge their citizenship rights or their capabilities.

Moderates did not necessarily recognize any culpability on the part of Mississippi's state government or its people for the violence that occurred there. A woman who met with Team 5 was labeled a moderate because she deplored the violence and acknowledged that black churches had been burned and some blacks had been killed. She would not go further, however. When a team member asked her who committed those acts of violence, the woman replied, "Well, who does these things in the North?" Of course, "criminals" do these things, she explained; but she would not admit the events were anything more than the work of "errant hoodlums."[17]

Another definition called into question was who qualified as a Mississippian. For example, one woman who had lived in Jackson all of her married life and had college-age children was not considered a Mississippian, and her opinions were not welcome.[18] Even natives were quickly disowned if they sympathized with blacks. A woman who attended the coffee with Team 6 was the wife of a retired Methodist minister and the former president of the state PTA, but when her son, a minister at Capitol Street Methodist Church, took an unpopular stand on civil rights, the church forced him to leave despite the family's long-standing ties to Jackson and Mississippi.[19] Olive Noble stayed with Ann and Sam Ashmore, the latter of whom was the editor of the *Mississippi Methodist Advocate,* during her visit with Team 7 and reported that even though the couple were native Mississippians whose ancestors had been early settlers and whose family had supplied the state with ministers for generations, they were constantly harassed, received obscene phone calls and threatening letters, and had their lives threatened. In addition to their stand on civil rights, their support of the NCC and the AAUW, both labeled communist organizations by racists, added to the controversy surrounding them.[20]

Newcomers experienced greater difficulties. A minister's wife who had lived in Jackson just a short time told Marjorie Dammann that her fifteen-year-old son had been "roughed up" by the police when he came out of a store. She too had frequently been followed by police, and she suspected the out-of-state license plates on her family's car made them suspect.[21]

Moderates and liberals found themselves isolated in the morass of mis-trust and hate. Following her visit to Mississippi, Henrietta Moore received a letter from her hostess Eleanor Fontaine, who said the Jackson hostesses discovered that those of them who had invited their "rather rabid friends" to meet the WIMS teams found that the "native white supremacists made them-selves rather obnoxious." Fontaine hoped that the experience would help the northern women understand the "problems of lonely moderates in the midst of seas of not-so-moderates."[22] Fontaine added that her family had enjoyed having Moore stay with them and that it had restored her sanity, explain-ing, "It is sometimes a very disturbing thing to live in Mississippi where all one's lifelong values seem to be held in no regard by the populace at large."[23] In this way, affirming the work of "lonely moderates" and opening dialogue with white supremacists, WIMS accomplished its primary goal of facilitating communication.

Segregationist white Jackson women could not comprehend why northern parents condoned their children's taking part in Freedom Summer and stay-ing with black families. The women questioned Team 2 about what kind of mother allowed such things, and Alice Ryerson replied that she was proud of her daughter for volunteering. The Jackson women were "shocked to the core" to discover that not only did she let her child take part, but her child was a *girl!*[24] They found it an "appalling idea that a girl was doing this and even more so . . . that she was living in a black family." This confirmed everything the Jackson women had heard about the volunteers and race mixing. On the positive side, however, it opened doors to a new conversation.[25]

Although they balked at Freedom Summer, a few Jackson women revealed that they had worked behind the scenes to keep the public schools open un-der the state desegregation order, they remained LWV members despite in-timidation, and they defended the two-party system in Mississippi, which was tantamount to advocating an overthrow of the government.[26] Such revela-tions indicate that even those who did not agree with COFO's methods might see the value in making changes to guard education and political freedoms.

Miriam Ezelle invited sixteen women to meet with Team 6, and thirteen women came. Team member Lucy Montgomery recalled that the team's "diplomacy was really put to the test" over the two and half hours of the gathering.[27] The group of Jackson women included the wife of a doctor, the wife of a retired minister, the president of the Galloway Memorial Methodist Church Women's Society, members of the Methodist WSCS, and a member of the national Girl Scouts board who was also the wife and sister-in-law of the Hederman brothers, owners of the *Clarion-Ledger, Jackson Daily News,* and local radio and television stations.[28] Ezelle announced to the gathering that she had taken an interest in civil rights and had been entertaining COFO volunteers and their mothers—news that shocked her daughter and friends in attendance.[29]

One of the adversaries confronted Jean Davis, president of a Chicago-area Girl Scout council, about why she had come to Mississippi. Davis explained that her daughter had volunteered with COFO and that even though Davis had qualms about her daughter's participation in Freedom Summer, "if she is involved, then I am involved." By coming to Mississippi, Davis could see for herself what was happening. She later said, "It became abundantly clear that there [was] a good deal of difference in the way people in the North and the people in the South raise[d] their children. . . . They really and truly couldn't understand how we as mothers could possibly let our children come down." The team tried several different tacks, including a biblical reference that had no effect, but they could not persuade the women to change their point of view. In trying to reach some sort of understanding, Davis asked, "Is there something we can do?" At that point Ezelle's daughter looked her in the eye and said, "Yes, you can go home, and take your daughter with you." This exchange reflected both the intensity of the feelings involved and the fact that northerners and southerners came to the problem from completely different perspectives based on attitudes that went beyond desegregation alone to include basic family values.[30]

The greatest hostility directed at the civil rights movement generally and the WIMS teams specifically occurred during this coffee. Henrietta Moore recalled that the Jackson women "had that cold angry look in their eyes that you read about."[31] Jean Davis explained that the women were on the defensive about Mississippi's reputation. They felt that the state was unfairly maligned in the press, and that people should come down to see for themselves. When Davis said that was exactly why she had come down to see her daughter, they immediately contradicted their position and dismissed her actions as inappropriate.[32] The southern women held firm to several contentions with which the northern women disagreed. Moore wrote, "They told us flatly that all Negroes are immoral, all have venereal diseases, and all were getting along just fine, being happily taken good care of by people like themselves [the Jackson women], until we northerners interfered. They knew the civil rights movement was communist led. Possibly the volunteer students and ourselves [mothers of COFO workers] . . . weren't actual communists, but we were definitely dupes."[33]

The Team 6 members found that the arguments of the Jackson women defied logic. They stated that blacks did not want integration, which northerners forced upon them, and then claimed that blacks' real goal was to socialize with and marry whites.[34] When they asked Miriam Davis how she would feel if her seven-year-old daughter grew up and married an African American, Davis replied that as long as they were compatible, the genetics would not concern her. She worried instead about "the hatred they would see in the eyes of those whom they met; the hatred they would feel everywhere, and the hatred which would be heaped upon their children."[35]

The debate over voting rights presented one of the most difficult southern positions for the northern women to understand. To the team, it seemed obvious that every individual should have the right to vote. The Jackson white women at the coffee thought that the majority of blacks lacked the proper education from which to make sound decisions. They did not want people voting who did not understand the Constitution, lacked basic reading skills, and could "barely make an 'x.'" They found no inconsistency in the fact that the State of Mississippi's education system ensured the poor literacy rates among blacks that were then used to deny them voting rights.[36]

The southern women also took issue with Jean Davis's plans to visit her daughter, telling her, "No self-respecting white southern women would do what you are going to do when you visit your daughter in Ruleville—we consider it downright immoral and we'll never do it."[37] As the women departed from the coffee, however, Miriam Davis observed that not one of them failed to express surprise that the COFO volunteers' mothers—Jean Davis and Henrietta Moore—looked so respectable, because, on the outside, no difference could be found between them and the Jackson women.[38]

The vast majority of Mississippians, including most women who met with the WIMS teams, belonged to churches and identified as devout Christians. Several of the white Mississippi women meeting Team 6 followed the thinking of their church boards, and in some cases their ministers, in supporting the exclusion of blacks from worship services. These included members of the Galloway Memorial Methodist Church WSCS, which created the first open break at the Jackson church by forming its own women's auxiliary independent of the national WSCS.[39] The society's "Information Bulletin 1" indicated that the new organization subscribed to "goals, ideals, and purposes" that would maintain the segregated southern way of life. Further, the auxiliary objected to the NCC's racial propaganda, its role in Freedom Summer, and its goal of "one worldism."[40]

Despite the local women's criticism, Jean and Miriam Davis visited Jean's daughter at the conclusion of the WIMS trip. In Ruleville, they attended a "basket-dinner" at a church where Fannie Lou Hamer spoke with her signature blending of religion and civil rights. Miriam reflected on the complexities of understanding the southern white women they had met who belonged to the Methodist Church and the auxiliary. "As I participated I thought of those white ladies at the coffee the day before who likewise [were] convinced that their point of view can be defended Biblically. How interesting that these two conflicting beliefs should be resting in the same cloak of religion."[41] Miriam Davis's musing reflected the religious debate heard across the state as ministers spoke out for and against civil rights.

Miriam Ezelle's family provides insight into the dynamics of differing opinions held by Mississippians within a single family, and how attitudes evolved for some but not others. Robert L. Ezelle Jr., Miriam's son, was the only board member to oppose the 1961 Galloway Church resolution giving ushers authority to turn away black worshipers.[42] Tougaloo College chaplain Ed King said Robert risked his life trying to change white Mississippi because he was a Christian and an American who believed in democracy.[43] During the mid-1960s, Miriam made a steady progression in her own thoughts on civil rights. In 1963, she seemed to object to the movement when she told then Tougaloo College president A. Daniel Beittel that she could not associate with the Council on Human Rights because it ignored freedoms she held dear, such as the rights of young people to be free "from being excited emotionally to take part in something they do not understand; and the right of the business man to run his own business according to his own best judgment, and to employ those who will best promote that business. My sympathies are with Negro 'moderates' who are being drawn into this *disturbance*."[44] Beittel agreed with her call for Jackson's mayor to establish a biracial committee to address the city's racial problems, but criticized her description of certain white university leaders, including Ed King, as "hothead[s]" who exercised "unbalanced judgment" regarding the movement.[45] In the spring of 1964, however, Ezelle decided she had an obligation to learn more about the people coming to Mississippi that summer, and quietly, she began inviting people to her home—students, a rabbi, and Team 6. Ezelle told Jean Davis that following the death of her husband, she had prayed for guidance about what to do with herself, and this answer had presented itself.[46]

Miriam Ezelle demonstrated a willingness to move toward acceptance of civil rights by her work with WIMS, but she held onto many old ideas. In October 1964, she wrote to Jean Davis about her objections to uneducated black voters, adding that white women had only been voting for twenty-four years and were better qualified. She further stated, "Negroes have no more right to demand that I associate with them than I have to keep them from associating with you. Not that I object personally to either association." She followed that with, "You should see my new maid. Do come back to meet her. You will love her—31 years old, 6 children, always with a smile and a good cleaner!"[47] While Ezelle was beginning to think about the changing role of blacks in southern society, she still subscribed to a racial hierarchy.

By 1965, Ezelle's stance took a more conciliatory tone. In a letter to Touglaoo's first black president, George A. Owens, she wrote, "We owe it to each other and our country to try to understand the reasons for different points of view and to forgive each other's mistakes; to rethink our own attitudes and to build on those principles and practices on which we agree."[48] She added that everyone who tries his or her best is "entitled to respect and fair treatment from others regardless of color because God indicated no color line. His requirements of men were named as justice, mercy, and humility."[49] Unlike Ezelle's son, her daughter who confronted Team 6 vehemently opposed desegregation and the civil rights movement. Ezelle said that even though her daughter was almost fifty years old, she had yet to realize that "the world never stands still." Ezelle believed that the young and the old bore the burden of moving Mississippi forward.[50]

At every coffee, the COFO students who had come to Mississippi became a flashpoint between the local women and team members. When asked about the volunteers, the white Mississippi women had a "flood of answers" about what the students had said and done, accusing them of being dirty, shameless homosexuals, communists, and beatniks.[51] Marie Barksdale of Team 5 observed that the "beatnik types" seemed to be in Jackson while the "ordinary college types" were in the rural areas, possibly explaining why so many Jackson women took offense.[52] Mississippians accused the students of interracial dating and sleeping together. Laya Weisner observed that "the women who talked loudest and hardest against the way the kids looked had never laid eyes on a COFO student." One woman, subscribing to the stereotypes, expressed certainty that she had seen a COFO student because she saw "a girl with long hair walking with a boy in blue jeans."[53] Priscilla Hunt theorized that the Mississippians looked for any excuse to criticize the students, whose appearance provided a convenient rationale.[54]

Most of the Wednesday women felt that the students dressed appropriately for the conditions in which they worked and lived.[55] Team members paid particular attention because of the complaints, and reported that the students represented a "cross-section of American youth," who were "clean with brushed hair, and tucked in shirts or dresses."[56] When Team 5 heard accusations of a volunteer's smelling bad, Florynce Kennedy felt it was expected in the Mississippi heat, given that the volunteer in question worked in Ruleville's agricultural community, which lacked proper bathing facilities. Marjorie Dammann wondered how the young women managed to look clean and crisp in the Delta dust.[57] Realistically, the students could not be dressed up all the time because they worked in the fields and lived with families of limited means who lacked hot water and had limited laundry and bathing facilities.[58]

At an interracial gathering in a private home attended by all the members of Team 2, the southerners expressed strong feelings that if the students dressed better they would be "more acceptable to the white community." Ruth Batson became impatient with this "petty criticism" and pressed the southern women to admit that "even if these workers were dressed as if they came directly from the pages of *Vogue* or *Esquire*, the basic problem would still be faced."[59] The subject was dropped. Ryerson said, "It was only us unstylish northerners who didn't think it [the students' appearance] was important."[60]

A few team members had opposing feelings about the COFO volunteers' appearances causing negative reactions from Mississippians. Jean Benjamin pointed out that the majority of students looked like the "decent, educated kids that they [were]—but the exceptions that look[ed] so 'beat' [gave] a horrible reputation to them all."[61] Kohlenberg believed the Mississippi white women took offense because they found the students' appearance disrespectful to southern custom and behavior standards, and she wondered if some of the black women might have felt the same way. Nevertheless, she also contended that revolutionaries should not be asked or expected to please those they oppose.[62]

WIMS based its methods on the participants' dressing and acting as proper ladies so they would not offend the southern women they met, and to distance themselves from the stereotypical view of civil rights workers. Therefore, the reactions of the Mississippi women to the COFO volunteers' appearance should not have come as a surprise to the team members—it violated the southerners' sense of decency. Rather than behaving as middle- or upper-class students from good schools, which most of them were, they projected a negative image. The fact that the Jackson women met with the WIMS teams—something the southern women would not do with the students—indicates that following protocol by dressing in white gloves and dresses accomplished WIMS's goal of opening doors closed to other activists. The southern women acknowledged that the northern women's appearance represented values that they shared.

The WIMS teams heard a frequent refrain from the Mississippi women, which blamed the North for racial unrest in the South. At the coffee for Team 5, a woman confronted them almost immediately, saying that Mississippi would not have any problems if the people had not come down from the North.[63] She told them that they knew nothing of Mississippi's culture or history, and that Mississippians had endured one Reconstruction and had no intention of undergoing a second one.[64] The team found it difficult to be "gentle," because the woman practically called them "barbarians." The Jackson woman attempted to impress the team by telling them that the local white women had children with degrees from Princeton and Harvard, but when Trude Lash politely indicated that some of the COFO students did as well, the woman dismissed the volunteers as communist beatniks. With references to the Harlem riots as evidence of northern divisiveness, the Jackson woman argued that blacks had lost ground since the civil rights movement began. Another woman was "impressed" when she heard Lash's German accent—but "for all the wrong reasons," Lash added. The woman said the Germans "knew how to keep order" and that "not all people were equal."[65]

Having the advantage of attending prior coffees, Goodwillie was able to make additional observations about the Team 5 coffee. She related the story of two women, Pat Terry of the local LWV, and a woman Goodwillie called "blue dress" who complained about losing her freedoms under the Civil Rights Act. Terry silenced the room by asking blue dress if the black man who could not find food or water for his family while traveling through the South was free. Seemingly at a loss, blue dress replied that it was "a very complicated problem." What made the exchange significant was that just the week before, at the coffee for Team 4, Terry had asked Diane Vivell if Vivell really believed blacks had been discriminated against. Thanks to the conversation at the earlier coffee, she had given that inquiry a great deal of thought and come to question the injustices endured by blacks, and she was willing to express that to other Jackson white women.[66]

As the women at the coffee with Team 5 continued their conversations, the southern women's positions shifted multiple times from supporting WIMS to blaming the North for the invasion. Goodwillie observed the conversation was like the Mississippi River itself, slowly weaving back and forth on its course toward the Gulf. As the southern women departed, they were warm and gracious and said they had enjoyed the get-together. Not an "easy enjoyment," Goodwillie wrote, " . . . in many ways it was a good battle hard fought." Most importantly, both sides emerged respecting the other, which was the only way they could begin to move forward.[67]

Another point of contention centered on the three civil rights workers. The Mississippi women who met with the first four teams found it difficult to accept, or admit, that Mickey Schwerner, James Chaney, and Andrew Goodman had been murdered—not surprising since the state's Senator James Eastland (D-MS) had informed President Johnson that he thought that their disappearance had been a publicity stunt.[68] The women who met with Team 2 said about seventy-five percent of Mississippians thought the men were hiding, and others believed CORE and the SNCC conspired to have them killed so that the federal government would "take over" Mississippi.[69] Marie Barksdale's African American hostess said she thought that the civil rights workers' disappearance was a hoax because she had read that (and perhaps wanted to believe it was so).[70] White Mississippian Florence Mars recalled that in Philadelphia, Mississippi, near where the men disappeared, those who did not believe it was a hoax feared saying so because it aligned them with COFO.[71]

Team 5 was the first team to visit after the discovery of the men's bodies and to hear the reactions of locals and movement workers. The earliest news reports contained only the bare facts without any human angle or commentary.[72] One woman at the Team 5 coffee "quickly brushed aside" the reports by saying the three men had "provoked their fate." She added, "Negroes are equal in the eyes of the Lord, but they will have to prove this to *us*. If you leave us alone with them, we'll teach them citizenship." Two of the three civil rights workers who disappeared had been Jewish, which alarmed Mississippi Jews. Some tried to distance themselves, such as one fourth-generation Mississippian who said, "Sure, I felt sorry for those boys . . . but nobody asked them to come down here and meddle with our way of life."[73] Lash observed that the blacks whom Team 5 met were not surprised by the news, while the whites tried to dismiss it, still hoping that it was not true. "This self-deception, which almost makes well-born Mississippians the victims of the terrorists, is like a wall around every white Mississippian," she stated.[74] In contrast, Francis Haight reported that the people working in the movement seemed to feel a "sense of relief" that the truth was now confirmed. Denials no longer carried any weight.[75]

When the conversations at the coffees got heated, the angels or the hostesses often came to the rescue. Florence Gooch, a self-identified liberal, hosted a coffee for Team 5. She purposefully chose guests who represented an array of views, except the worst reactionaries, hoping the invitees would be intrigued by talking with the "community-minded women of the North." All but one of the women came from long-standing Mississippi families, and their husbands were community business leaders.[76] Gooch was surprised that those who opposed the civil rights movement attended. When one attendee brought up the northern students, whom she called "disgusting," Gooch stepped in tactfully but firmly, never once deviating from her convictions. She steered the conversation to the WIMS team, explaining who they were and allowing "the conversation to develop again." This gave the Wednesdays women time to pause and "handle the attack with quietness rather than anger."[77]

The southern women did not stand alone in a steadfast belief in their convictions; the northern women were equally convinced they were right. Convincing the southern women to change their opinions required the Wednesdays women to approach them in a collaborative rather than a sanctimonious manner. Cowan, who had met with Lillian Burstein multiple times in the early stages of WIMS's development, described Burnstein as having "a heart of gold and no courage."[78] While the comment is true in a sense, it also reflects certain expectations or prejudices the team members brought with them about the southerners, despite every effort at objectivity. The WIMS participants expected the worst; they mistrusted anyone in law enforcement, and in some cases they were judgmental of those who held segregationist views.[79] Although objective observation was their goal, the emotional nature of the civil rights struggle, and the fact that the WIMS women had definite opinions or they would not have volunteered in the first place, made it impossible to be completely objective. Therefore, they found it imperative to appropriately temper the expression of their feelings to prevent closing rather than opening lines of communication with the southern women.[80] For example, white women told several of the WIMS teams about the devotion of their domestic help, who happily accepted gifts of hand-me-down clothes. One white woman commented, "My maid admires me so much, she wants to do everything just the way I do it." Lucy Montgomery of Team 6 noted that it evidently never occurred to the woman that this was the maid's method of deferring to her employer—"to survive by pleasing"—but Montgomery did not say so at the time.[81]

At the coffee for Team 6 where the guests became so hostile, Montgomery had her patience pushed to the brink when guests Mrs. Hederman, Mrs.

Crouch, and Mrs. Green insisted that Medgar Evers's assassination had been arranged by his own brother, that the blacks were happy with their lives and did not want to register to vote, and that no violence had occurred in the South before COFO had arrived. Montgomery labeled the trio delusional and "schizoid," saying it was like dealing with "patients in a mental hospital" and as if she was their nurse. The women blamed everything on a communist plot rather than concede when Montgomery pointed out the lack of logic in their arguments. Many white Mississippians accepted the connection between communism and civil rights because it had been ingrained as truth by the Mississippi Sovereignty Commission and those in power from the early days of the Cold War. Further, news media in Jackson controlled by the Hederman family portrayed this as the true state of affairs. What appeared "delusional" to Montgomery, a woman with northern sensibilities and preconceptions, instead reflected dominant political attitudes and the reported version of facts to Jackson women. This stark discrepancy illustrates the political and cultural divide between white women of the North and South that WIMS sought to address.[82]

The WIMS women also had their eyes opened by the southern women. After Ilza Williams, a member of Team 2, saw how blacks were treated as less than human, she came to understand why they struggled in the North. While previously she had questioned why southern blacks could not succeed in the North when she had managed to do so, she found that seeing firsthand the conditions under which they lived in Mississippi made her "more aware and tolerant" as she worked with blacks in her own community.[83] Peggy Roach of Team 3 had worked in the North and Midwest to alleviate poverty and discrimination, but in Mississippi, she was amazed that "black people didn't count for anything." Mississippians spoke of "being good to our blacks," but they did not treat them with dignity.[84] Seeing this lack of respect and the paternalistic attitudes led many team members to reevaluate how problems of racial inequity and poverty should be addressed.

Despite participants' preconceived notions, all the WIMS debriefings reflect that black and white team members acknowledged the inherent difficulty of the situation facing sympathetic white southerners. Nevertheless, some of the southern women believed that the northern women expected too much of them. Jane Schutt explained that most people coming down from the North could not understand the strong feelings about integration because they had no real experience with it. The movement had challenged long-held attitudes, beliefs, and customs that, as Jason Sokol notes, "divorced [southerners] from the myths of old." Southerner Barbara Brinson felt that many northerners believed everyone in the South was "ignorant . . . and didn't wear shoes." Lillian Burnstein asserted that many northern women thought that they "beat up a Negro every day, just for kicks, or had chickens in [their] back yards."[85]

Some of the southern women either expected this attitude or sensed it from a few of the WIMS women. Elaine Crystal got the impression that the team member she hosted in 1965 felt that the sympathetic southerners were not doing enough to change conditions in the South. A native of Iowa who moved to Mississippi in 1949, Crystal understood the situation from the perspective of someone who had lived on both sides of the Mason-Dixon Line: the women who came down did not understand why the southern women were not marching, but the northern women failed to realize that many southern women were doing the best they could.[86]

By contrast, Dorothy Stewart, an African American woman who spent her career in the Jackson public schools, observed that though the northern women might have arrived with paternalistic attitudes, by the time they left, everyone stood on equal footing. The team reports and debriefings support Stewart's conclusion. The WIMS women did, at times, criticize the southern women for moving too slowly, but they also developed an appreciation for the difficulty of the southerners' circumstances by meeting them and listening to their stories.[87] Kohlenberg recalled that her idea of the South changed because she heard the opinions of the southern women and saw the sincerity with which they expressed their feelings. "These were not ordinary bigoted, stupid, uniformed people," she observed.[88] Goodwillie believed that even though northern and southern women had expectations of the other, their meetings "enhanced mutual respect on both sides."[89] That respect was a first step toward opening lines of communication.

In a 1968 interview, Polly Cowan said she had grown sick of the phrase "building a bridge," which was a "fresh term" when they first used it; but she lacked a better choice of words. It is still difficult to find one that more appropriately describes what the Wednesdays women did.[90] Just as Clarie Collins Harvey had observed in Atlanta, prior to these gatherings the local women had no opportunity to come together in a setting that enabled them to feel safe engaging in an open discussion on civil rights. WIMS had built that bridge.[91]

The Mississippi women—black and white, of all faiths and classes—who came to meet with the WIMS teams were all products of Mississippi's long-standing racial traditions, the fear that engulfed the state, and the lack of communication. Further, the positions of churches—particularly white churches—played a pivotal role in determining the reactions of the citizenry to civil rights by skewing biblical principles to fit the hierarchy desired by the Citizens' Council and other racist and segregationist leaders. This led to an ever-widening division between black and white Mississippians. The views of white Mississippi women spanned the continuum of thought on civil rights. Some local white women reinforced the existing Mississippi way of life by perpetuating discrimination in their churches and their communities. Other whites reflected it in condoning the denial of civil rights to blacks and acquiescing to the fear of associating with people of another race. A small minority rebelled against it, although often quietly and from behind the scenes. Without taking these social relationships into consideration, the WIMS teams could not hope to open lines of communication to bridge differences or change attitudes.

The black women were less divided. Most agreed that religious tenets held all people equal in God's eyes, but they did not always agree on the best way to make that equality a reality in their daily lives. Mary Kyle estimated that only ten percent of the black middle class committed itself to working for civil rights, because "they would immediately be out of a job, and perhaps out of a life."[92] Her hostess frankly said that she would not help the movement publicly and her way of making a contribution was opening her door to Kyle.[93] The small black middle class had worked hard to get educations, good jobs, nice homes, and comfortable salaries; to turn their backs on that was not easy.[94] Priscilla Hunt noted, "You can't go to meetings and so forth if your husband is going to get fired."[95] By contrast, Ilza Williams found that poorer individuals she met, like Canton activist Annie Devine for example, felt they had nothing to lose by taking part in the movement.[96] Regardless of their class, all the black women whom the teams met were pleased that the Wednesdays women had come.

Despite the occasional confrontation, the WIMS teams experienced a number of victories as well. Ironically, one of the earliest came at the home of Lillian Burnstein, despite her protests that the program would cause problems. Burnstein did not want to miss the chance to host NCJW president Pearl Willen, a member of Team 2, and invited twelve Jackson Jewish women to meet her. Even though these local women were not proponents of integration, Willen felt they recognized that their moral obligation as Jews included a commitment to it.[97] Willen made inroads with the southern women by speaking frankly of the North's problems. The women agreed that outside help was necessary to bring about change in Mississippi, and the meeting provided them an opportunity to discuss what they could do to aid the process.[98] After

Willen returned to the hotel, Goodwillie gathered that the meeting was "tight and tired and defensive." Goodwillie wrote that she wished the WIMS women had gotten their "main purpose—support and education—across to the Jewish women," adding, "Maybe they feel just as strongly about getting their fatigue across to us."[99]

The LWV coffee attended by the white members of Team 2 offered an example of how this kind of interaction opened the doors to understanding. Unlike the other teams, Team 2 attended a coffee on Tuesday night before the Wednesdays women visited the Freedom Summer projects. Ryerson reported that initially the southern women who met at the home of Mrs. Rawls seemed unanimous—with the exception of Jane Schutt—in their disapproval of the Freedom Summer activities. But over and over the "air vibrated with ambivalence" like the ebb and flow of a tide, Ryerson wrote.[100] Mrs. Rawls, for example, tried to demonstrate how liberal she was but, at the same time, commented on the students' behavior and the ignorance of blacks and questioned why anyone would want to get involved in the movement.[101] Kohlenberg summarized what transpired when Schutt, after forty-five minutes, could no longer bear to listen to the criticisms and the statements regarding the fine life of Mississippi blacks. "She said, very quietly in a very broad accent, 'Now I just have to tell you ladies you are all wrong. . . . I was on the Civil Rights Commission . . . and listen[ed] to those people come and tell us how they were beat up, and how they lost their jobs, and what their troubles were.' . . . She also pointed out . . . [the students] were coming down because they believed in brotherly love, because they believed they could be helpful, because they believed that it was the job of the young as well as the old to help. . . . She talked for almost a half an hour in her quiet, persuasive way. . . . It just broke the log jam."[102]

Laya Weisner called Schutt's impromptu speech "the most exciting thing in the world," because all the other women who had initially seemed timid felt they could speak up. The team merely sat back and listened as the local women began sharing other stories of life in Jackson.[103] Until Schutt spoke, Kohlenberg stated, "They just couldn't understand what we thought we were doing and what our kids thought they were doing. . . . I don't think they thought we were making trouble, but they thought the whole Freedom Summer was a disaster for them."[104]

The more progressive white women welcomed the opportunity to talk freely with other white women, which was a "great relief" and encouraged them to be more open with each other. Trude Lash did not feel the women who met Team 5 were ready to work openly with black women, but she felt certain they would continue to do more soul searching on the issues.[105] Team 4 met at the home of Lenora Hudson, an active member of the Presbyterian Church; Mississippians Eleanor Fontaine and Ann Hewitt cohosted the coffee and helped lead the conversation. Two of the local women played bridge with Hewitt regularly but had no idea of her stance on civil rights. When team members Maxine Nathanson and Barbara Cunningham asked questions about the movement, the hostesses' answers appeared to be news to the local women.[106] Even for a liberal thinker like Hewitt, the WIMS visits provided an opportunity to broach the unmentionable subjects with her friends in a safe environment.

These women had, at last, opened a dialogue on race, but others went even further. Helen Meyner had worked with the national Red Cross and was the wife of a former governor of New Jersey when she volunteered for Team 7. She was slated to stay at the home of a Jackson Presbyterian minister and his wife, a breakthrough for WIMS. At the last minute, however, the couple sent word to Goodwillie that they had to withdraw their invitation for fear it would jeopardize the outcome of a vote on a controversial church issue. The wife, Barbara Hendrix, called Goodwillie later to express her regrets and embarrassment. Hendrix added, "You know we're not free, are we?" Goodwillie replied, "You're not any freer than the blackest man in this town." Several months later, Hendrix became a leader for change and organized WIMS's first multiracial lunch at the Sun-n-Sand Motor Hotel.[107]

In addition to attempting to bridge racial divisions, WIMS worked to bring women together within racial groups. Team 5's Marie Barksdale worked with Delta Sigma Theta to get the black sorority women more involved in the movement. Barksdale, Doris Wilson, and Aurelia Young of Jackson talked to ten members of the sorority and outlined a plan, with individual assignments, for the group to do 200 home visits over the course of a weekend. The following week when Dorothy Height came to Jackson, she met with the same women, who reported they had completed their assignments. The project renewed their enthusiasm and courage and deepened their involvement.[108] Under WIMS's influence, the women organized themselves and worked proactively with one another.

Wednesdays in Mississippi was always a woman-to-woman initiative—conceived by women, organized by women, reaching out to women—working outside the power structures of the male-led civil rights organizations. The WIMS strategy went beyond employing a gendered approach alone, however. The attributes that had kept women off the platform in rallies and out of the historical literature were the same ones that Height and Cowan sought to exploit as a source of power for WIMS. Cowan wrote, "High level women have unique abilities to offer people in troubled places. Initially, they have access to people—it is hard to turn away or ignore a 'tidy, smiling lady with white gloves and high heels.' When you combine experience, determination, knowledge, understanding and a desire to help—with femininity, you have a force to reckon with."[109]

Just as Dorothy Tilly found with the Fellowship of the Concerned, and as Height and Cowan discovered on their Selma trip, the intersecting identities of gender, age, and class provided a level of protection and acceptability that eluded other civil rights activists. Wearing white gloves and dresses, as was customary in the early 1960s, they—far from hiding their status—relied on being mostly middle-aged, middle-class and upper-class women to make their presence and their message less threatening and offensive. Although adopting these expected behavior patterns could have served to reinforce existing inequities, WIMS consciously chose to follow them as a method of infiltrating and tearing down those hierarchies, those of race specifically.[110]

Even though many southern women opposed northerners' coming to Mississippi, the WIMS women's aura of respectability served as an entrée to many white women who might otherwise have refused to meet with them, categorizing them as northern troublemakers. Trude Lash observed, "For the white women the realization that we were obviously middle-aged women with some standing in the community whose children were at the same colleges as their own created an uncomfortable challenge to firmly held prejudices. In this respect we were probably more effective than the COFO workers." This common ground made it difficult for many of the southern women to completely dismiss the WIMS team members in the same way they so often did the COFO students accused of being "communist-beatnik-prevert-Jews [sic]." The WIMS women did not march, demonstrate, or dictate terms. They merely sought to open a dialogue between women and affirm that respected people agreed with the same principles as the student activists and other civil rights proponents.[111]

Susan Goodwillie, Priscilla Hunt, and Geraldine Kohlenberg called this the "gentility factor." The white gloves were, in Goodwillie's words, their "most powerful weapon," a tool that enabled them to break through because it befuddled the racists who expected young trouble-makers.[112] It enabled the teams to travel into the black community to attend a dinner at Harvey's home, for example, without incident even when they were followed.[113] The WIMS women projected an image of class that the students did not, although most of the students were also middle-class. Age played a role in the image they portrayed, but it went hand in hand with respectability. As Kohlenberg noted, if they had gone as "thirty-six-year-old hippies," their appearance would not have had the same effect.[114] For a few WIMS women, "hippie" might have come closer to describing their true selves. Kohlenberg and Ryerson did not consider themselves proper ladies like their mothers' generation. Nevertheless, they took on that persona because the WIMS project required it.[115] Sylvia Weinberg echoed these sentiments. She wore dresses in Mississippi when ordinarily she spent most of her time in blue jeans. Denim, however, failed to convey to the southern women that the team members were women with good backgrounds, good educations, and good thoughts.[116]

While this strategy proved successful with the Mississippi middle-class women, age and class played differently to the students. Ryerson felt that their "gloves" created a barrier to understanding with the COFO students after a young woman acted "standoffish" with her until the woman learned Ryerson had a daughter volunteering in Mississippi. Ryerson had taken off her actual gloves but referred instead to her "metaphysical gloves." She concluded that "revolutionaries don't *ever* like ladies in white gloves," but she admitted she was happy to have the gloves to wave at unmarked police cars or trucks.[117]

In contrast to other civil rights organizations, the WIMS participants' quiet methods served as another means to foster success.[118] WIMS did not come down to shape up anyone; the women were invited by Mississippi women, and they came "to listen, to bear witness, to try to build bridges of communication but not to be rabble rousers." This under-the-radar operation worked, in part, because the Wednesdays women appeared to be individuals traveling apart from any organization. Today, this would be more difficult given mass media and social media outlets.[119] Goodwillie said the WIMS women were simply innocuous, and their gentility confused police and civil rights opponents monitoring their activity.[120] Ed King stressed the significance of the program and WIMS's approach to the movement: "The program was extremely important. . . . The whole thrust of what we were doing was not just the dramatic things, like going to jail or marching. We were trying to deal with every level of change that was needed, and Dorothy Height understood that."[121]

WIMS mirrored Height's personal activist philosophy. She was well aware that some blacks criticized her for taking too soft an approach, for working too well with white people, for not being radical enough, in the same way they had criticized Mary McLeod Bethune before her. The criticisms did not change her course, however. Instead, she reflected on words of wisdom she heard at the 1937 World Conference of Churches from John McMurray: "Go out and work for radical change, but don't try to just be radical . . . because nobody gets so tired as a tired radical."[122] Bethune influenced Height as well. Following Bethune's example, Height honed her quiet, persistent approach to leadership as president of the NCNW. This model contributed to WIMS's success in opening lines of communication and established the NCNW's staying power in Mississippi and as a national organization.

The Wednesdays women used a more circuitous, gentle, diplomatic approach to activism that mirrored the expected behavior of women at the time. Although she recognized her conclusion as a generalization, Kohlenberg believed that if men met in similar circumstances, they might think they had to take a position and defend it, while women of her generation did not feel that pressure and could take an indirect approach. Priscilla Hunt agreed, citing sociolinguist Deborah Tannen's theory of "rapport versus report."[123] Tannen argues that men and women's styles of communication differ, with women's conversations characterized by rapport, establishing friendships, finding and emphasizing common ground, and striving for solidarity.[124] Goodwillie, Hunt, and Kohlenberg agreed that Tannen's description of women's communication styles mirrored the approach taken by WIMS. Kohlenberg pointed out that WIMS's subtle approach was more "natural" to women of her generation and worked as an advantage to the project as a whole.[125]

Since the black Mississippi women met so few white women (outside of employers), and fewer still who offered them any sort of encouragement, they were thrilled to find support from the northern white women.[126] When Team 5 attended a lunch in Ruleville, the local black women appreciated having the opportunity to entertain the guests. The WIMS staff offered to assist them, knowing that Ruleville was a poor community; but one of the COFO volunteers explained that cooking was something the Ruleville women took great pride in doing, and to take that away from them would be insulting.[127] The visits demonstrated that outsiders were concerned about what was happening in the state and offered needed encouragement.[128] One woman told Mary Cushing Niles that the WIMS visit did the black women "a world of good" because it let them know that the northern women cared. She added, "We need to be reminded that we are part of the same country and world."[129]

The staff arranged for an interracial luncheon meeting at St. Paul's Church in Meridian for Team 3. About twenty black women came, but all the white women who were invited sent their regrets at the last moment. One white woman called in tears, saying how cut off she felt. When a black woman from the church offered to visit her, she accepted saying, "That would be wonderful! You could come to me, but I cannot come to you."[130] Geraldine Woods described the black women at the lunch as "friendly but quite guarded."[131] Some of them expressed displeasure that the COFO workers had come to the area, but few of these had visited the Freedom Summer projects.[132] The black women said that they had completely lost contact with whites, who were friendly in the past but changed their attitudes after the civil rights movement had brought reactionary forces against it to prominence. "Now they cross the street, even when they've known you for forty years," one woman lamented. Justine Randers-Pehrson corresponded with Mrs. A. W. Crump of Meridian, who wrote, "Your letter somehow touched my very heart. It gave me a needed lift. Sometimes I am so alone, but I have learned to live in a world all my own, since I was very young. My world does not permit even the thought of prejudice. . . . Your visit was the best thing which has happened in my life lately."[133] Crump added that she felt sure the next time WIMS traveled to Meridian that the white women would come to see them. Randers-Pehrson felt stunned "to be trusted in this way by southern Negroes who [had] every reason to draw away from anyone with white skin."[134]

Several team members expressed their surprise that so few blacks in Mississippi exhibited hate toward whites, and that they employed humor under such dire circumstances. Ann McGlinchy, a white member of Team 1, reported that a young black woman she met in Hattiesburg had just been released on bail for picketing the courthouse with twenty-five others. McGlinchy asked how the jailer had treated her and was amazed when the woman replied with no bitterness, "Well, he did beat up one of the girls, but he only spat on the rest of us."[135]

Marian Logan felt that the greatest thing the blacks in Mississippi had going for them was their sense of humor despite their circumstances. At a Jackson NAACP meeting, she observed that when the attendees discussed serious—even tragic—events, they put on a sketch using humor to dramatize the need for everyone to join the movement, particularly those who were "not following the line." She recalled the story of one maid who used a boycott to subtly exert pressure on her employer. The maid told the woman of the house that the black community was boycotting the Jitney Jungle grocery stores. When the employer did not reply, the maid repeated her statement multiple times. Finally the woman asked, "Are you trying to tell me that you don't want me to buy in Jitney Jungle?" The maid replied, "Oh, no Ma'am. I don't care if you buy any Jitney Jungle, all I am telling you is we're boycotting it; and if any food comes in here, you are gonna cook it." Logan imagined the wife trying to take over the cooking and cleaning chores, and the husband telling his wife to get the maid back no matter what it cost. Logan said of black Mississippians,

"I couldn't help feeling that they've got to win because nobody's got this kind of humor under such circumstances.... Who can laugh at a thing like this?"[136]

For southern black women, WIMS served as a source of encouragement and support that gave them hope that change might truly be coming, particularly for women in the Delta who only knew white women as employers. Hope came from knowing that black and white women in the North cared and worked on their behalf, as well as from discovering that women across town demonstrated a willingness to help. Civil rights activist and Mississippi's first black woman mayor Unita Blackwell of Mayersville said, "When Black and white women came together, it was, for us, strength. It was a feeling of we weren't alone. That group of Black and white women was something that we had not seen before."[137]

The black women in Jackson had a better idea of what the WIMS teams had come to accomplish and "delighted at the image of womanhood" they presented. The Jackson black women appreciated the interracial, interfaith gatherings, and hoped they would continue and grow larger.[138] Clarie Collins Harvey commented, "I must say that that kind of witness, ... with white women and black women who were there in the south and who were wanting good will to be administered, really made a difference and a change."[139] Dorothy Stewart spoke of the positive impact that interracial alliances had on women like Harvey, Blackwell, and Jessie Mosley. They "started to grasp a world that was outside of Mississippi, outside of Jackson, and they didn't want to be limited to just ... a little black neighborhood, a little black Mississippi." The NCNW, Stewart said, acted as the "catalyst" that helped women move beyond the "marginalized thinking" about what they could accomplish. Opening this door of opportunity carried immeasurable benefits for these women. They had faith in themselves and in the realization that neither they nor their children deserved to live under the current conditions.[140]

Slowly but surely, these efforts changed Mississippi and enabled women to move to a new level—and when they moved, so did the men and their families, Stewart argued. Lillian Burnstein and Janet Purvis, both white, made similar observations: by teaching and leading through example, and in doing what they thought was right, women significantly influenced the thinking of their families, their children, and their children's friends.[141] Team 7 members Priscilla Hunt and Edith Savage both contended that the women they met might influence their husbands, particularly with regard to acceptance of school integration.[142] Women played critical roles in getting important messages out to their communities and as voters. Not only did women cast ballots, they also encouraged their husbands to vote and taught their children the importance of voting as an element of citizenship.[143] By taking up the cause in ways that appeared to be women's work—through schools and church groups, for example—the women worked for change within the accepted bounds of womanhood. By teaching their children to think in new ways, they provided a legacy for future progress.

The team visits encouraged white Mississippi women to begin questioning what they heard about treatment of African Americans in the state and to assess the validity of their sources of information about the northern students. The WIMS women accomplished this by sharing their thoughts as parents of COFO volunteers, by reporting what they had seen while visiting the Freedom Schools, and by giving progressive-thinking white Mississippians the opportunity to speak out in support of change. Many of the Mississippi white women had turned a "blind eye" to the effects of Jim Crow. Height theorized that these women knew what was happening but felt no sense of "personal identification" with it. WIMS brought the oppression of blacks to the forefront and made white people aware of and interested in what was occurring on the other side of town. Janet Purvis agreed, saying, "It did keep everyone aware that there had not yet been a solution, and it had to be searched out." Further, Elaine Crystal observed, "Once we did start going to interracial places, and to meetings, we grew within ourselves, [in] our understanding of all the problems and opportunities." By summer's end, a few local white women had expressed an interest in accompanying the WIMS teams on their trips to the projects outside Jackson.[144]

The southern women had no awareness that northern teenagers frequently took part in summer mission trips sponsored by churches and other organizations to work in lower income areas in the North.[145] Henrietta Moore said the Mississippi women had a totally different outlook once they learned that some of these same students, including Moore's son, had worked previous summers teaching underprivileged blacks in Chicago and cities in the Northeast.[146]

Moore also had the opportunity to lead another Jackson woman to question the role police played in abusing the COFO volunteers. The woman told her that the link between "red-necks" and the police had no basis in fact, adding the police did "a splendid job." Moore replied that she only knew about the police in Greenwood where her son was beaten. The woman said, "Greenwood, I know it well," and carried on about her family living there before she realized exactly what had been said. She asked Moore for more details, still unbelieving but listening carefully. She took down the names of the assailant and the "worst" police officer so she could check into the situation and appeared genuinely "shocked."[147] This incident demonstrated the type of information exchange WIMS hoped to accomplish—the news came from a firsthand account, from a respected source, and caused the listener to question what she thought to be true. Had the woman heard a similar report from one of the COFO volunteers or read about the incident, she probably would not have given the story the same weight. Most likely she would have reverted to her statement that the reports were not true.

The most hostile gathering, the coffee attended by Team 6, also offered a note of hope for changing attitudes. After Lucy Montgomery made mention of blacks being made to feel inferior from birth, a chorus of denials rang out from the southerners saying that blacks were the ones who told their children to stay in their place, that blacks liked the social hierarchy, and that blacks knew that southern society's rules represented how blacks "ought to behave." But one woman, Mrs. Green, who sat in a corner, said, "Just think, a mother tells her child from the time it's born, you're inferior, you've got to stay down, you've got to stay in your place." Montgomery "hammer[ed] away" at her about whether or not Green thought that was right. Looking sympathetic, the woman said no, she thought it was "a terrible thing to be brought up this way." Green went on to say that she served on the state library board and that the American Library Association no longer recognized the state entity because of Mississippi's policies. She felt cut off and explained that performers and speakers refused to come to the state, which increasingly isolated its residents. Eventually Green broke from the opinions expressed earlier by her companions Hederman and Crouch, saying that something really had to be done.[148]

Some Jackson women expressed moderate positions that appeared quite liberal in Mississippi. Team 7 attended a "secret" interracial gathering of five white and four black women that Hannah Levin described as taking place on the "borderline between the Negro and white community," where white women who were sympathetic to civil rights could voice their true positions. After much discussion, a white woman in her fifties asked the group, "Well, really, are we any different from the people who hate, if we don't do anything?"[149] This brought home the reality that merely thinking that racial inequality needed to change was not enough; they had to take an active role to make it happen. Edith Savage, an African American team member, called this meeting the focal point of her visit. She believed that the white women deserved recognition because they had not met previously with black women, and that the team had encouraged them to move forward in human relations.

Savage wrote, "It may take years, and it may take just a short time. . . . But still, I feel this was a historical moment in our trip to Mississippi."[150]

In an early planning session for WIMS, Height cautioned the team members present not to expect to accomplish a great deal in one trip, but to see WIMS as "cumulative in its growth," giving them an opportunity to add women to the cause one, two, or three at a time.[151] At the WIMS orientation, Hannah Levin, a psychologist, stressed that changing attitudes is a gradual process and that the teams needed to encourage small steps while telling the southern women that changing attitudes in the North was also difficult.[152] During their visits, the WIMS teams met with about 300 women, almost half of them white, and Height observed, "As the summer progressed, an amazing number of local white women came forward, quietly and often apprehensively, to join our project. They said they decided to do so because they didn't want to rear their children in such a climate of hate; or because they knew integration was inevitable and they wanted to help make the transition as smooth as possible; or because they simply could no longer stand by, simply watching, as innocent people were harassed or even killed because they dared to try to register to vote."[153]

Slowly but surely, the WIMS women chipped away at the barriers to interracial cooperation, and in so doing, they impressed on the southern white women that they had nothing to fear by moving forward. [154] WIMS saw the change as a few southern women at a time joined the core group of angels, and the connections between black and white women were enhanced further as time progressed. After the teams had departed, many southern white women expressed their gratitude for the positive impact of the program. Miriam Ezelle wrote to Cowan, "I have been truly grateful to meet your visitors and to have had the privilege of entertaining such lovely women, who were sufficiently interested in Mississippi to take the trouble to come down to get acquainted with our problems and to want to help us in their solution. I feel very much richer thru [sic] knowledge of your efforts and your personalities. I went into it from the desire to give a better picture of Mississippi but I certainly gained more than I gave."[155] Florence Gooch concurred. "WIMS has brought me many new, but old (in the sense of familiarity) friends! It has also helped to bring some of us locally together and to make us feel not quite so isolated, knowing that other areas have problems and that to have a concern for people is to involve us beyond our own boundaries."[156] By aiding the WIMS teams, these women set an example for other Jackson white women to move forward on the civil rights issue. Through WIMS's efforts to facilitate

these contacts between local women, the cause as a whole moved forward as well.

Throughout the summer, Polly Cowan kept a tight lid on publicity about the project to protect the safety of the staff and teams. Through her media contacts, she arranged to release the story to UPI after the teams and staff were out of Mississippi and after the Democratic National Convention, which they hoped would improve readership. The *New York Times* and other national papers ran the story Sunday, August 30, 1964. Over the coming days a version of the story appeared in smaller papers, including the *Clarion-Ledger* on September 4, 1964. Listing the Associated Press as its source, the article included inaccuracies such as that the visits had lasted for several days and that the women had met in business offices to allay suspicions.[157]

Readers wrote vicious letters to the *Clarion-Ledger* editor in response. Mr. and Mrs. John Redding of Gulfport wrote to the "48 Northern women who in groups recently visited in Mississippi," telling them that they were misinformed about the lack of communication between the races in Mississippi. "The race subject is discussed openly and widely and constantly whenever and wherever parties or congenial company gather. Of course one could hardly expect the race subject to be discussed freely when antagonists are present. . . . If you think the Negroes you met bear much resemblance to the rank and file of Southern Negroes you are mistaken. Furthermore, we resent your implication that the white women who met with you represent the white people of Mississippi. They do not. Since when have Southern white women needed 'a bridge' built by highly educated Northern women in order to talk to Negro women?"[158]

Several months later, Jackson resident J. H. McDaniel sent an editorial to the *Clarion-Ledger* similarly addressed to the women who came "uninvited, unwanted, and uninformed" as part of the Mississippi "invasion." After accusing them of being part of a "communist conspiracy" to unseat Mississippi's congressmen, he summed up the teams' accomplishments as registering several hundred blacks to vote and integrating a few cafes. "On the debit side," however, he covered almost every racist train of thought the teams had hoped to combat and demonstrated his lack of understanding about WIMS by essentially crediting them with (or blaming them for) the entire Freedom Summer project.[159] Although WIMS made inroads in changing attitudes, some in Mississippi still had a long way to go; and some might never change.

Mississippi women were not the only ones to be affected by WIMS. The northern women returned home with a renewed commitment to helping the Freedom Schools, the community centers set up by COFO, and other projects

in the South and the North. As the women had agreed upon acceptance to the program, they began telling others about WIMS after the last team and staff left Mississippi. They spoke at their churches, clubs, and service organizations, and wrote articles about their experiences for local newspapers, alumni magazines, and organizational newsletters. Team members called the trip "the most meaningful thing I've ever done," "one of the most rewarding experiences I have ever had," "one of the most fantastic days of my life," "exhausting, exhilarating, scary, and yet hopeful," and totally life-changing—"I am not the person I was before going to Mississippi."[160] One woman also called it depressing, but added, "In fact, it was most rewarding frequently when it was most depressing."[161]

Homestays enriched the experience for the black Wednesdays women and the white members of Teams 6 and 7, who repeatedly commented on the rapport they developed with the Jackson women who hosted them. The WIMS women got a sense of the fear the local women felt at jeopardizing their jobs and positions in the community. All who stayed in private homes reported staying up until the wee hours of the morning to spend as much time as possible visiting with their host families, learning as much as possible about Mississippi life. The Jackson women, especially the whites, often felt the visits provided their first real opportunity to discuss their views on civil rights. Priscilla Hunt and Hannah Levin stayed at the home of Danelle and George Vockroth, whom Hunt described as having their hearts in the right place but nervous because of community pressure. Levin explained that they knew of every desegregation case but had no one else to talk to except in the most guarded way. Danelle Vockroth wanted to know what the Freedom Schools were really like and whether the students were beatniks.[162] Miriam Davis expressed the thoughts of many WIMS team members in saying, "Our hostess is a dear woman whom we love[d] instantly and to whom our visit was almost like a transfusion. What the conversation with her meant to us was equally gratifying."[163] Clarie Collins Harvey wrote of the change she observed in the Wednesdays women after their Mississippi experiences. "Some of you could just not believe—you told us on Tuesday night that what we said and what was in the papers couldn't be true, but Wednesday night when you came back, you were a different person because you lived through it."[164]

Height and Cowan hoped that the passionate response to the WIMS experience would spur the participants to action at home, and it did. Roach wrote, "You had to come away with your heart broken at what you had seen and know that you had to do something about it."[165] WIMS was not the sole reason they became more involved, but as Savage explained, "WIMS influenced

me to want to do more."[166] Johnson felt that WIMS offered a firsthand understanding of what blacks experienced in an environment where they could
not even protect their children.[167] Bourne commented, "The experience has
made me know again and in new ways how totally impossible it would be
for me not to be involved in social action—through the political structure, in
organized groups, and in personal relationships with others who can and will
work for constructive social change."[168]

Not only did WIMS deepen commitments to the civil rights movement,
but it made the northern women more productive in their work for it. Jean
Davis observed, "There is no doubt but that my trip deepened my personal
commitment and helps make me much more effective in talking with others."
Being able to say, "I was there," was "unbeatable" and enabled her to get others more involved.[169] Three elements stood out for Justine Randers-Pehrson:
the calm determination of blacks and the summer volunteers, the oppression,
and a realignment of her loyalties. She wrote, "Mississippi is somehow 'my
state' now—not the hated disquieting miasmic white state, but the staunch
Negro community that could enrich all America if only its forces could
flow."[170]

Team members contributed through a number of organizations to which
they belonged. Geraldine P. Woods of Delta Sigma Theta felt she benefited
from her teammates because they gelled and developed an openness with one
other. She also gained knowledge from the Mississippians she met, knowledge
that enabled her to guide the Social Action Commission and Deltas chapters
in thirty-eight states.[171] Priscilla Hunt felt that her greatest contribution came
through the YWCA, where she spent two years studying institutional racism
following the trip. After learning of the segregated facilities in Mississippi,
she encouraged her local YWCA group to put pressure on the national organization to end the practice and to study racism within organizations. The
study's results surprised many people who had not seen institutional racism
as a reason for the problems faced by blacks.[172] Olive Noble spoke to several
women's clubs in the Maplewood, New Jersey, area where she found opposition from more conservative attendees. Although she said it was difficult to
have the "courage to face the opposition . . . who feel you are a dreadful radical," her Christian convictions and the example set by Jane Schutt inspired
Noble to continue doing her part.[173]

The exposure the northern women had to their fellow team members also
enriched the experience. The only real criticism the Wednesdays women had
of the project was that beforehand they had not been given any biographical
information about their teammates. Nevertheless, the women learned a great

deal about each other, as one would expect of people thrown together for such an intense experience.[174] For example, Ryerson wrote, "For me, the most prejudice-destroying part of this trip was the experience of getting to know Sister Catherine [John]. What a nun! What a woman! What a liberated soul, and courageous liberal! I spent a lot of time with her, and, in my innocence, I had never known such people existed in the Catholic clergy."[175] Kohlenberg recalled that Wednesday night of their trip, Sister Catherine John sat barefooted as they had a "pajama party . . . talking way into the night," because they were reluctant for the experience to end.[176] "We became quite close and told each other a lot about our lives and particularly as concern[ed] things spiritual. . . . She seemed like a very individual kind of person . . . and I didn't know how that matched up with being a nun."[177] Narcissa Swift King corresponded with teammate Henrietta Moore about how the trip had broadened her base of friendships and how grateful she was the two had met. King asked Moore, "Has it happened to you as it has to me that you've made real friends, new ones, through the movement?" Although King had been warned that her civil rights work would cause her to lose friends, she had not lost any, and instead had cemented new alliances with people she had only known slightly or not at all.[178]

Cowan concluded that team members "became friends quickly in a way they might never [have] become friends if they had only worked together as school teachers in the same school." At home, the WIMS women worked together in ways they had not thought possible before the trip, and some remained life-long friends.[179] Such was the case with Josie Johnson and Maxine Nathanson. Nathanson missed the orientation before their trip and did not realize the black and white women had been instructed to stop interacting on the final legs of their journey to Mississippi. She felt hurt when she thought they had shunned her, but at the Freedom Summer projects, they were reunited like old friends. When Team 4 went to the Jackson airport to return home, they ordered breakfast, and then said, "Screw Mississippi," as they "boldly walked together to the plane."[180] On the return flight, rather than distancing themselves from one another, they got off in Memphis and St. Louis as an interracial group. "Not in a superficial way, we were all women, we were all wives and mothers," wrote Nathanson. Even though they each had different organizational experiences, the Wednesdays women shared an interest in the education and welfare of all citizens regardless of race or religion.[181]

The paranoia of Mississippians carried over to the team members. Ryerson reported, "We were astonished at how quickly we became suspicious of every expression on a white face—of every car and especially of every policeman.

Now that I am home, I jump at the sight of a white pickup truck or a state cop."[182] Kohlenberg added that even though the team members had a perfectly peaceful time in Jackson, "the simplest happening," from the stone-faced clerks at the hotel to a suspicious man in a car, took on the "most wildly melodramatic possibilities."[183] This caused Batson to comment on the bravery of the local women by comparison, who "acted like they had a job and they did it."[184]

Observing the civil rights struggle, the resistance of segregationist churches, and the inaction of other churches, both black and white, caused many Freedom Summer participants to question their own church's positions and how they as parishioners fit personally in that framework. Some fought for change from within, others walked away from their churches, and still others sought the answers within themselves. The number of signs advertising churches in the small towns between Jackson and Hattiesburg surprised Ruth Minor, a black member of Team 7. Despite professions of faith on the signs, Minor found that a very different picture emerged when she talked to ministers working with Freedom Summer, who said that it was appalling how many young people came to Mississippi with religious conviction and left with none. The ministers explained that after observing the oppression in Mississippi, one could understand how the young people lost faith when they saw no action on the part of the churches.[185]

The failure of the churches to align with civil rights led even the most devout to question the churches' official role. When Sister Catherine John visited the Holy Child Jesus Church and School, she was dismayed to find that the school, which represented her faith but not her order, was not reaching out to the unfortunate in the community or supporting the civil rights cause. She felt that the sisters there learned a great deal from the team's visit; however, it drew into question her own personal stance. She wrote, "As a Christian, I have been forced by the Mississippi experience to ask and re-ask some terribly searching questions about the relevance of institutionalized religion. I cannot find answers to my questions. I cannot forget Mississippi; I cannot forget Roxbury in Massachusetts and Watts in California. And, thank God, I cannot forget what these places tell me about our society. . . . Perhaps it will suffice to say that I am not the person I was before going to Mississippi."[186]

Inactive churches had the ability to affect even the most devout believers. In this case, though, rather than turning her back on her faith, Sister Catherine John was spurred to take a more vocal stand on civil rights as she carried the message to groups of nuns, to Catholic colleges, and to members of Congress. She sent a tape describing Mississippi's intolerable situation to her own religious order, which numbered approximately 600 sisters, and received numerous requests to speak to their groups. Lastly, she shared what she had learned with her students at Immaculate Heart College in Los Angeles, California, in the hope of teaching them the importance of working for change.[187]

WIMS changed how the team members looked at their own communities. Maxine Nathanson became more aware of the subtleties of discrimination in the North by comparison to its overt forms in Mississippi.[188] Ruth Batson thought of herself as a "red hot civil rights worker" at home in Boston, but when she saw the enormous problem in the South, she began to feel that she was not doing so much.[189] Ethel Hasserodt of the Passaic, New Jersey, YWCA wrote to Dorothy Height, "No matter how much I had read and heard about the difficulty of getting Negroes registered I simply did not know the depth to which our so called American democracy had degraded." She had appreciated neither the extent to which reprisals were a way of life in Mississippi, nor the courage exhibited by blacks "in the face of such gigantic obstacles."[190] Just before the final team arrived in Jackson, Goodwillie summed up her overall experience with the project. "My heart is heavy—I have learned a sadness this summer that will stay with me for a long time to come. . . . It is a 100-year-old sadness and it has ripened and mellowed and [is] not to be denied—it confronted us every day in Mississippi and will haunt us all the days of our lives to come. . . . I have learned a great joy too—a kind of deep joy that was equally new to me—a feeling that came with each glimmer of freedom, of equality, of humanness that creeps through the dark maze of Mississippi and sets our soul ablaze with hope."[191]

At civil rights meetings and rallies across the South, women and children made up the bulk of the audience, while men dominated the platform.[192] For the most part, black and white women followed social norms and deferred to male leaders regardless of the positions the women held in the movement and their level of responsibility. Because gender often excluded women from mainstream leadership positions, sociologist Belinda Robnett argues that many movement women served as "bridge leaders." These women composed a "strong grassroots tier of leadership that served as a critical bridge between the formal organization and adherents and potential constituents."[193] Robnett also identifies mainstream bridge leaders, who were usually white women working to make connections with other whites. The Wednesdays women served as bridge leaders in both senses—they brought diverse women together and gradually added "potential constituents" to the cause, and they created connections for the Mississippi women that aided the southern women's efforts. Goodwillie explained, "We were a link ... a transition from Mississippi to the larger world."[194] The northern women accomplished this by bridging the differences between progressive and conservative white women, and at the same time establishing interracial dialogue between black and white Jackson women. In both capacities, the WIMS teams acted as communicators and catalysts for change.[195]

Sociologist Jenny Irons contends that the cultural expectations for women to follow traditional gender roles meant that women brought skills to the civil rights movement that were different from those used by men—skills such as "maternalism, nurturance, and domesticity." As an example of "activist mothering," Irons cites the work of Aurelia Young, a music teacher at Jackson State College, who with her husband, civil rights attorney Jack Young, invited Team 3 to a gathering of local civil rights leaders and hosted members of Team 6 in her home. Irons argues that because the contributions of women like Young tended to be low-profile, the women received little recognition for their efforts, even though their work was pivotal to the movement's success.[196]

To accomplish WIMS's goals, the teams followed a similar pattern, engaging in women's work at the Freedom Schools and community centers, collaborating with local churches, and meeting over coffee in the homes of their southern hosts—all behaviors appropriate to middle-class, middle-aged women and mothers. The NCNW capitalized on this trend in its official statement: "As citizens, as mothers and as community leaders, southern and northern women are concerned for the safety of women and children who are engaged in voter registration drives and educational and cultural enrichment programs in Mississippi."[197] Josie Johnson theorized that women in the civil rights movement, like women who worked in churches, were accustomed to doing the hard work without getting recognition for it or being "publicly identified" as leaders.[198]

Unlike any other group operating in Mississippi during the summer of 1964, Wednesdays in Mississippi used the participants' gender, age, and class to bridge the divide across race, region, and religion. The WIMS teams set an example of how integrated groups of women could enjoy each other's company socially and work together effectively. Jean Benjamin felt that the fact that they did this with "total naturalness and lack of self-consciousness" had a positive effect on the women they met.[199]

The almost 200 black women who met with the WIMS teams directly, and the thousands of others who saw the Wednesdays women introduced at rallies, learned that black and white women outside the South cared about what happened to blacks in Mississippi.[200] Marian Logan felt such action was critical to preventing the same type of human rights atrocities that led to World War II. Sadly noting that Mississippi was "just not to be believed," Logan argued that her team had helped if only because they let black Mississippians know that they cared, and that other people cared too. She mentioned the babies the team saw in Palmer's Crossing with flies buzzing around them in the heat, but the crux of her argument had to do with the similarities she drew between Adolf Hitler and European Jews in the 1930s and 1940s, when people sat back and did nothing, and blacks in Mississippi in the 1960s. "Maybe what we're doing isn't much, but it's enough to let people know that somebody outside is watching them. . . . [Hitler] killed lots of people and everybody said, 'Isn't this terrible?' But, nobody really did anything about it . . . and if we don't do anything now, I'm telling you it's not going to be long it's going to be too late!"[201]

Many believed that outsiders who had come to Mississippi to work with the grassroots leadership held the key to the success of the civil rights movement in the state. WIMS team members and some of the southern women with whom they met agreed. Jay Shands, one of the Jackson hostesses, believed the people coming down helped to "jump start" the change. Lasting change would have to come from the heart, from blacks and whites, conservatives and liberals, living together over time.[202] Janet Purvis, also of Jackson, felt that the agitation kept everyone aware that they still needed to work out a solution to the problem.[203]

By making the trip, the Wednesdays women eased feelings of isolation in both black and white southerners and showed them new ways to work for change in their communities. The moderate whites saw that they were not alone in their thinking, and that others also worked behind the scenes for change, or, at the very least, believed the violence and discrimination against blacks needed to stop. In 1965, Florence Gooch observed what a difference those early inroads to interracial communication had made during WIMS's first summer in Mississippi: "WIMS gave me an umbrella for lunch at the Sun 'N Sand and for the afternoon tea at the Heidelberg, neither of which would have been easy—if, indeed, possible—the year before." Although she admitted that "social integration" would not be acceptable in Mississippi for a long time, "the visits of intelligent, dedicated women of both races" were part of the bridge that they would have to build together.[204]

CHAPTER SIX

Beyond Freedom Summer

"We have to stop thinking of 'outsiders' and think of 'allies.'
And we have to stop using the term 'coming in'—they're not
breaking in—we aren't closed."

—RUBYE LYELLS[1]

DRIVING POLLY COWAN AND ELLEN TARRY TO THE AIRPORT IN 1965, JULIAN Tatum, a sociology professor at the University of Mississippi, asked Cowan, "Do you see any progress in the state since last year?" Cowan said Tatum inquired "with such eagerness" that she did not have the heart to tell him no. She contemplated the question, saying she had "seen some change" and yet, "Some people and institutions were impaled on dead center."[2] Mississippi had taken its greatest steps forward since the end of Reconstruction almost a century earlier, but it also had a long way to go to catch up with the rest of the nation. The local women who had worked with Wednesdays in Mississippi hoped the program would continue to facilitate the state's progress.

Although the organizers intended WIMS to be a one-summer project, in November 1964, team members, Mississippi women, and government officials met to assess the degree of success achieved by WIMS's efforts and consider a path for the future. The Mississippi women "tipped the scales" when they "begged" the NCNW to continue the program.[3] The black Mississippi women unanimously favored WIMS's return. Lillie Belle Jones, who directed the Jackson branch YWCA, wanted team members to expand their reach, creating new opportunities for black and white women to interact.[4] White Mississippian Patt Derian commented that WIMS was "one more grain of sand that may ultimately produce the pearl."[5] The Mississippians, WIMS reported, felt that they had "gained insight into the true state of affairs within their law enforcement and judicial systems" from the northern women, and that WIMS had "started something invaluable."[6]

In the summer of 1965, WIMS featured interracial, interfaith teams paired with southerners by occupation, and by August, the success of its efforts to bridge the racial divide had become apparent. Derian, who later became President Jimmy Carter's assistant secretary of state for human rights and humanitarian affairs, wrote, "These ladies have established a pattern and method of activity that should not be allowed to disappear, rather it should be enlarged . . . all over the south certainly but also in other divided and simmering communities. A catalogue of Wednesday achievements probably cannot be compiled, simply because they did so much and the things that they did have yet to end . . . If you looked back over the last two years and marked every forward step in Jackson community relations, you'd find that a Wednesday lady has somehow been involved."[7] Derian, who moved to Mississippi from Ohio in the 1950s, had experience with many organizations to draw from when she assessed WIMS. She had worked with the American Civil Liberties Union, MPE, the YWCA, and Head Start; helped to establish Jackson's interfaith prayer group; and independently conducted housing inspections, after which she interceded with the city government on behalf of residents to resolve deficiencies, such as inoperable bath and kitchen facilities, and deteriorating contruction.[8] The job of achieving an integrated society remained far from finished, but thanks in part to WIMS's efforts, progress had begun.

For Mississippians, the civil rights movement in 1965 looked very different than it had the year before. The national leaders of the NAACP accused SNCC of being infiltrated by Chinese communists and divorced itself from COFO, creating a rift in the Mississippi movement primarily along class lines. By late July 1965, COFO had been abolished; and the following summer, fewer than 200 volunteers participated in programs run by the MFDP. Labor representatives invited middle-class black men to join them in forming an interracial group of Loyalist Mississippi Democrats to reunite with the national party; noticeably excluded from the new political alliance were sharecroppers, maids, and grassroots people like Fannie Lou Hamer who had paved the way for them through the MFDP.[9]

Social policy in Mississippi had shifted as well. During his State of the Union address on January 8, 1964, President Johnson announced that his administration declared "unconditional war on poverty."[10] The War on Poverty encompassed numerous social welfare programs advanced during Johnson's presidency but referred primarily to those under the Economic Opportunity Act of 1964 (EOA).[11] Title I of the act created the Job Corps, job training, and work-study programs; Title II provided for community action programs involving education; Title III introduced programs to fight rural poverty; Title IV offered employment and investment incentives for small businesses; Title

V initiated the Work Experience program for unemployed parents; and Title VI created Volunteers in Service to America (VISTA), based on the Peace Corps, to fight U.S. poverty.[12] Johnson selected Sargent Shriver to head the new Office of Economic Opportunity (OEO) to administer the program.

The anti-poverty programs created new opportunities and constraints for the civil rights movement.[13] While the programs offered relief and a chance for blacks to exercise some control over policy in their communities, the programs were not above political influence. For example, the EOA initiated Head Start in Mississippi; however, while the educational program met with success in helping children, it became embroiled in a political controversy over funding and control. Other programs also struggled to yield positive results as white Mississippians in positions of power attempted to block or control them.[14]

In 1965, WIMS continued to work on building bridges of understanding, but it employed new methods appropriate to the political and social changes that had taken place as compliance with the Civil Rights Act of 1964 became more widespread. Eight WIMS teams, totaling forty-seven women, went to Jackson and other Mississippi communities, including Philadelphia, Greenville, Greenwood, Mt. Beulah, Lexington, Edwards, and Oxford. Cowan again arranged team visits between northern and southern, and black and white women of various faiths, this time matching them by occupation. Most of the team members were teachers, but they also included social workers, librarians, psychologists, and a doctor. Additionally, WIMS helped track compliance with the Civil Rights Act by reporting abuses to national enforcement agencies.[15]

By 1966, the needs of Mississippians had evolved yet again. SNCC had no programs in Mississippi and only seventeen people working in the state. Black Power advocates called for the exclusion of whites from the movement, which caused many whites to distance themselves, even though Black Power did not garner much of a following among religious black Mississippians.[16] Also during this period, riots erupted in cities across the country, focusing the attention of both activists and the public on other areas and communities in need. In response to these changes, Wednesdays in Mississippi became Workshops in Mississippi to more specifically target the southern women's needs.[17] While WIMS had the specific goal of opening lines of communication between women to challenge white supremacy, Workshops aided the women who were racism's victims by addressing basic human needs such as housing, food, clothing, and employment. It created a bridge between government agencies and poor Mississippi women, giving them the knowledge they needed to make use of government assistance for their own advancement.[18]

The programs that grew out of the original WIMS concept created a ripple effect, expanding its positive impact. Even as the team members continued to present themselves as proper ladies engaged in women's work, they employed new strategies in response to Mississippi's evolving social climate, which now permitted interracial public gatherings. Their methods enabled them to move beyond being observers to directly participating in programs such as Head Start, the University of Mississippi Sumer Institute, the Philadelphia to Philadelphia Project, and WIMS's professional exchange. Workshops in Mississippi demonstrates that the NCNW continued to be a force in the civil rights struggle by adapting its program to meet the shifting needs of the times and the people, with classes on writing grant proposals and programs like Operation Daily Bread and Turnkey III.

In mid-November 1964, the NCNW held a two-day meeting at the Sheraton Park Hotel in Washington, D.C., uniting thirty northern and ten southern women who had taken part in WIMS, to discuss the value of the project and the NCNW's future direction in Mississippi. The meeting included representatives of the Civil Rights Commission, the Department of Labor, the Department of Commerce, and the Department of Health, Education, and Welfare (HEW). WIMS organizers and participants and government representatives addressed how the women could assist in implementing Title VI of the Civil Rights Act of 1964, which prohibited discrimination by government agencies receiving federal funds.[19]

The ten southern women offered a mixed assessment of WIMS. Patt Derian, who advocated the project's return, explained that it was "important for us to meet, northern and southern women together . . . to share in depth the significance of our experience . . . for determining new steps and future plans."[20] Another southerner, Jane Schutt, encouraged WIMS to return, to meet in integrated groups, to stay for longer periods, and to take their hostesses to multiracial lectures and any other place they could go in multiracial groups. She volunteered to arrange homestays for members of both races. A few southern white women were not so positive. They had read reports from team members and interpreted the evaluations as personal criticisms. They saw some of the Wednesdays women as unsympathetic to the southern white women's "special problems" and felt the northern women overlooked the South's "positive steps." When the northern team members condemned Mississippi, the southern women took offense because they believed the condemnation was aimed at them as well, even if that was not the intent.[21]

In the end, the positive evaluations carried the discussion, and the NCNW decided to return. Later Dorothy Height reflected on the decision to move forward, saying that African Americans had experienced so many instances of "rising expectations . . . almost immediately offset with disappointments" that it would have been wrong for WIMS to offer Mississippians hope for change and then leave them without realizing that potential.[22]

As she had done in 1964, Cowan made a trip to Jackson in March 1965 to reaffirm that the southern women welcomed the NCNW's help. Over five days, Cowan and NCNW staff member Hope Ackerman met with the local YWCA board, Millsaps College professors, school administration personnel, members of Delta Sigma Theta, WomanPower Unlimited, Father Bernard Law and Father James McGough, Julian Tatum, and members of Jackson's Unitarian Church. Cowan reconnected at luncheons, dinners, and meetings with friends from the previous year, including Lillian Burnstein, Mrs. A. B. Britton, Miriam Ezelle, Eleanor Fontaine, Florence Gooch, Clarie Collins Harvey, Mrs. Walter Neill, and Jay Shands. Two Jackson women admitted that the WIMS visits had a more far-reaching effect—North and South—than they had imagined.[23] The overwhelming consensus was that WIMS should return.

WIMS became a full-time NCNW program, and the headquarters moved out of Cowan's apartment to an office at 147 East 81st Street in New York. The NCNW employed a director to work with Cowan, and a researcher in Washington, D.C., to keep the organization abreast of legislation. Susan Goodwillie served as executive secretary. The annual budget quadrupled to $40,000, and the staff appealed to charitable foundations for grants. In 1965, thirteen foundations gave $19,850, and thirty-four individuals made contributions totaling $4,500.[24] Several 1964 team members assisted in fundraising, events for which included a United Artists film premier party and a benefit concert starring Coretta Scott King.[25]

In 1965, the veteran team members assisted in recruiting seven teams of forty-three women and a special team of four art teachers from thirty-six communities in eleven states and the District of Columbia. Area coordinators screened applicants with the final selection made by the New York staff. Although having interracial, interfaith teams remained important, the organizers concentrated more on choosing women with professional skills.[26] The women chosen were middle-class, mostly middle-aged, and "skilled in community relations and community action." They were effective communicators committed to solving civil rights issues in the North and the South.[27]

No longer required to separate the staff or teams by race, the organizers made a few adjustments to the project's logistics. The black member of the Jackson staff, Osceola Walden, a teacher and social worker, shared a house with Diane Vivell, the volunteer white staffer from 1964 who had returned to do legal research for the Lawyers' Constitutional Defense Committee (LCDC) in Jackson. The white staffer, Caroline Smith, a writer and researcher, lived in an apartment next to WIMS angel Ann Hewitt.[28] In 1965, all of the team members received invitations to stay in private homes. Team members did not necessarily travel to the same projects or meet with the same people because of the focus on professional exchanges. This made the structure of each visit less cohesive than in 1964 but offered the individual team members a greater array of experiences. The teams spent three days in Mississippi, but some stayed longer depending on their projects.[29] Because the organizers continued to have security concerns, one thing did not change: WIMS still notified the president, attorney general, and governor of its plans, in addition to maintaining weekly contact with the Department of Justice.

The team members' experiences in 1965 were subtly different from those of the previous year. A few commented that as they flew in and drove to the homes of their hostesses they found Jackson to be "in stark contrast" to the scars of violence they expected to see.[30] Rather than separating by race at the airport, the local staff waited together to meet the arriving teams. Ellen Dammond, a training supervisor for the YWCA and a member of its national board, wrote that the two staff women came forth "with such sure and steady strides" that she felt a "great sense of relief," in contrast to her expectations.[31]

The Wednesdays women still wore white gloves and dresses to be beyond reproach. Team member Carol Guyer of the Institute for International Education surmised, "A Northerner can get away with expressing highly iconoclastic ideas as long as she is neatly dressed, smiles, is gracious, and is a faithful church member!"[32] This continued to be true not just from the northern women's perspective but from that of the southern women as well. Florence Mars, a fourth-generation white woman from Neshoba County, Mississippi, wrote to Caroline Smith, "It is amazing what can be done if you wear white gloves. I do not wish to defend a society whose values are measured by white gloves and blue jeans, but in so far as they represent a certain strata of the society, it has some merit. . . . No one wants to dirty the white gloves."[33] Exploiting gender, age, and class continued to be an important aspect of the teams' success. Team member Marjorie Penney, an interpersonal-relations specialist, reported that the women she met in Jackson represented a "solid block of small power" and were "feminine women." She added, "I saw more flowered hats and white gloves [than] I've seen in many the day."[34]

Indicating not much had changed in how southern women presented themselves and how they communicated, Penney reported that most of the southern women appeared to have "an old-fashioned hold on their husbands" and shared "every living word" about WIMS with neighbors and close friends.[35] The WIMS organizers were delighted. Carol Guyer believed that the white women she met in Jackson and Greenville had "a very deep conviction about racial harmony and longed for support by their menfolk." When Guyer asked the southern white women, many of whom had developed an understanding of race relations through their churches, why they appeared to care more than white men, one responded, "Women are naturally more humane." This no doubt reflected both the reality of women's roles as family caregivers as well as the prevailing belief at the time that women and mothers were inherently more nurturing. Both Guyer and Caroline Smith noted that the "almost universal opposition by the men to interracial social events" remained an issue even as the women moved forward.[36]

By the end of summer, Cowan wrote, "It can be argued, with equal validity, that Mississippi underwent revolutionary change in the past year, *and* that it remains the most segregationist state in the Union. . . . Almost none of the WIMS 1965 projects could have been undertaken in 1964."[37] The staff resided interracially and the teams met and dined with local women in interracial groups without incident. Cowan called it breaking the "sight barrier," adding that the Jackson white women "saw that nothing happened to you when you had lunch together. . . . Then they moved to the next thing and the next thing. . . . When you can get used to seeing Negro and white people together, you get over that initial shock. Then it gets to a point where you don't see it anymore."[38] This freed women of different races to work side by side and to socialize, which created connections that "welded quite firmly." After one WIMS luncheon, a Mississippi woman said that coming to the gathering was the hardest thing she had ever done; but if she had not "moved" that far in a year, she would never have moved.[39]

The Wednesdays women noticed shifts in the attitudes of the southern white women. A black business owner who came with WIMS both summers, Flaxie Pinkett concluded that Mississippi had "come a long way" over the course of a year and noted that far more white women came to meet with the black women in 1965 than the prior year. The white women she met now echoed the sentiments the teams had heard from black women the first summer. "Both seemed interested in who we were and what we had to say; both seemed appreciative that we cared enough to come; both were relieved to have interested persons to discuss their problems with; and both gave promise of the determination for a better life for all people in Mississippi."[40] Likewise, Lorna Scheide, a member of the YWCA and LWV, observed that even though she still caught a "feeling of defensiveness," the Jackson women were "ready for a 'Next Stage'—i.e.: perhaps doing more widely with their new Negro friends."[41]

The Wednesdays women continued to be labeled outsiders in 1965, but the number of southern women welcoming their help grew. Cowan contended that the women who said they needed no help really had no interest in making changes at all. She added, "The truly dedicated insiders not only welcome help, from wherever it comes, but know they need it."[42] Penney noted that some of the southern women did not know where to begin in their communities or, in some cases, in their professions. Outsiders assisted them in taking the important first step.[43] Women in Greenville, including the wife of a prominent business leader, asked for more teams to be sent to their community.[44] Those who had seen progress wanted to continue bridging the racial divide. Jay Shands, a Jackson woman who worked with WIMS both summers, explained, "The ball is rolling and we don't want to go backwards."[45]

White supremacists continued to blame outsiders for the South's problems.[46] The Wednesdays women heard criticisms of the dirty COFO students and their behavior, which defied southern customs, along with accusations of communist infiltration in their ranks. Although Carol Guyer speculated that the southern women's disdain had more to do with the assumption that the students were subversive radicals than the actual activities in which they engaged, the rhetoric certainly carried enough power to restrict people's lives.[47]

The divorce proceedings of Danelle and George Vockroth, who had hosted Team 7 members Priscilla Hunt and Hannah Levin in their home in 1964, demonstrate how powerful accusations of civil rights activity could be. Although both husband and wife had expressed their feelings as frustrated moderates to the team the first summer, in 1965 George leveraged his wife's political activities against her in divorce court. A member of 1965 Team 4, Marguerite Cassell explained that George "properly impressed" the judge by telling him that Danelle was "running around to such Communist-front organizations as the Inter-Faith Council and the League of Women Voters," and that she had gone to work for the *Northside Reporter*, a liberal, pro-civil rights newspaper in Jackson.[48] In a time before no-fault divorces, the judge denied Danelle's request to end the marriage; however, since the couple had separated, he did grant her custody of their three children because of their young ages.[49] Despite the slurs by her husband, Danelle again welcomed WIMS teams in her home in 1965.

Fear remained the largest stumbling block to progress in the South for both blacks and whites.[50] Many acts of violence continued to go unresolved and unpunished.[51] Gladys Zales of Hadassah called her trip as a member of Team 2 a "journey into *fear* . . . that took on many voices and many forms." Zales added, "I saw it in the look of a mother, a husband. It was in the eyes, pursed lips—in the rigidity or the impress of a hand. I heard it expressed in whispers."[52] Not all fears had to do with physical attacks. At an afternoon meeting at Patt Derian's home, Hannah Levin, a psychologist and professor at Rutgers University, addressed the unease Mississippi women felt as they adjusted to the social ramifications of integration. The women present told Levin that they feared they saw "each other in the most stereotyped manners instead of widening [their] vision and beginning to notice new qualities and characteristics." Levin explained that they had no reason to feel guilty. They feared change, which did not indicate prejudice on their part but rather a natural human response to the new and the different. However, she stressed the importance of combatting the effects of fear "on their thinking and perceiving. . . . [By] increasing communication between whites and blacks, one gets knowledge of what's going on and the fear of the unknown lessens."[53]

Even though many white men continued to resist change, others expressed a willingness to move forward. The Jackson Chamber of Commerce came out in favor of compliance with the Civil Rights Act soon after President Lyndon Johnson signed the bill into law. Jackson's Mayor Allen Thompson, who personally found the law abhorrent, nonetheless stated the city would comply out of respect for law and order. In Philadelphia, Mississippi, assistant director of WIMS Margery Gross reported that the head of the local Rotary Club had stated, "We must overcome the sins of the past," referring to the racism in the community that had led to the murders of the three COFO workers.[54]

The Citizens' Council continued producing propaganda that fed on fear as businesses opted to comply with the new law. The council shifted its approach to generate support from the working class by appealing to class envy, even though many of Jackson's wealthiest citizens had stood with the segregationists and racists in the past.[55] Team member Josie Harbison, coordinator for Gray Ladies of the New Jersey Neuropsychiatric Institute under the Red Cross, reported that fliers distributed to people's homes stated, "The rich businessmen know that they can afford to live in wealthy areas of the city where the Negro cannot move. They have their rich private country clubs and golf links and swimming pools and private schools. They are selfish

and vicious in demanding that the white working-class mix with black un-
civilized animals so that they may make money off of their Negro customers."[56] With the defection of white businessmen in support of the Civil Rights
Act, blaming outsiders and communists alone for Mississippi's racial strife
no longer worked. Hence, upper-class Mississippians became the target of
segregationists, who hoped to increase their numbers by creating a class war.
Nevertheless, businesses increasingly chose to follow the law.

The most important and noticeable distinction between WIMS 1964 and
1965 was that the team members took an active role in working with the projects they visited. For example, rather than observing a Freedom School, they
assisted in preparing teachers to take part in Head Start to improve the education of disadvantaged children; instead of listening to reports on the status
of public education, they canvassed with local women to increase the number
of black children enrolled in integrated schools; and rather than restricting
themselves to social gatherings, they met with southern professional women
to create new networks benefiting both the southern women and themselves.

The EOA targeted the needs of the poor in several ways, but President
Johnson especially emphasized helping poor youth and pledged that the programs would insure that "poverty's children" would no longer be "poverty's
captives." He explained that the name Head Start was chosen to demonstrate
that the federal project would be a neighborhood effort that needed the support of volunteers to succeed. Lawmakers carefully crafted Head Start as an
experimental program in early childhood education, yet one that would yield
results.[57]

WIMS played a role in initiating Head Start in Mississippi and acted as
a catalyst in facilitating its programs in the state. Height was in attendance
when the White House announced the program just days before Cowan left
on her March trip to Mississippi. This gave WIMS the chance to introduce
Head Start to Mississippians before anyone else did. Having been briefed
by Height, Cowan used the trip to discuss Head Start with white and black
women in both segregated and multiracial groups. These women included
Hinds County's Head Start director Esther Sampson, a black social worker
who worked with WIMS in 1964, and Jackson's white assistant director Ann
Hewitt. The New York staff also began sending the women Cowan had met
materials on "pre-school education for culturally deprived children."[58]

The contacts WIMS made the year before enabled it to act as a liaison
between the black and white communities. Asked to serve on the board for
Head Start, Patt Derian and two other white women refused unless an equal
number of black women also served. WIMS provided them with a list of

black women leaders to contact.[59] Over the summer, the relationship that developed between Esther Sampson and Hewitt impressed the teams, and by September, the pair had the interracial board members meeting in each other's homes—something that would not have happened the year before without the impetus of a project like Head Start.[60] WIMS initiated the contact between the director, assistant director, and board members, while the program's goal of educating children gave them an appropriate venue for women and mothers to collaborate interracially. In this way, it mirrored MPE, which had worked across racial boundaries in 1964 to keep public schools open.

The Child Development Group of Mississippi (CDGM) administered the state's Head Start program, which was the largest in the nation. A group of private, public, and church organizations formed CDGM when the state government refused to apply for Head Start funds.[61] CDGM designed its curriculum to prepare children for regular school and provided them with two meals a day plus medical and dental care. Parents would receive counseling on how to improve the home environment. Head Start also offered employment opportunities to the many people required to staff the schools. Tom Levin, a New York psychoanalyst who had come to Mississippi in 1964, headed CDGM initially, responsible for its $1.5 million budget. The Delta Ministry, founded in 1964 by the NCC as a ministry of reconciliation to offer direct relief, partnered with Head Start from the beginning and offered space at its headquarters in Mt. Beulah.[62] Despite these ties to friends of the civil rights movement and the similarities between Head Start and the Freedom Schools, SNCC refused to endorse the project, which it criticized as an idea put forth by northern whites.[63] This did not deter many former SNCC workers, movement activists, and MFDP members from taking part, however.[64]

Two days prior to Head Start's launch, 6,200 students had enrolled in Mississippi's eighty-four centers, with ninety percent of the funds for the classes coming from federal grants and ten percent from local sources. In Jackson, 1,200 children enrolled in eighty classes at eighteen centers, taught by four white and seventy-six black teachers. Because state officials opposed Head Start's requirement that preschool classes be integrated, no public schools hosted classes. All met in parochial schools, black churches, community centers, and the predominantly white Unitarian Church.[65] Other obstacles included shootings and cross-burnings at facilities, and fires at a few buildings. Harassment by law enforcement resulted in a total of $1,000 in traffic fines the first week.[66]

WIMS helped prepare the Jackson Head Start teachers for their new assignments. A week before the schools opened, the special WIMS team of four art teachers arrived to train the Head Start teachers in creative art techniques used with young children.[67] The teachers appeared anxious to have "something extremely practical" to use in the classroom. The WIMS team provided them with context and activities that they could use confidently from the first day.[68] The team divided their responsibilities to conduct four workshops and demonstrate different art forms, including how to create projects using scrap materials.[69] The following week, it became apparent that both teachers and students had been deprived of the chance to experiment with art in Mississippi schools, but the WIMS women also found that their northern expectations did not necessarily fit life in the South. Initially Carol Guyer was concerned when three small girls used their straws and feathers to make feather dusters, suggesting they could imagine little more than their mothers' experiences as domestic servants, in contrast to northern children who made "birds of paradise and other fantasies." However, when the "children started tickling each other with great hilarity," Guyer realized that "a feather duster isn't necessarily a feather duster. It all depends upon your attitude."[70]

Because art instruction includes more than creating projects, the teams offered art appreciation programs to expand the horizons of Mississippi students and residents. During two weeks in Greenville, a member of the New York team developed a relationship with the Greenville Art Association, and they worked together to develop and fund programs to share art with the community. An art collector and member of the Chicago team created a slideshow of contemporary art by white and black artists. Following the presentation, the president of the Mississippi Art Society arranged to host a visiting exhibit at a local bank so that blacks who would have been turned away at a museum could attend.[71] Further, the team members searched out three foundations interested in funding a new integrated art museum in Jackson.

The Jackson Head Start directors emphasized the importance of parental involvement, and WIMS played a role in conveying that message. The New Jersey team met with three parent groups to suggest ways parents could encourage their children to "demonstrate at home what they had learned in school." The meetings pointed out to the WIMS teams the need for counseling parents in how to deal with children's normal problems.[72] Esther Higgs Cooke, a special service school teacher, helped parents understand their roles in preparing their children to attend public schools, explaining that parents must teach their children to care for their own physical needs independently, and must make them feel loved so that they do not engage in anti-social behavior to get attention at school. She added that the home atmosphere should instill in children a positive self-image to give them a sense of self-worth.[73] Cooke reminded the parents that "children are great imitators," and therefore that parents should "teach respect for law and order and for the rights of others"—an ironic lesson for a group of poor, almost exclusively black parents, whose rights had been ignored and abused for years.[74] Nevertheless, her suggestions were met with appreciation rather than resentment from the audience. This might have been because the parents were not sure what to expect at an integrated public school, and many lacked faith that their children would be treated as equals no matter how well prepared they were.

The vast majority of the Head Start centers had all-black student bodies because whites feared sending their children there. Patt Derian noted that for those parents, the medical and dental care often overrode their fear.[75] Dorothy Stewart, an African American educator in Jackson, recalled that having the northern women in Mississippi helped to ease the transition to an integrated staff and student body.[76] For example, WIMS found a white nursery school teacher in Iowa to join the Head Start project at Saints Junior College in Lexington, Mississippi, to integrate the teaching staff. The school served 140 children who lived on plantations in appalling conditions. It conducted its classes at night because the plantation owners refused to allow visitors or to let the children attend school during working hours.[77]

Adults across the state also benefited from the employment that Head Start provided in its centers. Local people worked as teachers, teachers' aides, janitors, maintenance personnel, cooks, servers, secretaries, and keypunch operators. It provided jobs for approximately 1,100 men and women at rates between fifty and sixty dollars a week. This compared to approximately three dollars a day paid to the average plantation worker (who might or might not work the whole week), and ten to fifteen dollars a week to domestics.[78]

Head Start received accolades from many sources. Derian called it "just about the best thing that could happen to children" because it introduced concepts to which people living in extreme poverty lacked access.[79] Likewise, Dorothy Stewart explained that northerners who assisted in implementing Head Start played an important role because Mississippians "were not sure that they wanted a program like this . . . with children and parents and community people being involved in the educational system."[80] Historian James F. Findlay quotes one Holmes County mother as saying, "It give the teachers and workers a chance to learn while they work with the children. Some people don't understand that it's very hard for our children to get along in Miss[issippi]. This program give them a great opportunity to be free of fear. . . . They are poor and this program give them food and great learning and new ideals and opportunity that they never had."[81]

Unfortunately, while Head Start met with success in the classroom, it became a political flashpoint for racists who attempted to undermine it.[82] All of Mississippi's members of Congress had voted against the president's poverty programs and opposed CDGM. Before the schools opened, a Jackson newspaper compared Head Start to Soviet Russia, Red China, and Hitler's Germany, concluding, "Here is one of the most subtle mediums for instilling the acceptance of racial integration and ultimate mongrelization ever perpetrated in this country." Senator John Stennis (D-MS), a member of the Appropriations Committee, accused CDGM of fraud, supporting the anti-war movement, and misappropriating Head Start funds to bail its staff out of jail and support the MFDP.[83] The senator claimed that CDGM used OEO money to underwrite "the extreme leftist civil rights and beatnik groups" in Mississippi, some of which he asserted had "definite connections with Communist organizations."[84] Sociologist Kenneth T. Andrews notes that the CDGM staff members' affiliations, past and present, with COFO, SNCC, CORE, NAACP, MFDP, the Urban League, and Delta Ministry made them targets.[85] The Mississippi Sovereignty Commission, which routinely monitored all such civil rights organizations, worked covertly to discredit CDGM and had informants on Director Tom Levin's staff who sent regular reports to Stennis and Senator James Eastland (D-MS).[86] Patt Derian theorized that Stennis was motivated by his constituents who thought the "white outside agitators" were "stirring up" the local blacks.[87]

The controversy over accusations of CDGM's misuse of funds spanned two years and proved to be the nation's largest involving Head Start, creating difficulties for President Johnson who needed southern senators' support for the War on Poverty and the Vietnam War. When OEO director Sargent Shriver opted to suspend funding to CDGM, Marian Wright Edelman, a CDGM board member and attorney for the NAACP Legal Defense and Educational Fund, assisted the organization in finding a new director and encouraging local leaders to fight within the system to continue receiving federal money for Head Start.[88] Led by Governor Paul Johnson, Mississippi Action for Progress formed in 1966 to apply for the OEO funds previously given to CDGM, and Shriver approved the shift.[89] Derian was surprised that the whites she spoke with in Issaquena County in the Delta region, whom she expected to support Eastland and Stennis, were "furious" at the loss of CDGM, because under the influence of that organization, "For the first time a lot of poor black people did not have to buy on credit. They were going in and paying with cash, and that amount of payroll pulled out of an impoverished county really made a difference." Those whites who benefitted from the improved economy let their congressional representatives know it.[90] Protests by blacks and some whites resulted in funds being restored to CDGM, although not at the previous level, and both it and MAP continued to operate in the state.[91]

Despite the political furor and harassment, the day-to-day operation of the Head Start centers continued. When the Mississippi legislature held up federal funds, the Presbyterian Church USA sent money to the schools. At least fifty of the centers serving over 3,000 children still met thanks to volunteer efforts. When one center burned down on a Sunday night, the children only missed one day of class. By Tuesday, they had reconvened in a makeshift facility with everyone in attendance. At one school, parents posted guards around the clock for the entire summer to protect their center.[92]

In the end, Dorothy Stewart said that Head Start not only worked, it "made a difference with the children."[93] Derian noted that the "children benefited unbelievably," and that the "adults were empowered."[94] Most surprisingly, the segregationist *Jackson Daily News* reported that the black and white staffs worked well together. This was a significant concession on the part of the newspaper, especially given that whites were teachers' aides, subordinate to black teachers.[95] While WIMS certainly could not take credit for the overall successes achieved by the Head Start program in 1965, it did play a significant role in getting it off the ground in Jackson and other communities across the state.

Looking to move forward following its struggles with desegregation, the University of Mississippi received a grant from HEW to conduct the "Special Training Institute on Problems of School Desegregation," an interracial meeting of teachers, principals, and superintendents of rural Mississippi schools. In the spring of 1965, Kate Wilkinson, a sociology graduate student who had befriended Goodwillie and Vivell in 1964, contacted WIMS for assistance in organizing the conference.[96] In response, the WIMS New York staff identified and screened possible lecturers on "community relations, psychology, sociology, teaching art and remedial reading." It obtained films, reference materials, and pre-publication books related to African American literature and civil rights work in the South, and created booklists for the participants. WIMS also arranged for the American Jewish Committee to make kits for them. Six WIMS team members and the Jackson staff served as specialists at the institute. For many of the 120 teacher-students in attendance, the institute was their first experience with prominent blacks, and the sessions helped change their "stereotyped concept of the Negro."[97]

Dorothy Height was the first black lecturer at the summer institute and the first black overnight guest at the university's faculty club. When she attempted to check in at the faculty club, the clerk called the institute's director, professor of educational psychology Roscoe Boyer, who gave assurance that Chancellor John D. Williams not only welcomed Height to the campus, but had invited her to his home for dinner. Height wrote, "As word of his approval spread across campus, it was like a miracle. The pervasive sense of unease seemed to dissipate."[98]

Height's lecture focused on the role that schools played in helping children achieve their full civil rights, and it quickly became clear that the local educators held many misconceptions. When Height quoted from a report of the U.S. Civil Rights Commission, many of the white attendees believed she read the words from a communist document. A white second grade teacher expressed her fear that the white children in integrated classrooms would sit on the same toilet seats as black children and "contract syphilis." It took Height's offering "an elementary lecture on the nature of venereal disease" for the woman to realize how unfounded her fears were. These open discussions began building bridges between those in attendance. Height recalled, "Nearly all of them recognized that it was the first time in their lives they'd heard a candid, nonbelligerent discussion of civil rights and desegregation."[99]

Even for those willing to change, it was not easy to make the transition. Height sat next to a white superintendent from Natchez, Mississippi, who had never shared a meal with a black person before, let alone a black professional woman. He told her that when he returned to his district, he planned to take no action to desegregate the schools; but he said, "I chose the best teachers and the best principals that I had, and brought them to this course. . . . They will begin things, and eventually I'll be able to say to the board of education, 'You see, this is what the people want.' When that time comes . . . I'll be ready, and I'll have the people on my staff ready to support it."[100] Though some Mississippians tried to block desegregation, others, like this superintendent, "saw its inevitability and were willing to think creatively about strategies that might sustain progress."[101]

After the institute, Roscoe Boyer wrote to thank WIMS, saying he found it ironic that as the director of the institute he was writing to another organization to express his gratitude for the success of his own conference. He noted, "Nevertheless, it was through your effort to marshal the forces of WIMS that the program succeeded." One black participant told him that she thought the attendees were now the best-informed people in the state as a result.[102] Chancellor Williams also wrote to thank WIMS, saying, "We had one of the most successful institutes in the country and, as a result, the entire state has benefitted."[103]

The fact that the university hosted the institute and its leadership offered positive feedback indicated a shift in the segregationist attitudes of earlier years; however, the director remained wary of the university being in the spotlight. Commenting on the importance of discussing civil rights in a "non-threatening, academic environment," Boyer concluded, "I am most grateful that all this has been accomplished without anyone wanting to demonstrate an invested interest in trying to popularize the institute through publicity. WIMS' cooperation in being a silent partner in the institute has been most gratifying."[104] As WIMS had found in meetings with local women the previous summer, the quiet approach had worked, providing an entrée to the university power structure and empowering the institution to move forward on civil rights.

Although WIMS did not initiate the Philadelphia to Philadelphia Project, WIMS played a role in it by uniting women from different parts of the state to work for change. Rudolf Gelsey, a Unitarian Universalist minister at the Church of the Restoration in the Germantown community of Philadelphia, Pennsylvania, conceived the idea for a program to reach out to the people of Philadelphia, Mississippi, following the murder there of the three civil rights workers in June 1964. He started by contacting Mississippi clergy.

Three weeks before Mickey Schwerner, James Chaney, and Andrew Goodman disappeared, Reverend Clay Lee had transferred to the First Methodist Church in Philadelphia, Mississippi, from Jackson's Galloway Memorial Methodist Church, hoping for a quiet pastorate after the intense infighting over integration at Galloway; but that was not to be. When Lee was approached in January 1965 to take part in the Philadelphia to Philadelphia Project, he thought it was "very noble" but also "unwise" because he feared locals would misinterpret the intent as northern interference. Despite his reservations, the project proceeded, and Lee agreed to act as a mediator between representatives of the northern and southern cities. He enlisted his congregant Florence Mars, and the two traveled to Philadelphia, Pennsylvania. Mars, a white businesswoman whose family had lived in Neshoba County for over a hundred years, had contacts in the black community and had increased Lee's sensitivity in racial matters.[105]

WIMS became involved through the Philadelphia, Pennsylvania, Women's International League for Peace and Freedom (WILPF), and team members networked with other activist women.[106] After a May 1965 meeting in which Lee told the organizers of the Philadelphia to Philadelphia Project that he did not think its goal of open and equal communication across race was realistic for his community at that time, he bowed to their insistence and asked Mars to work with WIMS as part of the project.[107] Eleven women on two WIMS teams, coordinated by Caroline Smith, took part in the Philadelphia to Philadelphia Project.[108]

After meeting Smith, Mars arranged for the two WIMS teams to visit with approximately fifteen women in Philadelphia, Mississippi, who might be willing to start a local organization like MPE.[109] Team member Margery Gross recalled that the Philadelphia women were white moderate Methodists, Baptists, and Catholics who wanted to "right some of the wrongs" of the past and were especially concerned about police brutality. While they made derogatory comments about COFO and the national press, most admitted that the civil rights movement and the murders had forced them to recognize what was happening in their area.[110]

Some of these women were nervous because they had family businesses, and others worried about what their husbands would think. Mars found that the women needed direction, telling her, "If we knew what to do, we'd try to do something." Patt Derian spoke to the group, and Mars credited that meeting with getting them organized and encouraging them to take action.[111] Intimidation could not easily be overlooked, however. Team member Marjorie Duckrey, a social worker and president of the Citizens' Committee on Public Education in Philadelphia, Pennsylvania, noted that Sheriff Lawrence Rainey and Deputy Sheriff Cecil Price, who had arrested the three civil rights workers, passed by "at least a dozen times" as the team sat in front of the COFO office. "As they passed, they left clouds of red dust to settle on the layer that had hardly settled from their last trip around," she said.[112]

The second WIMS team coming to Philadelphia, Mississippi, had a different sort of experience. Just before Mars was to meet with them, a sheriff's deputy arrested her for driving while intoxicated. The charges, which appeared to be harassment, were later dismissed. Nevertheless, local community-planning experts met with the WIMS team in Jackson rather than Philadelphia because of restrictions against interracial gatherings. During the meeting, the planning experts who came with WIMS provided the southern women with materials on community development.[113]

The two Philadelphia WIMS teams also worked with voter registration. One woman they accompanied to register was Lillie Jones, nicknamed "the biggest little woman in the world" after she persuaded the U.S. postmaster general to arrange mail service for her neighborhood. A registrar repeatedly turned Jones away in 1964; when a WIMS team came with her to the courthouse in 1965, the same registrar treated her graciously and registered her. Teary-eyed, Jones left the courthouse with what she called "somebody-ness"—her voter registration.[114] Although many factors led to this change, WIMS's presence demonstrated that people outside Mississippi continued to monitor infringement on the rights of blacks there. One team member commented that Jones taught her a lesson on the importance of understanding the southern struggle, and how to see even "meager" gains as a "beautiful thing."[115]

WIMS's contributions to the Philadelphia to Philadelphia Project became evident in several areas. Florence Mars wrote to Caroline Smith, "Where the evil forces have such an overbearing head start, the kind of help you are offering is of indispensable value. There has seemed no way to marshal the positive forces—but they are here."[116] Six Mississippi women who met with Margery Gross insisted on inviting others to meet that afternoon at the home of Millie Hallowell, who lived next door to Sheriff Rainey. Although the invitees seemed reluctant to act (perhaps because of their location), they showed concern "about the total lack of involvement of the men," who were "money mad" and willing to stop at nothing to protect their financial security.[117] Although not liberal by northern standards, these women showed a willingness to move forward and asked WIMS to provide materials on organizing community action groups.[118] WIMS also brought the Philadelphia, Mississippi, women into contact with Jackson MPE women. The Philadelphians then started a local MPE chapter, organized a car pool to minimize harassment of black high school students, arranged for tutors for them, and coordinated with the parents of black children to act upon complaints.[119] Prior to WIMS acting as a liaison, MPE had failed to make a connection with the Philadelphia women.

The WIMS visits to Pax Christi Center and St. Francis Mission opened the door to working with Mississippi Catholics and created a bridge between Jackson Catholic women and the mission. In 1964, Natchez-Jackson Diocese Bishop Richard Gerow refused to give permission for the Maryknoll Sisters to join the WIMS teams in Mississippi or for team members to meet with local Catholic groups. One nun, Sister Catherine John of the Sisters of the Immaculate Heart, did come, as did Peggy Roach, executive assistant of the NCCW, who met with Father Bernard Law and the bishop. As a result of those efforts, in 1965 Father Law asked WIMS to send a team to visit the mission located in an impoverished area of Greenwood.[120]

Pax Christi grew out of the efforts of Father Nathaniel Machesky, a white Franciscan friar from Michigan, and Kate Foote Jordan, or "Miss Kate," a white widow from a prominent family in Greenville, Mississippi. After receiving permission to open the mission for blacks in Greenwood, Father Machesky and Father Bonaventure Bolda established St. Francis Mission and School in the former Blue Moon café and nightclub in 1950. The town only had two black Catholics at the time, but the priests went door-to-door and encouraged parents to send their children to the mission school, promising them a good education. In September 1951, the school opened with twenty-two students in kindergarten through second grade. Within two weeks, the enrollment had grown to fifty-five, and the school continued adding grades each year through the eighth grade.[121] Jordan had converted to Catholicism in 1951 and devoted her life to serving the poor. In 1952, in conjunction with the mission, she founded Pax Christi, a secular institute of religious women. The members lived a lifestyle similar to that of nuns. They remained unmarried, vowed poverty, and committed to aiding the poor; but unlike nuns, they renewed their vows annually. They wore light blue uniforms and immersed themselves in Greenwood's black community. By the mid-1960s, the group included twenty dedicated members, two of whom were black.[122]

By the time of the WIMS visit, the mission school had 400 pupils and had expanded through the twelfth grade. Over the years, the mission had moved to larger facilities and included Head Start, a credit union, a used clothing store, recreational activities for children and a teenage night club, a library, a clinic, a boy's day camp, little league baseball, and a community newspaper called *Center Light,* which reported events to the black community not covered in the *Greenwood Commonwealth.* Staffed mostly by white Mississippians, the mission also relied on fifty interracial, interfaith volunteers from eighteen states, who were students, priests, and nuns, for its day-to-day operation.[123] As director, Jordan worked to change the ways of the racist community. This no doubt presented challenges since Pax Christi had no communication with the white section of town, a "stronghold of white supremacy." The mission received threats from the Klan, and the WIMS team observed that bullets remained lodged above a doorway where someone had shot into the building. The nuns reported having "doors slammed in their face" at the Catholic church in downtown Greenwood. Regardless, Jordan, preaching her "3 C's—community conscience, communication, and courage," encouraged the children to heed the words of a young mission priest who said, "Let us pray for the White Citizens' Council and the Ku Klux Klan. For those that love us and those that hate us. Let us pray."[124]

For years, Father Machesky had followed the direction of Bishop Gerow in keeping a low profile on civil rights. Sociologist Paul T. Murray notes the priest said, "We preached it [racial equality], but we didn't feel we could demonstrate." Machesky found such protests incompatible with the peaceful teaching of his order. Jordan, likewise, did not care for the "permissive lifestyle" of many of the young women in the civil rights movement. Nevertheless, the mission supported the movement by distributing food to local blacks, hiring blacks, and opening its facilities for use by the MFDP.[125] In 1967, however, Father Machesky moved to the forefront of civil rights when he and two other clergymen formed the Greenwood Movement, which sought to generate jobs and respect for African Americans. The men launched an eighteen-month boycott to force local businesses and city leaders to hire more blacks.[126]

A WIMS team from Virginia and Washington, D.C., stayed overnight at the mission and created a bridge between locals and the mission's leadership in two distinct ways. First, WIMS team members and local women discussed the similarities between the problems faced by Greenwood's residents and those of the Citizens for Better Education in Washington, D.C., demonstrating that the South was not alone in its problems. The team suggested ways for the community's private citizens to pool their efforts toward a common goal. Second, when the team returned to Jackson, they visited with fifteen Jackson Catholic women and one man at their church to tell them about the mission. The Jackson Catholics had no prior knowledge of its existence, but hearing that Greenwood Catholics had "closed their homes and church to the nuns at Pax Christi" spurred them to action. Ten of them committed to visiting the mission and attempting to break through to the white community there.[127]

In another example of WIMS's work for education, Team 7 participated in house-to-house canvassing to persuade Jackson's black families to enroll their children in integrated schools. The previous year, Jackson's public schools had integrated the first grade; in 1965, the Jackson school board's plan called for integrating the first, second, third, and twelfth grades. (Although the first grade had been integrated officially in 1964, only about three percent of those black students eligible to enroll in white schools had done so.) The canvassing organizers reported that the multiracial WIMS team lent a "special significance" to the effort and emphasized "the importance of school integration in Jackson from a national as well as a local point of view."[128]

Reverend Stevens of the LCDC instructed the team members to present themselves with an opening remark stating that they were "working for better education in Mississippi." Frances Perkins, a lecturer on preschool education at Tufts and Brandeis Universities, found that this approach often led to a warm welcome. Stevens suggested that they stress that "white schools [had] better education by virtue of a lower teacher to pupil ratio, better equipment, . . . foreign languages beginning a year earlier, the availability of Latin, separate junior and senior high schools and better opportunities for scholarship aid." The Wednesdays women informed families that no incidents "of any consequence" had occurred when schools integrated in 1964. Further, the team explained that the children were eligible for free tutoring and transportation, and that the people organizing these services had scheduled an orientation to acquaint the students with procedures for scheduling them, arranged for friendly white students to welcome them, and planned to organize periodic meetings for high school students to share their experiences.[129]Team member Mary Cannady, a social worker and director of the district office of Family Service of Philadelphia, Pennsylvania, described the many-faceted reactions of both Mississippians and team members to the experience. "We enjoyed canvassing the homes, talking with the 'ordinary' people. Some of the Negro team members were a little surprised by what they found, the great social distance. . . . There was polite acceptance of what we had to say. . . . There were apathy, resignation, indifference, and even enthusiastic acceptance. Many times, what seemed like a noncommittal reception, when explored sympathetically, turned out to be a deep feeling, usually of fear, which I was not quite prepared for. These mothers were mortally afraid of harm coming to their children, or they had deep feelings that their children were inferior and could not compete."[130]

School desegregation had been stalled in the South for over a decade following the *Brown* decision, and it seemed that at last progress had begun. Constance Curry, who worked with the NAACP Legal Defense Fund and the AFSC to desegregate schools across the region, estimated that in 1965 alone, the efforts of the two organizations had resulted in the registration of 4,000 black students in all-white schools.[131] By becoming directly involved in canvassing for school segregation, the team members felt they had helped make a difference and had gained a better understanding of the problems faced in integrating schools.

In 1964, the WIMS teams discovered that heightened racial tensions caused by the civil rights movement had resulted in increasing isolation of Mississippi professional women, a circumstance that the 1965 WIMS structure was designed to address. The teams not only worked to change attitudes about civil rights, but also dealt with the backlash the movement had created. Restrictions on interracial meetings systematically excluded black women from participating in professional organizations. White women too suffered because they did not have the benefit of their black colleagues' experiences, and because some national organizations excluded Mississippi chapters from participating based on the state's racist policies. Therefore, the chance for southern professional women to meet with northern professionals provided a "heartening experience." Following the WIMS visits in 1965, many made plans to meet at national conventions, and northern women invited the southerners to speak at events in the North.[132]

In other cases, WIMS stepped in where Mississippi welfare and education officials failed to provide resources to daycare centers and teachers. For example, Carol Guyer reported that a Greenville woman who had run a daycare facility for twelve years and served on the Delta Ministry board and the Mississippi Council for Human Relations had no knowledge of the funding available from government and non-profit organizations.[133] WIMS supplied the daycare director with details on how to apply for these funds. In a second instance, team member Sue Miller, a remedial reading teacher, instructed Mississippi classroom teachers in methods to improve language development and reading skills. While quiet during the question and answer period of Miller's presentation, many black teachers came forward enthusiastically to look at educational material picturing black and white children interacting.[134] The northern women filled in the gaps left by the state government and pushed Mississippi to meet its obligations to its children.

The Wednesdays women also opened lines of communication between social workers in the state. Team 2 met with three white social workers and five of Mississippi's six black social workers, in their first integrated meeting. Team member Helen Stanford, a psychiatric social worker with Planned Parenthood, noted that the southern women exchanged ideas and feelings that they had not shared prior to the WIMS meeting. As northern and southern women discussed their mutual problems integrating the agencies they worked for, Stanford noted that the group did not speak about how wonderful life was in the North and how poor it was in the South, but engaged in a "mutual sharing." All agreed to meet again at the next national social workers' convention.[135]

Mississippi librarians stood out as a group of professionals cut off from their national organization. Georgia, Alabama, Louisiana, and Mississippi had withdrawn from the American Library Association, refusing to comply with the organization's anti-discrimination policies.[136] Team 7 met with representatives of the Mississippi Library Commission, the Jackson Library and Jackson Municipal Library System, the Jackson State College Library, a former librarian of Jackson's first black branch library, and librarians from Jackson's black schools. The team then researched what federal funds were available to train these librarians and provide other services. Even though the Civil Right Act of 1964 had passed, branch libraries remained segregated by virtue of the fact that they stood in segregated neighborhoods.[137]

The WIMS teams acted as a bridge between communities and county library services. The counties used bookmobiles, which many blacks did not know they could use. In addition, Mississippi's library commission hired twenty to thirty high school seniors each summer to work on the bookmobiles, both to provide the students with employment and to encourage them to enter the library field. Until the WIMS teams began investigating the status of library services, no black librarians had any idea this program existed. "It is theoretically open to all Mississippians and this was the first time they had ever heard of it," exclaimed team member Guest Perry, a white librarian from Watertown, Massachusetts. Betty Barnes of Team 7, a freelance researcher and editor, commented that prior to her trip to Mississippi she thought that "poor communication" there referred to a lack of sensitivity and a failure to understand. She did not realize that one group of people could "so successfully" keep the "simple facts of life" from another group.[138]

WIMS also sought to improve the quality and availability of medical care for individuals working in the civil rights movement. While Mississippi generally lagged behind other states in quality of care, the care available to civil rights workers was even worse. Team member Dr. Anne Keller, a pediatrician from Philadelphia, Pennsylvania, met with Dr. Alvin Poussaint, the recently appointed southern field director of the Medical Committee for Human Rights, a national organization assisting civil rights workers who needed medical help. Keller wrote, "I was depressed at the meagerness of the medical presence in Jackson." She described the clinic where he worked as "a small dirty little office with no equipment." Dr. Poussaint, an African American and a recent graduate of Cornell Medical School, was limited because the segregationist in charge of medical licensing in Mississippi had not granted him a license. Poussaint provided Keller with a list of the equipment the clinic needed, which included a car. Upon Keller's return home from Mississippi, she contacted Dr. George Wilson of the Philadelphia Medical Committee for Human Rights who arranged for the car and needed supplies to be sent to Jackson.[139]

Psychologist Dr. Hannah Levin came to Mississippi with WIMS in 1964 and 1965, which enabled her to see both the change and the stagnation with regard to racial attitudes. Along with her WIMS colleagues, she met with psychologists at the Mississippi Summer Institute. Although the team members learned a great deal about mental health services in Mississippi, perhaps their greatest contribution was in helping other northerners understand the southerners' thought processes. At the debriefing Levin attended in 1965, she reported that southern whites asked questions like, "We know we must love children, but do [we] have to touch them?" Levin noted, "It gives you an understanding of the vice that they've been brought up in. They're trying to break through. It isn't hate. It's like a rigid die that their mind has been set in." She explained that it was easier for northerners to be liberal because they had not been brought up to "see the world in black and white," as southerners had.[140]

Looking to help the unemployed as well, WIMS offered aid to Jane Schutt and Helen Burney, who led the Job Corps training program in Jackson Sargent Shriver had identified the Job Corps as an important part of the EOA's strategy to end poverty within a generation, by giving people the skills they needed to succeed in the workplace. Historian David Zarefsky notes that the prevailing belief was, "Once the poor had acquired training and work habits, jobs surely would be available."[141] WIMS's connection to job training began with the 1964 WIC meeting in Atlanta, which led to the formation of Women in Community Service (WICS), an organization designed to address desegregation, voter registration, poverty, illiteracy, education, unemployment, housing, and hunger, and which became affiliated with the Job Corps.[142]

The national Job Corps focused primarily on the unemployment of men, assuming that women were in the workforce only until they married or became pregnant. As a result, women represented only twenty-five percent of the participants nationally. Gender exclusion made the efforts of WICS all the more important as it worked to screen women and refer them to other programs if they did not qualify for the Job Corps.[143] Team member Esther Higgs Cooke called the Jackson Women's Job Corps program "the most ambitious, heart-rending, frustrating effort I have ever witnessed," noting that Schutt and Burney worked against "monumental odds to register and process applicants," as the "lone standard bearers." Schutt and Burney received no help from the city government, social service agencies, or the medical profession. When the two women managed to interview and process young women, they could not find doctors to complete the medical portion of the application.[144] As a result of Cooke's observations and the insistence of Jackson WICS president Jessie Mosley, WIMS requested federal funds for a full-time staff salary.[145] Here WIMS identified the need for government intervention and helped in applying for the proper assistance.

Monitoring compliance with Title VI of the Civil Rights Act of 1964 stood out as one of the important goals of WIMS in 1965.[146] The New York

WIMS staff acted as liaisons between the local communities, team members, and government enforcement agencies. The WIMS staff fielded complaints from local women and had team members investigate; often Mississippians called to ask whether the act applied to particular situations. In all of these circumstances, the staff would either refer the callers to the proper government agencies or report the infractions themselves. For example, WIMS functioned as a watchdog to insure that a dormitory being built with federal funds at the University of Southern Mississippi became an integrated facility. WIMS reported segregated school textbooks, and informed the appropriate departments of discrimination in housing, employment, and availability of government services.[147]

In other instances, the WIMS teams checked on the compliance of businesses. The women called on three national companies that maintained different hiring practices in the North and South, urging them to comply with Title VI.[148] Team member Ellen Tarry reported to her host, Walter Lipscomb, who worked in public relations for Coca Cola, that WIMS had received a report indicating that the company had integrated teams manning their delivery trucks, but that white men did all the paperwork while black men did the strenuous labor. Lipscomb later informed Cowan that, even though work still needed to be done, the company president had taken action to begin hiring blacks in all departments, including one in sales and one as a supervisor in an unspecified department.[149] Whether these efforts changed the attitudes of business leaders is unclear, but they did change business procedures, creating new opportunities.

WIMS interceded with ABC to have local stations broadcast a documentary on ecumenism. The local stations had told Catholic officials that they could not broadcast the show due to previous commitments. Although the push to air the documentary appeared to focus on religion rather than race, local Catholics had supported civil rights, albeit quietly, by integrating church services and parochial schools, and as a result they were targeted in the literature of racists groups. By reporting the incident to ABC, WIMS in essence challenged the segregationist owners of Jackson's two television stations, the CBS affiliate owned by Citizens' Council members Robert Hederman and Tom Hederman Jr. of Jackson, and the NBC affiliate owned by Clint and John Murchison of Dallas, Texas.[150] ABC did not have an affiliate in Jackson at the time and depended upon one of the two stations to air its programs. After hearing WIMS's complaints on behalf of Mississippi Catholics about the failure to air the documentary, ABC informed WIMS that a local station had since broadcast the program. Cowan saw this as "one small success" in

WIMS's efforts to "influence the communications industry to take a more progressive attitude." Whether owners and managers of the local station that eventually aired the documentary changed their attitudes is uncertain, but they clearly adjusted their practices.[151]

Although the 1965 trips centered less on breaking down racial barriers than those in 1964, the social climate had not changed entirely, and meetings with small groups of women continued to play a crucial role in changing attitudes and gathering converts to the civil rights cause. Florence Gooch wrote to Susan Goodwillie that only through these gatherings would the number of Mississippi women involved increase. She added that she had received valuable information on employment studies for the LWV from team member Marguerite Cassell, information Gooch would not have found had it not been for WIMS.[152]

The interfaith composition of the teams remained critical. Marjorie Penney said of Mississippi's religious fervor, "This 'closed society' is church centered in ways that we can hardly understand. Our mother[s] could have, our grandmothers could have, understood very easily, but there is a tightness, a parochial-mindedness that even as a Baptist . . . I have never experienced."[153] Penney made these observations after attending a meeting of church women at the home of Miriam Ezelle, which included mostly Baptists and Methodists, a few Presbyterians, one or two Episcopalians, one Catholic, and one Jew. Penney advised that if WIMS wanted to make strides, it needed to find women who speak "church women's language . . . Baptist and Methodist women's language—because there is a vocabulary."[154]

The interfaith movement continued to grow, as did attendance at interracial meetings. The national chairman of Christian Social Relations of CWU, team member Elizabeth Haselden, expressed her surprise at seeing approximately one hundred people at an Interfaith Prayer Fellowship meeting, some twenty percent of them black.[155] With Ann Hewitt as president of the state CWU and Jane Schutt as president of the Jackson chapter, CWU set an example by holding its 1965 annual state meeting at a Jackson hotel with seventy-five black women in attendance. The hotel would have prohibited the integrated meeting in prior years.[156] Episcopal churches had quietly integrated in the early 1960s, but the Episcopal churchwomen who met with team member Jean Frey, national resolution chairman for CWU, found that they could do more. After hearing Frey's report on the activities of her Chicago-area church, they saw the value in unifying rather than remaining "compartmentalized in their own churches," and later held the first city-wide integrated meeting of Episcopal churchwomen.[157]

Even for denominations that remained resistant to change, the WIMS visits offered encouragement to the moderates and liberals among them. Marjorie Penney recalled that one woman, for whom the Baptist Church was "the core of her life," cried for over an hour as the two talked about their churches. The woman called Penney the next day to apologize and explained that she, her husband, and a man from Wisconsin were the only "liberal-minded" people in her church's 3,000-member congregation. She told Penney, "I just said to my husband that I couldn't stop crying because I knew she understood—she's a Baptist like we are."[158]

Where the Jewish community had been open to WIMS in 1964, the 1965 team members received a mixed reception. Team member Gladys Zales, chairman of purchasing for Hadassah, met with twelve Jewish women whom she initially found openly hostile, telling her she should have gone to Harlem instead.[159] Caroline Smith reportedly observed that "there was rudeness at the beginning of the meeting that she wouldn't have believed if she hadn't been there."[160] This shift in attitude evidently took place in response to an increase in anti-Semitic literature appearing in Jackson, which the local Jewish women blamed on the interference of "Jewish 'do-gooders' from the North."[161] Nevertheless, in the following weeks, four Jewish team members were housed in Jewish homes. Rabbi Perry Nussbaum and his wife, who had hosted a team member the previous year, met with Team 4 members Buddy Mayer, wife of the president of Rothschild Enterprises, and Selma Taub, a teacher for disadvantaged children. Mayer found Nussbaum abrasive, while Taub found him "very pleasant and quite enlightening." The women especially disagreed on what the rabbi intended when he asked, "Just what is the purpose of the WIMS coming down here?" Taub saw this as an innocent and earnest question, but Mayer perceived it as an attack, perhaps because the rabbi was well acquainted with the project. The final consensus of the Jewish Wednesdays women was that the "Jewish community would not obstruct but neither would it lead the cause of integration."[162] This marked a setback from 1964.

In 1965, WIMS helped Jackson's Unitarian Church make strides with its Wednesday Night Forum, a weekly discussion open to anyone, by providing speakers from its last three teams.[163] One team spoke to a full house on a variety of topics, including prenatal clinics, a film about Africa, early childhood education, building community centers to alleviate juvenile delinquency, and ways to combat human relations problems.[164] When the program ended, audience members expressed their appreciation that the WIMS team cared enough to come. A male Jackson realtor approached team member Shirley Lipsey to say, "It's the women like you who are going to make a difference.

The men can't do it."[165] Although some businessmen had taken a stance upholding the new civil rights law, the perception remained that women were the vanguard of the movement. Regardless of who led the way, Smith noted, "The value of an open forum in a divided society with limited communication cannot be overstated."[166]

The liberal stance of the Unitarian Church in Jackson did not go unpunished. On August 22, 1965, Reverend Donald Thompson was shot outside his home following threats on his life because of the church's integration policy. At the debriefing for Team 5, Mildred Pitt recalled words of his that she had heard just two weeks earlier: "If the few of you here don't speak out, nobody else will. Okay, so maybe you're afraid, and maybe you don't know what's going to happen to you, but you're the saving grace." Pitt added that she had not thought much about it at the time but had not stopped thinking about it since.[167] Prophetically, Rev. Thompson had asked Marjorie Penney to "tell the people in Philadelphia, Pennsylvania, that this Philadelphia-to-Philadelphia project is not right. It's extremely dangerous."[168] The shooting of Rev. Thompson increased fear among both blacks and whites and demonstrated that supporting civil rights still carried serious consequences.[169]

Social change occurs gradually as a result of many different impulses. Mississippi may have been moving at a "snail's pace," but at last reformers had begun to make a difference, as Esther Sampson noted.[170] When the Wednesdays women met with their counterparts across the state, they played a role in those forward steps. Hannah Levin explained that if people began to work together, they would start to socialize in time.[171] In 1965, WIMS moved beyond merely opening dialogue to directing that dialogue toward specific goals that would make Mississippi a better place for its citizens. The team members acted as bridges between women in Mississippi and the North, between women in Jackson and other cities across the state, between women in various organization and religious groups, and between those in need of services and the appropriate government offices. When organizations refused to meet across racial lines, and when national organizations excluded Mississippians, WIMS opened dialogue to find common ground.[172]

Inspired by the success of Wednesdays in Mississippi, Marian Wright Edelman used the WIMS model for a pair of projects sponsored by her non-profit child advocacy group, the Children's Defense Fund (CDF). Edelman had moved to Washington, D.C., and established CDF in 1973 after being frustrated by the fight for political control of CDGM. At the turn of the twenty-first century, CDF gave its mission a new moniker: Leave No Child Behind. Its goal continues to be ensuring that every child has a "*Healthy Start, a Head*

Start, a *Fair Start,* a *Safe Start,* and a *Moral Start* in life and successful passage to adulthood with the help of caring families and communities." Wednesdays in Washington and Wednesdays at Home became the centerpieces of the organization's effort to mobilize women, parents, grandparents, people of faith, youth, and other concerned citizens to demand that government leaders protect the interests of all children. The two programs set aside Wednesday as the day to send emails, letters, and faxes, and to make phone calls or personal visits to push for support of children's initiatives.[173] For example, students at Syracuse University formed Students United for Child Advocacy to organize fellow students around issues like child welfare and to meet with local and congressional leaders to promote change. As part of Wednesdays at Home the Syracuse students encouraged others to take grassroots action on behalf of underprivileged children.[174]

In 1966, the changing needs of Mississippi women dictated that adjustments be made, and WIMS reached its conclusion. Among the state's poor, the need for food, housing, jobs, and education replaced the call for desegregation of public accommodations and voter registration. Biographer Kay Mills observed that the movement was "evolving into quiet organizing around economic and educational issues."[175] If the NCNW wanted to remain a force in the fight against racism and poverty, it had to change its approach too. Wednesdays in Mississippi became Workshops in Mississippi, with a new thrust and a new format. Although the NCNW no longer conducted team visits, northern women continued to collaborate with southern women through Workshops. The NCNW's goal became reaching and assisting more "hard-core poor women."[176]

The Workshops organizers listened to what Mississippi women told them was needed. Fannie Lou Hamer said, "We need food. . . . Jobs are gone. The cotton fields are gone. . . . There's no place for tenant farmers, and there's no industry, and we need to be able to feed ourselves and take care of our children." Others said, "We hear the government's supposed to have a lot of help for us, including Social Security, but we don't know where it is." Some had Social Security withheld from their paychecks, which, as the NCNW found when checking their accounts for them, the employers had never reported or never paid to the government on the employees' behalf. Workshops responded to these "express needs of the people," creating fluidity in the project's focus, which evolved over time.[177]

Hamer insisted early on that Workshops include poor white women, who suffered equally with poor blacks. One white woman, Sally Carson, told the Workshops organizers, "Bad off as we are, at least if you all didn't come down for Mrs. Hamer, we'd have nobody coming for us." The 1960 Mississippi census data indicates the severity of poverty for both races: 193,065 non-white families and 172,131 white families earned incomes below the national poverty level of $3,000. While the total number of poor blacks and whites was relatively close, only 41 percent of poor white families made less than $1,000 per year in 1960, compared to 53 percent of poor non-white families. Moreover, only 43.3 percent of Mississippi's white families lived below the poverty line, as opposed to 85.5 percent of the state's black families. [178] Height reflected on this paradox of poverty: "While the majority of the [nation's] poor are really white, our problem is that the majority of the black are poor."[179] As a result, through Workshops the NCNW addressed poverty as a universal problem, of no racial, regional, or religious boundaries.

The early workshops demonstrated the Mississippi women's interest in receiving the NCNW's help and defined its direction. The first Workshops meeting took place in Jackson in November 1966. WIMS called on local women to help with the planning; they came from Biloxi, Canton, Clarksville, Corinth, Greenville, Greenwood, Hattiesburg, Jackson, Laurel, Mayersville, McComb, Oxford, Philadelphia, and Wesson. Although the organizers expected twenty-five women, sixty women arrived from fifteen cities across Mississippi. Height recalled, "They spoke of the responsibility of women who had a better education and a good job to work for the general good, because they had access to information and knew how to use it."[180] They wanted better housing, community centers, and free school breakfast and lunch programs.[181]

The second workshop, co-chaired by Canton civil rights activist Annie Devine and Mississippi NCNW president Jessie Mosley, took place in Oxford, Mississippi, in January 1967. The program focused on writing grant proposals and included presentations from federal officials, the Southern Regional Council, and professors at Mississippi's leading colleges and universities. To facilitate participation, the NCNW paid travel and babysitting expenses for the attendees and reimbursed those who paid for substitutes at their places of employment. Workshops requested that each community send two women who could then teach others the skills they had learned.[182] Forty-three women attended from Brandon, Batesville, Biloxi, Bolton, Blanton, Carthage, Corinth, Courtland, Greenville, Greenwood, Jackson, Laurel, McComb, Magnolia, Moss Point, Okolona, Oxford, Quitman, Ruleville, and Vicksburg.[183] The speakers expressed amazement that the attendees had "outlined, drafted, and critiqued" proposals for day care centers, school meals, community centers, and programs for teen girls by the time the workshop ended. The event demonstrated that Workshops could help poor rural

Mississippians meet specific needs by "tapping available federal resources"—by making them aware of federal aid they qualified for and instructing them on how to apply for it.[184]

Although Lyndon Johnson had initiated the War on Poverty in 1964, it took the stark reality of seeing poverty firsthand for many to truly understand its impact on the lives of Mississippians. In April 1967, Marian Wright Edelman testified before the Senate Subcommittee on Employment, Manpower, and Poverty, which was meeting in Jackson. Asserting that Johnson's poverty legislation had done little to change economic conditions for Mississippi's poor, she challenged the committee to go to the Delta with her and see the living conditions there. They did, and they were appalled. John Dittmer reports that Senator George Murphy (R-CA) asked Johnson to "declare an emergency situation exist[ed] in these areas." Senator Robert Kennedy (D-NY), after seeing the lethargic children with thin arms, sunken eyes, and swollen bellies, called it "a condemnation" of Congress, who had failed to provide measurable relief to the state's poor. This was particularly troubling considering the OEO reported that same year that it had spent $75 million on programs in Mississippi, the most of any state. In July, doctors testified that the children were "suffering from hunger and disease and directly or indirectly they [were] dying from them." Governor Paul Johnson attempted to counter the criticism by saying, "Nobody is starving in Mississippi. . . . The nigra women I see are so fat they shine."[185]

Coinciding with the subcommittee meeting in Jackson, several of the southern black and white women who took part in Workshops traveled to New York for a meeting to discuss the project's future direction. This was in keeping with the NCNW's desire to involve those most likely to benefit from the program in its planning, and thereby to improve Workshop's effectiveness. The meeting convened at the home of Marian Logan and discussed the progress of Workshops and its upcoming summer meetings; included were presentations by Ruth Batson, who worked on numerous anti-poverty agendas, and Annie Devine, who served on the Workshops Steering Committee.[186]

Resistance from local officials continued to be a problem for Workshops, as it had been in earlier years of the civil rights movement. The NCNW held a third workshop in Indianola, Mississippi, in June 1967, at the request of the Department of Agriculture, with Hamer and Height as hosts and discussion leaders. The attendees included thirty-one poor women, fifteen representatives from all levels of government, and nine members of the Sunflower County Community Action Program, an umbrella organization for various anti-poverty programs.[187] When Height and Cowan arrived in Indianola, they received word that county clerk Jack Harper Jr. had contacted Governor Johnson, who arranged for OEO to withdraw funds for the program. He accused the NCNW of being a "subversive group" bringing outsiders to the state. Cowan said, "We're not going to turn back." She insisted she would find the money. Among the many donations in 1967, the largest came from the Louis and Pauline Cowan Foundation, which donated $12,500.[188]

The 1967 summer workshop focused on "Closing the Communication Gap." As the meeting progressed, it became increasingly apparent that communication—and therefore learning—was not a one-way street; the northern women and government representatives had as much to learn from the southern women as the reverse. When a government official responsible for food stamps told the group he had searched the county and not found anyone who was hungry, a "belligerent" older woman stood up and said, "Mister, you're looking at her now." The Food Stamp Act of 1964 had given counties the option to shift from distributing free federal surplus commodities—staples such as flour and milk—to food stamps that were funded by the federal government and purchased by the poor for use in specified grocery stores. The stamps entitled their buyer to receive additional stamps at no charge; however, many of the people had no income with which to purchase the stamps in the first place, even at a rate of two dollars per person. The government officials did not understand until the women pointed it out to them that the system made it impossible for the women to feed their families if they had literally no money to buy the stamps initially. Unemployment in rural Mississippi counties had risen dramatically following passage of the Food and Fiber Act of 1965, which paid plantation owners to reduce cotton production. Seasonal work dropped by seventy-five percent between 1965 and 1967. Further, when minimum wage expanded to cover agricultural workers in 1966, many farmers stopped hiring day labor to chop cotton and switched to herbicides, affecting an estimated 50,000 families. By 1967, half of the counties in Mississippi had moved to food stamps, leaving 64,000 people without access to free food.[189]

After a home economist from the U. S. Department of Agriculture at the workshop gave a presentation to the poor black women using flannel-cloth visual aids of a middle-class white family, the black women were convinced the government had no help to offer them. Hamer became angry with the government representatives, but Cowan assured her that the WIMS organizers had tape recorded everything to corroborate the promises of assistance made by officials at the meeting, and that Cowan would send a copy to the Agriculture Department in Washington. The tape later circulated around that department as a lesson in "how not to handle people."[190] Clearly the southern women were not the only ones to benefit from the exchange of information at the workshops, and the NCNW later arranged meetings between the Mississippi women, the Department of Agriculture, and the OEO. Height and Cowan insisted that the government representatives treat the local women as equals and consider them "consultants." The 1967 summer workshop received endorsements from the national Community Action Program and the Department of Agriculture as an example of how community action agencies and technical action panels could get services to low-income people.[191]

Cowan, too, faced a learning curve. When she suggested to Hamer that they conduct a seminar on family planning, Hamer reportedly explained, "Child, our young ones are our money. We got no other. When we'se out picking cotton, the more in the family the more the money." Hamer added sadly, "The cotton picker has taken it away from us. The younger ones know that. But us older ones still think like we used to."[192] Although Hamer had been the victim of a "Mississippi appendectomy," or forced sterilization, the NCNW records do not indicate whether she revealed this fact to Cowan, who dropped the idea of family planning.[193] The conversation served as a vivid reminder, though, of how poor southern women viewed life through a different lens than those in the North, poor or not.

Workshops led to increased mutual respect between Mississippi women and government representatives, who both demonstrated an "eagerness to close the communication gap." Everyone present at the workshops gained a clear understanding that the entity delivering services and the recipient had to work together to solve problems in order to maximize the programs' benefits. Harper, the county clerk who had derailed the Workshops funding, attended the summer 1967 workshop and listened to the stories of hunger, inadequate health care, and general poverty. At the meeting's conclusion, he grudgingly conceded, "[Fanny Lou Hamer] has brought us all together to look at what's going on, and there's some things we can work on. Some things we may not be able to do much on, but we can try." Organizations like the OEO began to seek the NCNW's advice on what programs would be the most beneficial to Mississippi women and in identifying participants to attend them. Height found that Workshops "provided a bridge" between the government agencies and the Mississippi women, and that it supplied the women with the tools for their own advancement.[194]

After the initial Workshops meetings, the NCNW continued moving toward programs directed at specific needs. Hamer repeatedly stressed to Height the need to relieve the hunger of poor rural Mississippi families.

Hamer told Height how Thelma Barnes, a black woman running for Congress from Washington County, had lost the election despite the area's being seventy percent black. People explained that they wanted to vote for Barnes, but someone paid them twenty dollars to vote for the white candidate. Additionally, on the election day the white landowners offered jobs that kept blacks in the fields, preventing them from casting ballots. Having witnessed the long, hard battle black Mississippians had waged to gain the vote, Height was incredulous that the so many blacks had chosen work or money over voting. Hamer explained, "You see, Miss Height, down where we are, food is used as a political weapon."[195] But, people's having adequate food would change that, even if the people did not have jobs. "When you've got 400 quarts of greens and gumbo soup canned for the winter, they can't tell you what to say or do. ... [A pig and a garden] would not only help them break the chain of political oppression, giving them some dignity and freedom, but would give them food for themselves and their families, helping relieve the terrible problem of starvation and malnutrition."[196]

From this conversation grew the ideas for pig banks and community gardens. Working for the YWCA, Height had witnessed the success of the Heifer Project, which the YWCA had co-sponsored with fourteen national and religious organizations to distribute livestock around the world and train the recipients in caring for the animals, in order to improve the socioeconomic status of women. By receiving a cow, a woman had the benefit of its milk, both for sale and for consumption by her family.[197] Height believed a pig bank could yield similar results.

The pig bank started with fifty-five pigs, fifty white Yorkshire sows and five burnt-brown Jersey boars chosen by Willis McAlpin of the Heifer Project in Prentiss, Mississippi. He chose young sows because the idea was to breed the pigs rather than butcher them immediately for food. Each family who took a pig agreed to donate two pigs from each litter back to the bank so that the number of available pigs grew. With sows averaging five litters of six to eight piglets, the NCNW expected the original sows to yield approximately 2,000 pigs. At a year old, the pigs would weigh about 225 pounds and yield 125 pounds of meat. The pigs were kept on a farm about a mile outside of Ruleville. Local women built a fence and a "small sturdy building with a cement floor and a red roof" to shelter the pigs. In fact, the pigs had a sturdier home than some of the women. Outside of the building someone wrote a dedication in cement with her finger: "Mrs. Fannie Hamer, October 11, 1968."[198]

The project in Ruleville met with such success that it spread to other counties and communities. Bolivar County had two receiving stations for the pigs and served Shelby, Cleveland, Gunnison, Mound Bayou, and Rosedale.[199] By its third year, the pig bank program had produced between 2,000 and 3,000 pigs, benefitting 300 families. By 1973, another 600 families had participated.[200] The concept even found its way to Swaziland, after the king of that country saw the pig banks featured in an NCNW film.[201]

Height came to see hunger as "a violence" in people's lives, and the NCNW addressed the issue through Workshops and fighting for federal reform. Assistance came slowly, however. Ethel Gadison, a black woman from Mississippi, pushed for community gardens, which she argued could keep 200 families alive while they waited for government action.[202] Many in the rural counties did not own land, and others had more produce than they could consume. By joining forces they could exchange food and services. Further, working together boosted their confidence, and being part of a national organization empowered them.[203]

The NCNW purchased seeds, rented large plots of land, and organized gardens in three southern counties, Sunflower and Bolivar Counties in Mississippi and Macon County in Alabama. Hamer played a pivotal role in organizing the project at the local level. The southerners grew an assortment of greens and vegetables. The growers agreed to donate ten percent of the crops to the sick and elderly, and they shared the rest among members of the cooperative. The NCNW built a house in each county as a food center, where the participants delivered the crops and women did canning. Those women who had the facilities at home also used their own kitchens for canning.[204] Cowan arranged for Spiegel's to donate freezers, where the food could be stored until needed. The first harvest produced approximately 2,000 pounds of canned vegetables, the work of 300 men, women, and children performing a variety of tasks, benefitting 250 families. Older people, too weak to do the physical labor, kept the accounts.[205] This structure permitted everyone to contribute in some way to the food's production and to feel that they had earned their share.

Focusing on children, Workshops sponsored a study, "Their Daily Bread," through the Committee on School Lunch Participation. The NCNW petitioned Orville Freeman, secretary of the Agriculture Department, to increase the allocations of federal aid to Mississippi's poor. Coordinating the implementation with local officials, Freedman provided $1 million in a supplemental food package and food stamps to new and expectant mothers, infants, and young children who were not otherwise eligible for assistance. In another example of the NCNW successfully interceding on behalf of Mississippi's children, the Agriculture Department's deputy assistant secretary indicated that it was investigating the hike of Canton school lunch prices from twenty cents to thirty-five cents after receiving a report from the NCNW.[206]

Hamer acted as an anchor for many of the activities conducted through Workshops that directly affected her life and the lives of poor women and families she met every day. The NCNW paid Hamer for her work and wisdom, demonstrating the organization's desire to keep local control in the hands of those most in need.[207] When the NCNW donated clothing, Hamer distributed it off of racks in her home. She spearheaded the Fannie Lou Hamer Day Care Center in Ruleville, which the NCNW supported, to provide childcare for women who worked in a small garment factory in nearby Doddsville.[208] Another area Hamer insisted needed attention was housing. Women like Leola Williams of Greenwood wrote to Height, asking her to intercede with the Department of Housing and Urban Development (HUD) because local officials were apathetic toward the deplorable conditions there. Williams estimated that ninety percent of Greenwood blacks lived in substandard housing, with ten to twelve people occupying two- and three-room "shacks."[209] Height admitted, "I never would have thought of getting into housing, but it was they who said, 'We just don't have a place to live.'"[210] Thus the NCNW moved into new territory once again.

To tackle the problem of inadequate housing, the NCNW worked quietly, as it had in the past, while producing results that had a substantial impact on people's lives. Height assembled an interracial team that included the white housing specialist Dorothy Duke, and Unita Blackwell, a former sharecropper who had worked in the civil rights movement with Hamer. Blackwell had first come into contact with WIMS in 1965 when the Wednesdays women posted bail for her. She met Height at a Workshops meeting the following year. Hamer recommended Blackwell for a new position the NCNW was creating to assess and address housing needs in Mississippi, and Height liked the idea of including a local woman. When Height approached her about joining the NCNW effort, Blackwell explained that she did not know anything about housing. Height replied that she surely knew what it was like to need a good house, and Blackwell said, "Now that's the gospel truth," agreeing to take part.[211]

Under Duke and Blackwell's direction, the organization initiated Turnkey III. Sponsored by HUD and the Ford Foundation, the project enabled low-income families to buy rather than rent housing. Families who qualified for public housing moved into the new houses with no down payment on the condition that they perform maintenance, providing "sweat equity." With support from the Mississippi Home Builders Association, Hancock

Bank of Gulfport, and First National Bank of Biloxi, the NCNW organized a homebuyers association and the new homeowners received training in how to "manage and maintain their homes on a cooperative basis."[212] To ensure Senator James Eastland did not block the effort, Blackwell approached his chauffeur to intercede on the project's behalf. The driver told her that the senator "just nodded positively" in response, which indicated that he "would not oppose it but did not want to go on record as supporting it." HUD initially suggested the NCNW approach OEO, calling the project "too people oriented," according to Blackwell. Eventually, however, HUD allotted $3 million to finance 200 three- to five-bedroom homes with garden plots in a wooded area north of Gulfport, Mississippi, called Forest Heights. The neighborhood included a day care center, recreation center, and community services.[213]

Turnkey III featured three unique qualities that stood out in comparison to other housing programs: the financing, the training provided to residents, and the creation of homeowners associations. Under Turnkey III, a builder agreed to construct a home using specified plans at an agreed-upon price. The local housing authority then purchased the home for a family. Through their homeowners association, the neighborhood families performed property management and maintenance tasks, which reduced the costs to the housing authority. The amount saved was then credited to the families, along with the amount of the federal subsidy normally paid under the Housing and Urban Development Act of 1965. When the credit equaled the remaining debt on the home, the family became the homeowner and received a deed. Families that chose to move before paying off the balance received the accumulated credit. A homeowner could also pay off the balance early.[214] The training program taught residents, most of whom had little formal education, about mortgage financing, budget keeping, home-maintenance skills, and other aspects of homeownership. The training included a nine-hour pre-occupancy course and twenty-two hours of post-occupancy instruction. This latter segment incorporated principles of "self-government" and management to prepare the residents to create and administer their own homeowners association. The NCNW insisted that a private entity outside of HUD conduct these sessions so residents did not see this as a landlord-tenant relationship.[215]

The story of Forest Heights resident Ike Thomas dramatically demonstrates the power of homeownership. In 1969, Thomas risked his life to close the floodgates to Forest Heights during Hurricane Camille, a Category 5 storm with winds of 200 miles per hour and a storm surge estimated at over twenty feet, which took the lives of 140 people on the Gulf Coast. Following the storm, HUD secretary George Romney toured Forest Heights, the only intact neighborhood in Gulfport, and asked Thomas why he had taken such a chance. Thomas explained he did it because, for the first time in their lives, he and the other residents had "something of their own." HUD later created a film called *Something of Their Own* that showed the determination of the families in Forest Heights to improve their lives.[216]

The housing initiatives stand out among the most important programs to come out of WIMS because they continue in effect today, providing affordable home ownership to those who could not achieve it otherwise.[217] By June 1972, Turnkey III's efforts had produced 6,637 homes in eighty-five municipalities. As a result, OEO and the Ford Foundation supported the NCNW's home ownership programs in Raleigh, North Carolina; St. Louis, Missouri; San Antonio, Texas; Elizabeth City, New Jersey; Oklahoma City, Oklahoma; and New Orleans, Louisiana, totaling 18,761 units estimated at $407 million. The NCNW continues to operate the original Forest Heights project and received a grant from the Bush-Clinton Katrina Fund to help the Turnkey III families in the Gulfport area hard hit by Hurricane Katrina in 2005.[218]

While blacks and whites in Mississippi worked together successfully in many workshops programs, other interracial efforts in the state began to disintegrate. In 1966, SNCC voted to expel whites from the organization, a decision not everyone agreed with. Fannie Lou Hamer, who had worked long and hard with SNCC since it came to Mississippi, resigned in protest. The first white woman in SNCC to work in a field project, Penny Patch, echoed the problem that many had with Black Power, the sudden exclusion from the movement in which the white SNCC workers had invested so much personally and emotionally. While she had always accepted the emergence of black political and economic power as a goal of the civil rights struggle, Patch explained, "I was desolate and full of rage—rage at the system, at the country, at all the white people who opposed change or did nothing. And I was full of rage at my own beloved SNCC community for what felt like a betrayal." The move by SNCC not only excluded whites, but shifted the organization's focus from the nonviolence of Martin Luther King Jr. to Black Power and the Black Panther Party, creating a newly divisive mood across the country.[219]

Even after the separatist Black Power movement emerged, the NCNW continued to work interracially in Mississippi. Height contended that the term Black Power connoted an "objective that is—or should be—foreign to us: violence and the implicit domination of the fight for freedom by the black man." The goal was neither black power nor white power, which both fostered color barriers. Instead Height argued, "The kind of power we seek is the power of freedom in a colorless society—the power to help build a constructive nation . . . together with our fellow Americans."[220] Cowan called "whitey go home" the "worst period." Her son, Paul Cowan, wrote that she "felt uneasy with the polarization that . . . often communicated strong anti-white feelings." He believed it hurt her more than most people because it affected her daily life working as the "only white official in a black organization."[221] It took Height's coaching for Cowan to understand what Black Power represented and be persuaded to stay involved through the period. Cowan recalled, "White people by the droves cut off their support, moral and financial. It was difficult, but if you could overcome your hurt and see that it was the result of young black people trying to overcome their own years of being hurt, if you could understand that and take a lot of guff, you could come out on the other side a stronger person."[222]

As with members of many civil rights organizations, the WIMS women were saddened by the shift, but also understood the reasons behind it. Geraldine Kohlenberg remembered "feeling a kind of loss." Where she had felt attached to the "nobility" of nonviolence, Black Power seemed more threatening, at least in its rhetoric, though not necessarily physically frightening. The rejection of whites left one wondering where a well-intentioned, liberal white woman fit in the movement. While acknowledging that blacks needed an outlet and could not internalize their frustration indefinitely, Kohlenberg had admired the nonviolent movement that "sort of sanctified" the black community, which remained steadfast and strong. Kohlenberg reflected that "suffering has a kind of glamour that rage does not." Priscilla Hunt felt that Black Power hurt the cause more than helping it, by making it too easy for critics of the civil rights movement to say, "They are dangerous; they should all be locked up." Even whites who had taken part in the movement found that Black Power pushed them beyond their ability to sympathize. Hunt added, however, that some had to take a more active role in the protest movement, because "not everybody is made to just quietly have stones thrown at them walking over bridges." Susan Goodwillie contended that Black Power turned many people away from the movement, but that it was the logical next step.[223] Although Height received criticism for working too closely with whites, the NCNW continued to advocate interracial cooperation under her leadership.

By the latter half of the 1960s, the organizations that originally took part in Wednesdays in Mississippi continued to support the NCNW initiatives, but their focus no longer centered on Mississippi. For example, the NCNW, NCJW, NCCW, and CWU participated in WICS and through it, the Job Corps, but the efforts took on a national scope.[224] In this way, the push to relieve poverty might have actually hurt poor Mississippians as they moved out of the spotlight, and as attention focused on other areas that competed for funds, volunteers, and the assistance of social service programs. All of these changes prompted Fannie Lou Hamer to tell Dorothy Height that while many groups came to Mississippi to work for civil rights, the NCNW stayed long after the high-profile part of the struggle was over.[225]

Conclusion

*"The 1960s gave many of us an opportunity to fight injustice and to
work for freedom. Freedom for black people is a step toward freedom
for all people. . . . This effort for a national liberation encouraged
many white people to join the battle knowing that no one of us can be
free until all of us are free."*

—POLLY COWAN[1]

IN JUST EIGHT WEEKS' TIME, BETWEEN MAY 1964 WHEN POLLY COWAN AND
Shirley Smith traveled to Mississippi to confirm that the NCNW's help was
still welcomed and the arrival of the first WIMS team in July, the organizers
of Wednesdays in Mississippi designed and implemented the only civil rights
program organized for women, by women, as part of a national organization, and the only program directed at helping Mississippi women during
Freedom Summer. Dorothy Height and Polly Cowan shared a belief that the
cornerstone of civil rights was the mutual respect and acceptance as equals of
people of extreme differences. Knowing that a truly integrated society could
not be achieved in an environment of racial hostility that prevented normal
human interactions, they devised a plan to change that environment—a plan
for which their own relationship served as a model. Cowan's daughter, Holly
Cowan Shulman, recalled Height saying that WIMS "simply started from one
woman's thoughts and another woman's vision—women 'who did not wait
for an organizing committee,' but simply dug into the job they saw before
them."[2]

Under the auspices of the National Council of Negro Women, Height
and Cowan created WIMS, a collective of women united to build bridges of
understanding. Participants came from different parts of the country, representing different races, ethnicities, religions, ages, and classes. They sought to
soften the white women's attitudes towards the sweeping social changes taking place in Mississippi and across the country, to illustrate by example that

white Mississippians had nothing to fear from working and socializing in interracial groups, and to raise awareness in the North of the struggle taking place in the South. Even though the teams met with women from varied socioeconomic backgrounds, the NCNW recognized that it could not accomplish its goals without gaining the support of the southern white middle class, and it directed the bulk of its early efforts toward this group.

Unlike the high-profile organizations working in the state, WIMS participants employed a quiet approach, purposefully exploiting their gender, age, and class to open doors closed to other civil rights activists. As they traveled around the state, the Wednesdays women projected an image of stature and motherhood, showing that their concern for children was uppermost in their minds and that they had come to the South to learn. They worked woman-to-woman to open lines of communication between black and white women in Mississippi across race, region, and religion, in order to find common ground between the different groups and to ease the transition to an integrated society. By doing this, WIMS opened the door for Mississippi women—who had begun the summer fearful of reprisals, uncertain of what the future held, and skeptical that anything would make a difference in race relations—to take their first steps toward reconciliation.[3]

As the Wednesdays women traveled the state and visited the Freedom Summer projects, they accumulated a body of knowledge to use in conversing with southern women about what they had seen when the two groups met over coffee. This was essential to allaying white southerners' fears about the civil rights movement. The team members became the eyes and ears of the Mississippi white women who could not talk with civil rights activists or see the projects for themselves. Fear, the teams found, was the biggest stumbling block to progress—fear of physical and economic retribution and fear of the unknown. Another critical element, overlooked in discussions of women in the civil rights movement, was how the struggle played out in the churches, across all denominations, reflecting and even directing what took place in the community. Particularly in white churches, segregationists often overruled ministers in interpreting beliefs and setting policies. The Wednesdays women employed the knowledge they gained in each of these areas when they conversed with their southern counterparts to open lines of communication.

In addition to opening dialogue with the southern women, the WIMS visits encouraged Mississippians to act. In communities across the state visited by WIMS teams, white women gradually began to host and participate in interracial meetings. They spoke out more openly for integrated schools, churches, and other public facilities. While fear continued to be a major obstacle, many women began to venture into new areas as they observed others doing so without retribution. African American women also found new avenues for activism, and new allies in the northern women and in a few southern white women.

Even though WIMS did not operate the Freedom Schools, its efforts at funding and supplying the schools certainly had a positive impact on the students and serves as one example of how WIMS aided Mississippians. Activist Unita Blackwell explained the impact on her son: "Thirty-five years later, Jerry still talks enthusiastically about his freedom school experience—how considerate and kind his teachers were, how they didn't try to pour information into his head in a strict controlling way but got him involved in learning and how much he learned."[4] COFO volunteer Mike Miller reported years later, when the student-teachers returned to the towns where they had worked, that some of them met former Freedom School students who had become city council members, mayors, and chiefs of police. He said that they "all spoke of how the freedom schools had opened their minds to the possibility of being first class citizens."[5] WIMS's support helped to keep the schools viable and promoted education.

In its second year, WIMS facilitated education and social programs through a professional exchange that established patterns of interracial cooperation. The teams assisted Mississippi women in initiating the Head Start program and took part in the Mississippi Summer Institute and the Philadelphia to Philadelphia Project, all designed to create racial justice. The WIMS team members who were teachers, librarians, social workers, psychologists, and doctors connected with their southern counterparts to help the southern professionals increase their effectiveness. These efforts assisted black professional women who were isolated from their peers, and poor southern blacks who were systematically excluded from exercising their rights. Jackson educator Dorothy Stewart noted that women like Height and Mississippi NCNW president Jessie Mosley taught her that she could do whatever she chose to do. They "gave us some shoulders on which to stand, they gave us some strength to go up that ladder that we're still climbing. . . . Most of all, they taught us that, yes, we can, we can do it, and we must do it."[6]

As the social climate in Mississippi thawed, Workshops in Mississippi replaced WIMS to address poverty in the state. It began with teaching poor Mississippi women how to write grant proposals to obtain the government funds to which they and their communities were entitled. Beyond that, Workshops initiated programs to tackle specific needs, such as Operation Daily Bread to focus on hunger and Turnkey III to address housing. Today the NCNW continues to work with programs that grew from these early efforts.

For the Wednesdays women, the intensity of the experience molded a group of strangers into a team, giving them a basis of strength from which to continue the fight at home. They spoke at their local churches, clubs, and service organizations, and they wrote articles about their experiences for local newspapers, alumni magazines, and organizational newsletters. Because no two of the almost one hundred women who traveled to Mississippi the first two summers moved in the same civic and social circles, the women initiated different actions at home, from elementary tasks to fundraising for the NCNW's Mississippi projects to complex political maneuvering.[7] Each successive visit by WIMS and its successor Workshops compounded this ripple effect.

The effects of WIMS expanded beyond the immediate benefits seen in Mississippi and the northern communities, with one of the most important being the legacy of activism passed on to future generations. Historian Holly Cowan Shulman says her mother Polly Cowan's "prophetic Judaism" to seek justice and help those in need carried over to her children and grandchildren, who "worked toward that goal in politics, law and the rabbinate, through writing and art, education and the academy."[8] Shulman's younger sister, Liza Cowan, said her own radicalism was inspired by their mother, who ironically had a hard time accepting it in her daughter. Liza Cowan reflected, "The white gloves don't work anymore, but there is nothing quite as amusing as expressing outrageous ideas while twiddling one's pearls."[9]

Many team members had long family histories of social activism; others were the first generation to set such an example. In both cases, activism inspired the northern women to have both pride in their children's social consciences and trepidation for their safety. Geraldine Kohlenberg's daughter played an active role in the peace movement during the Vietnam War; but when Kohlenberg expressed concern about her daughter's safety, her daughter replied, "Well you went to Mississippi in 1964, and Dad went on the March on Washington, so what did you expect me to do?"[10] Sylvia Weinberg said that the WIMS experience became integrated into her personality and influenced her decision-making. As a result, she took her grandchildren to a peace march at the United Nations. One grandson later wrote to her explaining how the experience affected his life and his understanding of what it meant to be part of a social movement in which he believed.[11]

The exploitation of gender, age, and class and the under-the-radar approach to opening dialogue among women were keys to the success of the

WIMS model. Though operating incognito has become increasingly difficult with the growth of professional and social media in an electronic age, the strategy of quietly connecting with people informally continues to be valuable, as exhibited by organizations that use similar models today. For example, team member Kohlenberg cited an Episcopal priest who took part in discussions between women on both side of the abortion issue. The result did not necessarily lead to a change in anyone's position, but it did open the discussion and increase the women's understanding of one another's positions. Similarly, staff member Susan Goodwillie identified Women for Peace of the Women's Federation for World Peace, which unites Jews and Palestinians, Christians and Muslims, blacks and whites, and Americans and Arabs through conversation and their common bonds as women. Members of the organization travel around the country in teams to discuss the world situation, their differences, and their overriding desire for peace and understanding.[12] Small conversation groups "create an environment of trust and information," which overcomes the misinformation about society's most important issues and helps people of different experiences to understand and appreciate each other.[13]

WIMS offers a new paradigm through which to analyze civil rights activism. It challenges our earlier view of Freedom Summer activists as predominantly young student radicals and demonstrates the effectiveness of the quiet approach taken by middle-aged women presenting themselves as proper ladies. Although Dorothy Height and the NCNW have been dismissed by some as too cautious, this study confirms that the NCNW involved itself in civil rights work, promoting integration and black voting rights as well as addressing education, poverty, hunger, housing, and employment. With its unique approach of quietly sending women of stature in interracial, interfaith teams, Wednesdays in Mississippi, and through it the NCNW, served as catalysts for change by opening lines of communication across race, region, and religion. In doing so, the Wednesday women reached into the community like the "long-handled spoon" that Clarie Collins Harvey had envisioned, "stirring up" the southern women and bringing them together in ways they had been incapable of doing alone.

Appendix

WEDNESDAYS IN MISSISSIPPI TEAMS—1964

Team #1—New York/Hattiesburg
Jean Benjamin
Polly Cowan
Dorothy Height
Marian Logan
Ann McGlinchy

Team #2—Boston Area/Canton
Ruth Batson
Sister Catherine John Flynn
Beryl Morris
Geraldine Kohlenberg
Alice Ryerson
Laya Wiesner
Pearl Willen
Ilza Williams

Team #3—Washington Area/Meridian
Flossie Dedmond
Wilhelmina Hetzel
Mary Cushing Niles
Flaxie Pinkett
Justine Randers-Pehrson
Margaret Roach
Dr. Geraldine P. Woods

Team #4—Minneapolis Area/Vicksburg
Virginia Bourne

Barbara Cunningham
Josie Johnson
Mary Kyle
Maxine Nathanson

Team #5—New York/Ruleville
Marie Barksdale
Lilace Reid Barnes
Marjorie Dammann
Frances Haight
Ethel Hasserodt
Claudia Heckscher
Florynce Kennedy
Trude Lash

Team #6—Chicago Area/Canton
Etta Moten Barnett
Jean Davis
Miriam Davis
Narcissa King
Lucy Montgomery
Henrietta Moore
Arnetta Wallace
Sylvia Weinberg

Team #7—New Jersey/Hattiesburg
Jane Gardner
Priscilla Hunt
Dr. Hannah Levin
Helen Meyner
Ruth Minor
Olive Noble
Edith Savage

WEDNESDAYS IN MISSISSIPPI TEAMS—1965

Special Team of Art Teachers—Cambridge
Rita Delisi
Mary Austin

Laura Avery
Marla Higgins

Team #1—New York City
Polly Cowan
Ellen Dammond
Carol Guyer
Dr. Molly Harrower
Ellen Tarry
Gladys Zales

Team #2—Philadelphia
Jean Dillinger
Margery Gross
Dr. Anne Keller
Marjorie Penney
Henrietta Smith
Helen P. Stanford

Team #3—New Jersey
Esther Higgs Cooke
Blanche Goldstein
Josie Harbison
Dr. Hannah Levin
Sue Miller
Loran Scheide

Team #4—Chicago
Marguerite Cassell
Dorothy Dawson
Diana Guyer
Elizabeth Haselden
Buddy Mayer
Dorothy Jones Singleton
Selma Taub

Team #5—Washington/Virginia
Virginia Bushrod
Bee Foster

Jean Frey
Jane McClary
Flaxie Pinkett
Mildred Pitt

Team #6—Philadelphia
Ruth Bacon
Gertrude Barnes
Rae Cohn
Marjorie Duckrey
Shirley Lipsey

Team #7—Boston
Betty Barnes
Mary Cannady
Rae Dudley
Faith Griefen
Frances Perkins
Guest Perry
Frances Tillson

Acknowledgments

THIS BOOK COULD NOT HAVE COME TO FRUITION WITHOUT THE MANY people who have supported me throughout the process. I want to thank those who have read the manuscript and offered invaluable suggestions, including Landon Storrs, Nancy Beck Young, Linda Reed, Gail Murray, Julie Cohn, Bernice Heilbrunn, and Kristen Contos Krueger. Also thanks go to Joe Pratt who taught me what it means to be a writer and editor.

Along this journey, I met wonderful people who have also become friends, beginning with Polly Cowan's daughter, Holly Cowan Shulman, who made many connections for me. Collaborating with Marlene McCurtis of the WIMS Film Project enriched my work and always energized me. She has preserved the stories of northern and southern women whose voices would have been lost otherwise.

One of the greatest thrills was getting to know Priscilla Hunt, Susie Goodwillie Stedman, and Gerry Kohlenberg Zetzel. They are remarkable women who not only travelled to Mississippi with WIMS but remained committed to helping others throughout their lives. They are inspirations, and I thank them for sharing their stories with me.

Many thanks go to archivists Kenneth Chandler, National Archives for Black Women's History at the Mary McLeod Bethune Council House in Washington, D.C.; Debra McIntosh, J. B. Cain Archives of Mississippi Methodism at Millsaps College; Anne Webster, Mississippi Department of Archives and History; Jennifer Brannock and Cindy Lawlor, McCain Library and Archives at the University of Southern Mississippi; Sara Hutcheon, Schlesinger Library at the Radcliff Institute for Advanced Study at Harvard University; Joellen ElBashir, Moorland Spingarn Research Center at Howard University; and Brenda Galloway-Wright, Urban Archives at Temple University. Thanks also to Dorothy Ferebee biographer Diane Kiesel, who shared her findings on the NCNW's Selma trip.

A special thank you goes to Craig Gill, Robert Jefferson Norrell III, and the University Press of Mississippi for making my dream a reality—to honor the WIMS women in celebration of WIMS's fiftieth anniversary.

To my husband, Tom, thank you for your patience all the evenings and weekends I had my head in a book or brought drafts to bed. Thanks, too, to Tom, Travis, Austin, Tracey, Tiffany, and Trudy for your support and encouragement.

Notes

ABBREVIATIONS

Adams Faculty Papers	John Quincy Adams Faculty Papers, Millsaps College Archives, Millsaps-Wilson Library, Millsaps College, Jackson, Mississippi.
Ashmore Papers	Sam E. and Anne Lewis Ashmore Papers (1960–1966), M100, J. B. Cain Archives of Mississippi Methodism, Millsaps College Archives, Millsaps-Wilson Library, Millsaps College, Jackson, Mississippi.
Batson Papers	Ruth Batson Papers, 1919-2003, MC 590, Schlesinger Library, Radcliffe Institute for Advanced Study, Harvard University, Cambridge, Massachusetts.
BWOHP	*Black Women Oral History Project: From the Arthur and Elizabeth Schlesinger Library on the History of Women in America, Radcliff College,* vol. 5, ed. Ruth Edmonds Hill (Westport, CT: Meckler, 1991).
COHCH	Center for Oral History and Cultural Heritage, McCain Library and Archives, University of Southern Mississippi, Hattiesburg, Mississippi.
Cowan Papers	Polly Cowan Papers, National Archives for Black Women's History, Mary McLeod Bethune Council House, Washington, D.C. All references are to Series 1, Box 1.
CRDP	Ralph J. Bunche Collections, formerly the Civil Rights Documentation Project; Manuscript Division, Moorland Spingarn Research Center, Howard University, Washington, D.C.
CRMC	Civil Rights and Methodism Collection, Mississippi Department of Archives and History, Jackson, Mississippi.
CWU Records	Church Women United Records, 1902-2004, General Commission on Archives and History: The United Methodist Church, Madison, New Jersey.
J. B. Cain Archives	J. B. Cain Archives of Mississippi Methodism, Millsaps-Wilson Library, Millsaps College, Jackson, Mississippi.

Johnson Papers	Johnson (Paul B.) Family Papers, Collection M191, Special Collections, McCain Library and Archives, University of Southern Mississippi, Hattiesburg, Mississippi.
Mantinband Papers	Mantinband (Rabbi Charles,) Papers, M 327, McCain Library and Archives, University of Southern Mississippi, Hattiesburg, Mississippi.
MDAH	Mississippi Department of Archives and History.
Millsaps	Millsaps College Archives, Millsaps-Wilson Library, Millsaps College, Jackson, Mississippi.
MMC	Moses Moon Collection, audio tapes 1963–1964, Smithsonian Archives Center Institution, National Museum of American History, Collection #AC0556, Reference Box 3 (original Box 9), #5 SE1.2, N47.
NABWH	National Archives for Black Women's History, Mary McLeod Bethune Council House, Washington, D. C.
NCNW Papers	National Council of Negro Women Papers, NABWH. Unless otherwise indicated, all references are to Series 19.
OHH	UH—Oral History of Houston, Houston History Archive, M. D. Anderson Library, University of Houston, Houston, Texas.
Owens Papers	George A. Owens Papers, Tougaloo College Archives, L. Zenobia Coleman Library, Jackson, Mississippi, Mississippi Digital Library.
Schutt Papers	Jane M. Schutt Papers, T/028, Series 1.1, Tougaloo Collection, Mississippi Department of Archives and History.
SSC	Albert and Shirley Small Special Collections Library, University of Virginia, Charlottesville, Virginia.
Stennis Collection	John C. Stennis Collection, Congressional and Political Research Center, Mississippi State University Library, Starksville, Mississippi.
WIMS Film	Wednesdays in Mississippi Film Project under the direction of Marlene McCurtis, Dean Schramm, Joy Silverman, and Cathee Weiss.
WIMS OH	Wednesday in Mississippi Oral History Interviews, at Albert and Shirley Small Special Collections Library, University of Virginia, Charlottesville, Virginia.

CHAPTER ONE

1. Charles Mantinband, "A Message for Race Relations Sabbath 1962," issued by the Committee of Justice and Peace of the Central Conference of American Rabbis, Mantinband Papers, Box 1, Folder 1, USM.

2. "WIMS Team #1," Team Debriefing transcript, 1964, NABWH-001-S15-SS5-F17-S1, Folder 17, Side 1, NCNW Papers, Series 15, Subseries 5, 1, 26.

3. Dorothy Height, *Open Wide the Freedom Gates: A Memoir* (New York: Public Affairs, 2003), 165; Pauline Cowan, interview by John Britton, March 8, 1968 (hereinafter Cowan interview, 1968), CRDP, 20, 27; Susan Goodwillie Stedman, interview by Holly Cowan Shulman, October 20, 2002 (hereinafter Stedman interview, 2002), WIMS OH, 43–44. Susan Goodwillie Stedman married after her involvement with WIMS and is referred to as Susan Goodwillie; interviews are referenced by her name as recorded at the time.

4. A few organizations attempted to work within the boundaries of southern protocol, including the Southern Student Organizing Committee, the Delta Ministry Project, and Operation Compliance. See Gregg L. Michel, *Struggle for a Better South: The Southern Student Organizing Committee, 1964–1969* (New York: Palgrave McMillan, 2004); Mark Newman, *Divine Agitators: The Delta Ministry and Civil Rights in Mississippi* (Athens, GA: University of Georgia Press, 2004); and Kimberly E. Nichols, "'Service for All Citizens': Operation Compliance and the 'Opening of Public Accommodations to All,' 1964" (M.A. thesis, University of Memphis, 1997).

5. Church Women United formed in 1941 as United Church Women. Its name changed to Church Women United in the mid-1960s and it is referred to by that name throughout to avoid confusion.

6. Barbara Ellen Smith, ed., *Neither Separate nor Equal: Women, Race, and Class in the South* (Philadelphia: Temple University Press, 1999), 17–18.

7. Smith, *Neither Separate nor Equal*, 17–18.

8. Geraldine Kohlenberg Zetzel, interview with author, July 6, 2011 (hereinafter Zetzel interview, 2011), OHH, 17–18; B. E. Smith, *Neither Separate nor Equal*, 17–18.

9. Jason Sokol, *There Goes My Everything: White Southerners in the Age of Civil Rights, 1945–1975* (New York: Alfred A. Knopf, 2006), 59.

10. Sokol, *There Goes My Everything*, 56–57.

11. Charles M. Payne, *I've Got the Light of Freedom: The Organizing Tradition of the Mississippi Freedom Struggle* (Berkeley: University of California Press, 1995), 7.

12. This figure represents 539 blacks, 42 whites, and the highest number of lynched women in any state during the period. "Lynchings, by State and Race, 1882–1968," The Charles Chesnutt Digital Archives, www.chesnuttarchive.org/classroom/lynchings_table_state.html; Lynne Olson, *Freedom's Daughters: The Unsung Heroines of the Civil Rights Movement from 1830–1970* (New York: Touchstone, 2001), 173, 200; Nicholas Mills, *Like a Holy Crusade: Mississippi 1964—The Turning of the Civil Rights Movement in America* (Chicago: Ivan R. Dee, Publisher, 1992), 18.

13. Dorothy I. Height, interview with Polly Cowan, February 11, April 10, May 29, October 6, November 10, 1974; February 2, March 28, May 25, October 5, 1975; February 1, May 31, November 6, 1976, BWOHP, 172; John Dittmer, *Local People: The Struggle for Civil Rights in Mississippi* (Champaign, IL: University of Illinois Press, 1995), 109, 215; Bruce Watson, *Freedom Summer: The Savage Season That Made Mississippi Burn and Made America a Democracy* (New York: Viking Adult, 2010), 18, 24

14. Census 1900, Social Explorer Dataset (SE), digitally transcribed by the Inter-university Consortium for Political and Social Research, edited and verified by Michael Haines, compiled, edited, and verified by Social Explorer; Census 1960, General Population Characteristics, Mississippi, www.census.gov.

15. Mary Cushing Niles, "Report on Trip to Mississippi—July 21–23, 1964," Folder 279, NCNW Papers, 7; Justine Randers-Pehrson, "Report of a Team Member: 'Wednesdays in Mississippi,'" 1964, Folder 304, NCNW Papers, 6; "WIMS Team #3," Team Debriefing transcript, 1964, NABWH-001-S15-SS5-F42-S1, Folder 42, Side 1, NCNW Papers, Series 15, Subseries 5, 51.

16. "Wake Up Mississippi!" September 13, 1964, clipping, CRMC, Series 1.

17. "Mississippi's Inheritance to Its Youth," author unknown, n.d., Ashmore Papers, Box 2, Folder 2.

18. Myrlie B. Evers, with William Peters and introduction by Willie Morris, *For Us, the Living* (Garden City, NY: Doubleday, 1967), 235; Dittmer, *Local People*, 89.

19. Anne Moody, *Coming of Age in Mississippi* (New York: Bantam Dell, 1968), 286–291.

20. Ed King Jr., interview with John Jones, November 8, 1980, Folder 1, Ed King Collection (hereinafter King interview, 1980), MDAH, 11; Dittmer, *Local People*, 116.

21. King interview, 1980, 45–46.

22. King interview, 1980, 43, 45–46.

23. John F. Kennedy, "Radio and Television Address to the American People on Civil Rights, June 11, 1963," John F. Kennedy Presidential Library and Museum, www.jfklibrary.org/Research/Ready-Reference/JFK-Speeches/Radio-and-Television-Report-to-the-American-People-on-Civil-Rights-June-11-1963.aspx; Dittmer, *Local People*, 109, 166–167, 173; Taylor Branch, *Parting the Waters: America in the King Years, 1954–1963* (New York: Simon & Schuster Paperbacks, 1988), 825–827.

24. Taylor Branch, *Pillar of Fire: America in the King Years, 1963–1965* (New York: Simon & Schuster Paperbacks, 1998), 77; Height, *BWOHP*, 172; Height, *Open Wide the Freedom Gates*, 143; Michael O'Brian, *John F. Kennedy: A Biography* (New York: Thomas Dunne Books, 2005), 847.

25. Branch, *Parting the Waters*, 889–891; Dittmer, *Local People*, 173.

26. Sokol, *There Goes My Everything*, 56–57.

27. Yasuhiro Katagiri, *The Mississippi State Sovereignty Commission: Civil Rights and States' Rights* (Jackson, MS: University Press of Mississippi, 2001), 5.

28. Linda Reed, *Simple Decency & Common Sense: The Southern Conference Movement, 1938–1963* (Bloomington, IN: Indiana University Press, 1991), 158, 159.

29. Sokol, *There Goes My Everything*, 85.

30. Reed, *Simple Decency & Common Sense*, 159.

31. Clay F. Lee, interview with Orley B. Caudill, July 8, 1980 and July 23, 1980 (hereinafter Lee interview), F341.5.M57, vol. 186, COHCH, 31.

32. Gene Roberts and Hank Klibanoff, *The Race Beat: The Press, the Civil Rights Struggle, and the Awakening of a Nation* (New York: Alfred A. Knopf, 2007), 348.

33. Susan Goodwillie Stedman, interview with author, July 8, 2011 (hereinafter Stedman interview, 2011), OHH, 6; Steven D. Classen, *Watching Jim Crow: The Struggles Over Mississippi TV, 1955–1969* (Durham, NC: Duke University Press, 2004), 52–53.

34. Ellipses in original. Patt Derian to Polly Cowan, January 7, 1965, Folder 275, NCNW Papers.

35. Roberts and Klibanoff, *The Race Beat*, 84; Charles W. Eagles, *The Price of Defiance: James Meredith and the Integration of Ole Miss* (Chapel Hill: University of North Carolina Press, 2009), 179.

36. "Hazel Brannon Smith," Encyclopedia of Alabama, www.encyclopediaofalabama .org/face/Article.jsp?id=h-1826.

37. John R. Rachal, "'The Long Hot Summer': The Mississippi Response to Freedom Summer, 1964," *The Journal of Negro History* 84, no. 4 (Autumn 1999): 331.

38. Clarence James Goodwillie to John Morley Goodwillie, June 10, 1964, in possession of Susan Goodwillie Stedman; John Morley Goodwillie to Clarence James Goodwillie, June 21, 1964, in possession of Susan Goodwillie Stedman. See also www.history .uh.edu/cph/WIMS/.

39. Stephanie M. Wildman with Adrienne D. Davis, "Making Systems of Privilege Visible," in *White Privilege: Essential Readings on the Other Side of Racism*, 2d ed., ed. Paula S. Rothenberg (New York: Worth Publishers, 2005), 95, 99; Stedman interview, 2011, 17.

40. Charles Mantinband, "Rabbi in the Deep South: A Mississippian Shows the Way; How to Be True to One's Belief—and Survive—in an Area of Racial Tension," *Anti-defamation League of B'nai B'rith Bulletin*, May 1962, Mantinband Papers, Box 2, Folder 2, 3.

41. Stedman interview, 2011, 6.

42. Susan Goodwillie, letter to "Dear Friends far away," July 30, 1964, in possession of Susan Goodwillie Stedman.

43. "WIMS Team #3," Debriefing, Side 1, 63–64.

44. Trude W. Lash, Project: Wednesdays in Mississippi (WIM) Report, 1964, Folder 306, NCNW Papers, 13; "WIMS Team #5," Team Debriefing transcript, 1964, NABWH-001-S15-SS5-F18-S2, Folder 18, Side 2, NCNW Papers, Series 15, Subseries 5, 66–67.

45. WIMS made every effort to keep identities confidential. Debriefing audio tapes usually mention southern participants as "Mrs." followed by a surname and preceded by a clarification of whether using names on the tape was acceptable. Very few references include first names of the women or their husbands. The transcripts of all the 1964 debriefings tapes transcribed that year used "Mrs. A.," "Mrs. B.," and so on to designate individual women. On numerous written reports, names are crossed out and illegible, even names of women who operated openly. No complete list exists of the women who met with the teams or served as hostesses. With a few exceptions, the white women identified as attending the coffees are not mentioned in the Mississippi State Sovereignty Commission documents. Most likely, they did not openly support civil rights, they did not associate with individuals who supported civil rights, or they opposed it.

46. Newman, *Divine Agitators*, 53.

47. Jenny Irons, "The Shaping of Activist Recruitment and Participation: A Study of Women in the Mississippi Civil Rights Movement," *Gender and Society* 12, no. 6, Special Issue: Gender and Social Movements, Part 1 (December 1998), 696; Stedman, interview, 2011, 5.

48. Janet Purvis, interview with Marlene McCurtis, January 22, 2008 (hereinafter Purvis interview, 2008), WIMS Film, 08:46:51–08:47:59.

49. "WIMS Team #5," Debriefing, Side 1, 24–25.

50. Vicki L. Crawford, Jacqueline Anne Rouse, and Barbara Woods, eds., *Women in the Civil Rights Movement: Trailblazers and Torchbearers, 1941–1965* (Bloomington: Indiana University Press, 1990), 3–5.

51. Victoria Gray Adams, "They Didn't Know the Power of Women," in Faith S. Holsaert, Martha Prescod Norman Noonan, Judy Richardson, Betty Garman Robinson, Jean Smith Young, and Dorothy M. Zellner, eds., *Hands on the Freedom Plow: Personal Accounts by Women in SNCC* (Urbana, IL: University of Illinois Press, 2010), 237.

52. Clarie Collins Harvey, "Women in the Civil Rights Movement—Trailblazers and Torchbearers," October 12–15, 1988, Racism—Assignment: RACE, 1224-4-2:13, CWU Records, UMC, 7.

53. Charles M. Hills, "Affairs of State: Agitation's Aftermath," newspaper clipping, 1963, Schutt Papers, Box 1, Folder 55,

54. Wilma Clopton and Jay Shands, interview with Marlene McCurtis, January 24, 2008, transcript, (hereinafter Clopton and Shands interview), WIMS Film, 15:19:38–15:21:07.

55. Florynce Kennedy, "Once upon a Week," *The Queens Voice*, October 9, 1964, Folder 232, NCNW Papers. A memo dated September 27, 1964, in the Mississippi Sovereignty Commission records indicates that the bomb "may have been caused" by the Sanders' housing "freedom workers" in their home. Sovereignty Commission Online, MDAH, 9-31-2-50-1-1-1.

56. King interview, 1980, 66.

57. "Boycott gets publicity; 31,000 letters sent to white community," March 2, 1964, *Mississippi Free Press*, 1.

58. Randers-Pehrson, "Report of a Team Member," 1.

59. "Wednesdays in Mississippi—Team #1," 14; Polly Cowan, "Women in Mississippi (WIMS) Preliminary Report," 1964, Folder 280, NCNW Papers, 26–27; Kojo Nnamdi, "Wednesdays in Mississippi: An Interview with Guests Susan Goodwillie, Priscilla Hunt, Mildred Pitt Goodman, Doris V. Wilson, and Russlyn Ali," *Public Interest,* WAMU, American University Radio, Washington, DC, 2001 (hereinafter Nnamdi interview, 2001), cassette.

60. Association of Citizens' Councils, "The Citizens' Council," n.d., Johnson Family Papers, M 191, Series II, Subseries 8, Box 124, Folder 12.

61. Gary Phillip Zola, "What Price Amos? Perry Nussbaum's Career in Jackson, Mississippi," in *The Quiet Voices: Southern Rabbis and Black Civil Rights, 1880s–1990s,* eds. Mark K. Bauman and Berkley Kalin (Tuscaloosa, AL: University of Alabama Press, 1997),

245. See James W. Silver, *Mississippi: The Closed Society* (New York: Harcourt, Brace & World, 1964), 41.

62. Florence Mars, *Witness in Philadelphia*, with Lynn Eden, foreword by Turner Catledge (Baton Rouge, LA: Louisiana State University, 1977), 76.

63. "Testing of 'Rights' Law Continues Across Dixie: Council Urges Walkout; Jackson CC Gives Integration Protest," *Clarion-Ledger*, July 7, 1964, 1.

64. "Rep. Williams, Calls CR Body a 'Gestapo,'" newspaper clipping, n.d., Schutt Papers, Box 2, Folder 51; M. Carl Hollman, press release from the U.S. Commission on Civil Rights, October 5, 1962, Schutt Papers, Box 2, Folder 9.

65. Jane M. Schutt, "Statement by the Mississippi Advisory Committee to the U.S. Commission on Civil Rights," April 17, 1963, Schutt Papers, Box 1, Folder 2, 1-2. The statement refers to specific abuses that occurred over a fourteen-month period ending in January 1963 and reported to the U.S. Civil Rights Commission by the Mississippi Advisor Committee. Schutt Papers, Box 2, Folder 22.

66. Prathia Hall, "Freedom Faith," in *Hands on the Freedom Plow*, 178.

67. "WIMS Team #3," Debriefing, Side 1, 65.

68. Height, *Open Wide the Freedom Gates*, 114.

69. Priscilla Hunt, "De-briefing—Wednesdays in Mississippi," September 24, 1964, Folder 308, NCNW Papers, 8.

70. Miriam Davis, "Report on Wednesday, August 12, 1964 in Mississippi," n.d., Folder 307, NCNW Papers, 4–5; Maxine Nathanson, Report, 1964, Folder 305, NCNW Papers, 2.

71. "WIMS Team #2," Team Debriefing transcript, 1964, NABWH-001-S15-SS5-F20-S1-S2, Folder 20, NCNW Papers, Series 15, Subseries 5, 96.

72. Priscilla Hunt, phone interview with author, October 6, 2008; "Wednesdays in Mississippi—New Jersey Team to Hattiesburg," n.d., Folder 308, NCNW Papers, 8–9; "WIMS Team #7," Team Debriefing transcript, 1964, NABWH-001-S15-SS5-F38-S2, Folder 38, Side 2, NCNW Papers, Subseries 5, Series 15, 1–3; Polly Cowan, "Wednesdays in Mississippi—Report From Polly Cowan, Project Coordinator," 1964, Folder 277, NCNW Papers, 4; Height, *Open Wide the Freedom Gates*, 183.

73. NCJW, News for Publicity Chairman, "NCJW Head Takes Part in Wednesdays in Mississippi," September 4, 1964, Folder 303, NCNW Papers, 3.

74. "WIMS Team #2," Debriefing, 21–23.

75. Derian, letter to Cowan, January 7, 1965.

76. Randy J. Sparks, *Religion in Mississippi*, Heritage of Mississippi Series Vol. II., (Jackson, MS: University Press of Mississippi, 2001), xi.

77. David L. Chappell, *A Stone of Hope* (Chapel Hill: University of North Carolina Press, 2004), 105-106.

78. Douglas W. Johnson, Paul R. Picard, Bernard Quinn, *Churches & Church Membership in the United States: An Enumeration by Region, State and Country* (Glenmary Research Center: Washington, D.C., 1971), 5–8. There were approximately 670,000 Southern Baptists, compared to 214,000 United Methodists.

79. Zola, "What Price Amos?" 238.

80. Samuel S. Hill Jr. with Edgar T. Thompson, Anne Firor Scott, Charles Hudson, and Edwin S. Gaustad, *Religion and the Solid South* (Nashville, TN: Adingdon Press, 1972), 24–25.

81. Priscilla Hunt, Susan Goodwillie Stedman, and Geraldine Kohlenberg Zetzel, interview with author, July 7, 2011 (hereinafter Hunt, Stedman, and Zetzel interview, 2011) OHH, 48.

82. Carol Bergmark, "Chronology of the Civil Rights Struggle—1953–1970," Robert Bergmark Papers, F14, Box 2, Folder 5, J. B. Cain Archives. Episcopal priest Duncan Gray became one of the earliest supporters of desegregation in a 1956 speech delivered at Mississippi State College. Rachal, "'The Long Hot Summer,'" 330.

83. M. Davis, "Report on Wednesday, August 12, 1964," 3; Aaron Henry, "Freedom Views," July 18, 1964, *Mississippi Free Press*, 4.

84. Paul Harvey, "God and Negroes and Jesus and Sin and Salvation: Racism, Racial Interchange, and Interracialism in Southern Religious History," in *Religion in the American South: Protestants and Others in History and Culture*, eds. Beth Barton Schweiger and Donald G. Mathews (Chapel Hill, NC: University of North Carolina Press, 2004), 284–285

85. P. Harvey, "God and Negroes and Jesus and Sin and Salvation," 284–285.

86. Decell Memorial Methodist Church Board, January 27, 1963, Ashmore Papers, Box 1, Folder 3.

87. Jane M. Schutt, interview by Leesha Faulkner, October 3, 1994, and October 10, 1994 (hereinafter Schutt interview, 1994), COHCH, 24.

88. Sparks, *Religion in Mississippi*, 230, 234.

89. Charles Mantinband, "In Dixieland I Take My Stand," First Annual George Brussel Memorial Lecture, April 16, 1962, Stephen Wise Free Synagogue, New York City, NY, Mantinband Papers, M327, Box 2, Folder 2, 10.

90. Alex D. Dickson, Jr., "Sermon Preached in the Parish Church of St. Columb's on October 14, 1962," Schutt Papers, Box 1, Folder 36, 2, 4.

91. Paul Harvey, *Freedom's Coming: Religious Culture and the Shaping of the South from the Civil War through the Civil Rights Era* (Chapel Hill, NC: University of North Carolina Press, 2005), 2; P. Harvey, "God and Negroes and Jesus and Sin and Salvation," 286.

92. M. Davis, "Report on Wednesday, August 12, 1964," 3; Bertist C. Rouse to Sam Ashmore, n.d., Ashmore Papers, Box 1, Folder 4. Most segregationists referred to Old Testament passages Deuteronomy 7:1–3, Joshua 22:12–13, and Ezra 9:12 regarding God's warning to the Israelites. Others referred to Acts 17:26, where God specifies the boundaries of the nations of men. Fannie Lou Hamer held that this also applied for integrationists because it indicated God "made of one blood all the nations of men." Chappell, *A Stone of Hope*, 112.

93. Roy Wolf to Sam Ashmore, January 3, 1963, Ashmore Papers.

94. Ephesians 6:11–12, King James Version; P. Harvey, *Freedom's Coming*, 198.

95. Galatians 3:26–28, King James Version; "Mississippi's Inheritance to Its Youth."

96. 1 John 3:9–11, King James Version; "Mississippi's Inheritance to Its Youth."

*

97. Purvis interview, 2008, 08:33:31–08:43:19.

98. Mantinband, "A Message for Race Relations Sabbath 1962," 1; Charles Mantinband, "The Horns of a Dilemma," *Central Conference of American Rabbis, 1964*," 242.

99. Charles Mantinband, "The Church and Race Relations," (PhD diss., Burton College and Seminary, Manitou Springs, Colorado, December 1958), Mantinband Papers, M327, Box 1, Folder 13, 72–73, 84–85.

100. Perry Nussbaum to Sam Ashmore, February 20, 1963, Ashmore Papers, Box 1, Folder 4.

101. Perry E. Nussbaum, oral history, August 5, 1965, Perry E. Nussbaum Papers, 1947–1972, MC 430, Box 4, Folder 6, American Jewish Archives, Cincinnati, Ohio.

102. Perry Nussbaum to Sam Ashmore, February 20, 1963, Ashmore Papers, Box 1, Folder 4.

103. The United Methodist Church formed in 1968 when the Methodist Church and the Evangelical United Brethren Church joined as one.

104. "Born of Conviction," *The Mississippi Methodist Advocate,* January 2, 1963, 2.

105. James B. Nicholson, "Real Issues for these Times," n.d., Ashmore Papers, Box 1, Folder 2, 1.

106. Reiff, "Conflicting Convictions," 162, 166–167, 172–173; Glenn Miller to Sam Ashmore, January 10, 1963, Ashmore Papers, Box 4, Folder 1.

107. Guinn Memorial Methodist Church Board to *Mississippi Methodist Advocate*, n.d., Ashmore Papers, Box 1, Folder 3, 1.

108. Kemper County Laymen of Methodist Church to *Mississippi Methodist Advocate*, January 12, 1963, Ashmore Papers, Box 1, Folder 3.

109. Reiff, "Conflicting Convictions," 166, 170.

110. Bill Selah to Sam Ashmore, Ashmore Papers, Box 1, Folder 2.

111. Dean M. Kelley to Edward W. McRae, January 30, 1963, Ashmore Papers, Box 1, Folder 4.

112. Lawrence W. Rabb to Sam Ashmore, January 7, 1963, Ashmore Papers, Box 1, Folder 4.

113. "Homecoming Next Sunday: Galloway Methodists Begin a Year-long Celebration," November 7, 1965, SF: Jackson Churches Methodist Galloway Memorial 1836–1976, MDAH.

114. P. Harvey, *Freedom's Coming,* 64; W. J. Cunningham, *Agony at Galloway: One Church's Struggle with Social Change* (Jackson: University Press of Mississippi, 1980), 23; Sparks, *Religion in Mississippi,* 158, 161–162.

115. Ray E. Stevens, ed., "Galloway Church History 1956–1965: Book One," June 1, 1996, J. B. Cain Archives, 155.

116. Cunningham, *Agony at Galloway,* 124. Episcopalian and Lutheran churches also admitted blacks. Sparks, *Religion in Mississippi,* 244.

117. W. J. Cunningham, interview with Orley B. Caudill, August 6, 1981 (hereinafter Cunningham interview, 1981), F341.5.M57, vol. 242, COHCH, 24.

118. Cunningham, *Agony at Galloway,* 19, 46; Sokol, *There Goes My Everything,* 104, 3, 5–6, 14, 15, 19

119. Cunningham interview, 1981, 24, 26.

120. Curtiss Paul DeYoung, Michael O. Emerson, George Yancey, and Karen Chai Kim, *United by Faith: The Multiracial Congregation as an Answer to the Problem of Race* (New York: Oxford University Press, 2003), 69.

121. Cunningham, *Agony at Galloway*, 24.

122. Cunningham interview, 1981, 28, 30–31.

123. "Church Mixing Blocked: Ushers Bar Way Of Two Bishops At Service Here," *Clarion-Ledger*, newspaper clipping, March 30, 1964, Local Churches: Galloway UMC, Box 27.1, J. B. Cain Archives; Cunningham, *Agony at Galloway*, 55–56; Branch, *Pillar of Fire*, 264.

124. Cunningham, *Agony at Galloway*, 29, 145; "Homecoming Next Sunday"; "Methodist Group Elects Officials," newspaper clipping, n.d., Local Churches: Galloway UMC, Box 27.1, J. B. Cain Archives. Under pressure from the board, Cunningham finally tendered his resignation in December 1965, effective June 1966. On January 10, 1966, the Galloway board voted 65 to 40 to open its doors to blacks, reflecting the changing times. By the 1980s, African Americans still failed to worship at Galloway regularly or in significant numbers. Cunningham interview, 1981, 33, 42; Stevens, "Galloway Church History," 221; Sokol, *There Goes My Everything*, 106.

125. Richard Aubrey McLemore and Nannie Pitts McLemore, *The History of the First Baptist Church of Jackson, Mississippi* (Jackson: Hederman Brothers, 1976), 222, 268.

126. Patt Derian, interview with Betsy Nash, December 17, 1991 (hereinafter Derian interview, 1991), Stennis Collection, 7–8.

127. Purvis interview, 2008, 08:33:31–08:34:02.

128. Charles Molpus to Bernard F. Law, September 27, 1963, Schutt Papers, Box 2, Folder 16.

129. Hunt, "De-briefing—Wednesdays in Mississippi," 8.

130. Sparks, *Religion in Mississippi*, 235.

131. William A. Osborne, *The Segregated Covenant: Race Relations and American Catholics* (New York: Herder and Herder, 1967), 89.

132. Claude Sitton, "3 Hotels Register Negroes in Peaceful Jackson Test," July 6, 1964, *New York Times*, 1.

133. Rachal, "'The Long Hot Summer,'" 329–330.

134. Nathanson, Report, 4.

135. Nussbaum, oral history, 13, 4, 14; Zola, "What Price Amos?" 236.

136. Bauman and Kalin, *The Quiet Voices*, 6.

137. Matthew Frye Jacobson, *Whiteness of a Different Color: European Immigrants and the Alchemy of Race* (Cambridge, MA: Harvard University Press, 1998), 188; David R. Roediger, *Working toward Whiteness: How America's Immigrants Became White: The Strange Journey from Ellis Island to the Suburbs* (Tuscaloosa: University of Alabama Press, 2005), 27, 116.

138. Debra L. Schultz, *Going South: Jewish Women in the Civil Rights Movement* (New York: New York University Press, 2001), 21.

139. Clive Webb, *Fight against Fear: Southern Jews and Black Civil Rights* (Athens, GA: University of Georgia Press, 2003), 197.

140. Mantinband, "In Dixieland I Take my Stand," 10.

141. Lillian Burnstein, interview with Marlene McCurtis, January 22, 2008, transcript (hereinafter Burnstein interview, 2008), WIMS Film, 06:49:14.

142. Nussbaum, oral history, 6–8.

143. Nussbaum, oral history, 6–8, 40–41; "Names of Jews Running the United Nations," n.d., Johnson Family Papers, M 191, Series II, Subseries 7, Box 110, Folder 5.

144. Schultz, *Going South*, 18; Webb, *Fight against Fear*, 80.

145. Webb, *Fight against Fear*, 150–151.

146. Nussbaum, oral history, 29.

147. Allen Krause, "The Southern Rabbi and Civil Rights" (M.A. thesis, Hebrew Union College-Jewish Institute of Religion, Cincinnati, Ohio, 1967), Mantinband Papers, M327, Box 1, Folder 7, 306–307.

148. Schultz, *Going South*, 95, 100.

149. Charles Mantinband, "From the Diary of a Mississippi Rabbi," *American Judaism*, Winter 1962–1963, 9. The diary entry is for October 2, 1962.

150. Bettye Collier-Thomas, *Jesus, Jobs, and Justice: African American Women and Religion* (New York: Alfred A. Knopf, 2010), 313.

151. Collier-Thomas, *Jesus, Jobs, and Justice*, 410.

152. Collier-Thomas, *Jesus, Jobs, and Justice*, 311.

153. C. Harvey, "Women in the Civil Rights Movement," 1; Janine Marie Denomme, "'To End This Day of Strife': Churchwomen and the Campaign for Integration, 1920–1970" (PhD dissertation, University of Pennsylvania, 2001), 1.

154. Collier-Thomas, *Jesus, Jobs, and Justice*, 367.

155. Denomme, "'To End This Day of Strife,'" 171, 173. The Field Foundation gave CWU $66,000 to launch Assignment: RACE.

156. C. Harvey, "Women in the Civil Rights Movement," 5. That same year, Schutt attended a Fellowship of the Concerned meeting in Atlanta with M. G. Haughton, a black woman and minister's wife from Jackson, where they too discussed creating the prayer group. C. Harvey interview, 1965, 25.

157. Schutt interview, 1994, 5.

158. Denomme, "'To End This Day of Strife,'" 248–249.

159. Susan Lynn, *Progressive Women in Conservative Times: Racial Justice, Peace, and Feminism, 1945 to the 1960s* (Brunswick, NJ: Rutgers University Press, 1992), 46–49.

160. Lynn, *Progressive Women in Conservative Times*, 46; Height, *Open Wide the Freedom Gates*, 114–116.

161. Evelyn Brooks Higgenbotham, *Righteous Discontent: The Women's Movement in the Black Baptist Church, 1880–1920* (Cambridge, MA: Harvard University Press, 1993), 2.

162. Rosetta E. Ross, *Witnessing and Testifying: Black Women, Religion, and Civil Rights* (Minneapolis: Fortress Press, 2003), xiii, 13–15, 11–12.

163. Ross, *Witnessing and Testifying*, 51–52, 32, 80; Grace Jordan McFaddin, "Septima P. Clark and the Struggle for Human Rights," in *Women in the Civil Rights Movement: Trailblazers and Torchbearers.*

164. Ross, *Witnessing and Testifying*, 47, 32; Barbara Ransby, *Ella Baker and the Black Freedom Movement: A Radical Democratic Vision* (Chapel Hill: University of North Carolina Press, 2003).

165. Ross, *Witnessing and Testifying*, 174.

166. Hall, "Freedom Faith," 172, 180.

167. Denomme, "'To End This Day of Strife,'" 140; "Diane Nash," *Women and the Civil Rights Movement, 1954–1965*, eds. Davis W. Houck and David E. Dixon (Jackson: University Press of Mississippi, 2009), 156.

168. P. Harvey, *Freedom's Coming*, 170; Ross, *Witnessing and Testifying*, 111.

169. Chappell, *A Stone of Hope*, 72–73, quoting Fannie Lou Hamer interview, Project South, Stanford University, MFDP, chapter 55, 4–8, 14–15.

170. Chappell, *A Stone of Hope*, 71–72; Ross, *Witnessing and Testifying*, 114.

171. Sparks, *Religion in Mississippi*, 224, 226.

172. King interview, 1980.

173. Watson, *Freedom Summer*, 52.

174. Vicki Crawford "African American Women in the Mississippi Freedom Democratic Party," in *Sisters in the Struggle: African American Women in the Civil Rights-Black Power Movement*, eds. Bettye Collier-Thomas and V.P. Franklin (New York: New York University Press, 2001), 123–124; Dittmer, *Local People*, 102–103; "Prospectus for the Mississippi Freedom Summer," Schutt Papers, Box 1, Folder 32.

175. Crawford, *Sisters in the Struggle*, 123–124; Dittmer, *Local People*, 103, 210, 219; Payne, *I've Got the Light of Freedom*, 201, 300.

176. Steven F. Lawson and Charles Payne with an introduction by James T. Patterson, *Debating the Civil Rights Movement, 1945–1968* (Lanham, MD: Rowan & Littlefield Publishers, Inc., 1998), 30, 126; Dittmer, *Local People*, 210, 219.

177. King interview, 1980, 77–78.

178. Height, *BWOHP*, 172; Dittmer, *Local People*, 109, 173, 213, 215–218; Olson, *Freedom's Daughters*, 200, 299; Branch, *Pillar of Fire*, 240; Reed, *Simple Decency & Common Sense*, 165; Claude Sitton, "Mississippi Is Gripped by Fear of Violence in Civil Rights Drive," *New York Times*, May 30, 1964, NCNW Papers, Folder 197.

179. Tom Ethridge, "Mississippi Notebook: About 'Summer Project Mississippi': FBI Chief Warns of Red Influence," March 31, 1964, *Clarion-Ledger*, Johnson Family Papers, Series II, Subseries 9, Box 141, Folder 8.

180. "A Major Purpose of Invaders Is to Attract Federal Occupation," newspaper clipping, *Clarion-Ledger*, June 30, 1964, Schutt Papers, Box 1, Folder 56.

181. Sokol, *There Goes My Everything*, 3, 56–59.

182. Mike Miller, "Mississippi Musings: Freedom Summer Revisited (Civil Rights Movement in the 1960s)," *Social Policy* 25, no. 1 (Fall 1994): 46–61; Height, *Open Wide the Freedom Gates*, 167.

183. Henry Hampton and Steve Fayer with Sarah Flynn, eds., *Voices of Freedom: An Oral History of the Civil Rights Movement from the 1950s through the 1980s* (New York: Bantam Books, 1990), 188.

184. Dittmer, *Local People*, 244.

185. Hampton, Fayer, and Flynn, *Voices of Freedom*, 187; Stedman interview, 2002, 30; Susan Goodwillie, "Laws recently passed or still pending in the Mississippi State Legislature," memorandum to Shirley B. Smith, March 18, 1964, Folder 72, NCNW Papers; Rachal, "'The Long Hot Summer,'" 320.

186. Dittmer, *Local People*, 259; N. Mills, *Like a Holy Crusade*, 86.

187. Sitton, "Mississippi Is Gripped by Fear of Violence"; "Police Fear Crisis in Jackson, Miss.: Force Strengthened to Bar Any Negro Demonstrations," clipping, *New York Times*, March 8, 1964, Folder 232, NCNW Papers, 52; Height, *BWOHP*, 184; Crawford, *Sisters in the Struggle*, 123–124; Ransby, *Ella Baker and the Black Freedom Movement*, 299, 306; Hampton and Fayer, *Voices of Freedom*, 187; Stedman, interview, 2002, 30; Olson, *Freedom's Daughters*, 299.

188. Katagiri, *The Mississippi State Sovereignty Commission*, 158–159.

189. Erle Johnston Jr., memo to A. D. Morgan, June 26, 1964, Johnson Family Papers, Series II, Subseries 10, Box 144, Folder 7.

CHAPTER TWO

1. Height, *BWOHP*, 172.

2. Dorothy Height, interview with Holly Cowan Shulman, October 16, 2002 (hereinafter Height interview, 2002), WIMS OH, 13; Height, *Open Wide the Freedom Gates*, 138–142; Height, *BWOHP*, 168–170; Holly C. Shulman, "Polly Spiegel Cowan: Civil Rights Activist, 1913–1976," 2004, Jewish Women's Archive, http://jwa.org/weremember/cowan; Holly Cowan Shulman, *Wednesdays in Mississippi: The National Council of Negro Women and the Civil Rights Movement in Mississippi during Freedom Summer, 1964* (Washington, D.C.: National Park Service, Mary McLeod Bethune Council House, forthcoming), 11–12.

3. Polly Cowan, "Chapter I," autobiography fragments, Folder 8, Cowan Papers, 3; Stedman interview, 2002, 28.

4. Height interview, 2002, 13; Height, *Open Wide the Freedom Gates*, 138–140; Cowan, "Chapter I," 4; Shulman, "Polly Spiegel Cowan: Civil Rights Activist"; Shulman, *National Council of Negro Women*, 11–12; Cowan interview, 1968, 20, 27, 4.

5. Paula Giddings, *When and Where I Enter: The Impact of Black Women on Race and Sex in America* (New York, 1984), 213.

6. Deborah Gray White, *Too Heavy a Load: Black Women in Defense of Themselves, 1894–1994* (New York: W. W. Norton & Company, 1999), 148–149, 177; Giddings, *When and Where I Enter*, 202, 213.

7. Height, *Freedom Gates*, 1–2, 18–19, 25, 28–30, 40–41, 84–85; Height, *BWOHP*, 36.

8. Height, *Open Wide the Freedom Gates,* 30-32.

9. Height, *Open Wide the Freedom Gates,* 79, 82–85, 155–156; Shulman, *National Council of Negro Women,* 7; Height, *BWOHP,* 37.

10. Polly Cowan, "Why Me?" autobiographical essay, Folder 7, Cowan Papers; Isaiah 1:17; Cowan interview, 1968, 35–36; Shulman, *National Council of Negro Women,* 8–9, 3–4; Shulman, "Polly Spiegel Cowan."

11. Cowan, "Why Me?"; Cowan interview, 1968, 35–36; Shulman, *National Council of Negro Women,* 8–9, 3–4; Shulman, "Polly Spiegel Cowan"; "Our History," *Straus News,* April 29, 2004, www.strausnewscom/articles/2004/05/18/about_us/history/about01.txt; Fern Marja Eckman, "Closeup: For the Rights of Youth," newspaper clipping, n.d. Folder 17, NCNW Papers.

12. Shulman, *National Council of Negro Women,* 8–9, 3–4; Shulman, "Polly Spiegel Cowan."

13. Dorothy Height, "'We Wanted the Voice of Women to be Heard': Black Women and the 1963 March on Washington," in *Sisters in the Struggle,* 85–88.

14. Height, *Sisters in the Struggle,* 85–88; Height, *Open Wide the Freedom Gates,* 145–146, 157–158; Cowan, "Chapter I," 7; Dorothy Height, interviewed by Holly Cowan Shulman, January 24, 2003 (hereinafter Height interview, 2003), WIMS OH, 41–44; Height, *BWOHP,* 173.

15. Susan Goodwillie, "Profile of Susan Goodwillie," Folder 208, NCNW Papers.

16. Stedman interview 2002, 6; Susan Goodwillie, interview with William Chafe, January 22, 1989, "The Reminiscences of Susan Goodwillie" (hereinafter Goodwillie interview, "Reminiscences"), Lowenstein Oral History Project, Oral History Research Office, Columbia University, New York, 3–4.

17. Stedman interview 2002, 8–11; "Profile of Susan Goodwillie."

18. Stedman interview, 2011, 26–27.

19. Height, *Open Wide the Freedom Gates,* 157–158; Cowan, "Chapter I," 10; Height interview, 2003, 41–44; National Council of Negro Women Education Foundation, "Wednesdays in Mississippi, 1964," Folder 270, NCNW Papers. Although the WIMS records state that 300 children and young people were arrested, other evidence indicates a total of 350 arrests, 250 of which were children under sixteen. "Gregory Reputed on Way Here for Parley Tonight, Weekend Activities Remain Question," *Selma Times-Journal,* October 4, 1963, A1-2; J. Mills Thornton III, *Dividing Lines: Municipal Politics and the Struggle for Civil Rights in Montgomery, Birmingham, and Selma* (Tuscaloosa: University of Alabama Press, 2002), 454.

20. Cowan, "Chapter I," 7; Height, *Open Wide the Freedom Gates,* 157–160; NCNW Education Foundation, "'Wednesdays in Mississippi' 1964," 3; Stedman, interview, 2002, 15, 8.

21. Polly Cowan, "Chapter 2, Selma, Alabama," autobiography fragments, Folder 10, Cowan Papers, 10.

22. Height, *Open Wide the Freedom Gates,* 157–158; Cowan interview, 1968, 6.

23. Cowan, "Chapter I," 12.

24. Cowan, "Chapter I," 16–17, 7; Height, *Open Wide the Freedom Gates,* 157–160; NCNW Education Foundation, "'Wednesdays in Mississippi' 1964," 3; Stedman interview, 2002, 15; Cowan interview, 1968, 7–8; Susan Goodwillie Stedman, interview with Marlene McCurtis, 2008 (hereinafter, Stedman interview, 2008), WIMS Film, 04:35:52–04:37:49.

25. James Forman, Moses Moon Collection (hereinafter MMC),40:19; "Register and Vote urges Comedian Dick Gregory, Calls for Large Turnout Monday at Courthouse," *Selma Times-Journal,* October 6, 1663, A1-2; "Leaders urge big turnout in Selma," *Birmingham News,* October 6, 1963, A-2.

26. "Dorothy Height," in *Women and the Civil Rights Movement,* 221–223; "Register and Vote urges Comedian Dick Gregory," A1-2.

27. Dorothy Ferebee, MMC, 40:50.

28. Ferebee, MMC, 40:50.

29. Polly Cowan, MMC, 45:40; "Register and Vote Urges Comedian Dick Gregory," A1-2.

30. Dick Gregory, MMC, 48:49; "Leaders Urge Big Turnout in Selma," A-2.

31. Forman, MMC, 26:40.

32. Shulman, *National Council of Negro Women,* 9; Cowan interview, 1968, 7; Height, *Open Wide the Freedom Gates,* 158; NCNW Educational Foundation, "'Wednesdays in Mississippi' 1964," 3; Cowan, "Chapter I," 18.

33. Cowan interview, 1968, 8–9; "Register and Vote Urges Comedian Dick Gregory," A1-2; Shirley Smith, "My Southern Journey," a confidential memo to Mrs. Harris, Mr. Horton, and Mrs. Peterson, October 10, 1963, Folder 11, Cowan Papers, 2. Newspaper reports confirm approximately forty "possemen."

34. Cowan," Chapter 2," autobiography fragments, 18–19; "Hall Arrested," *Selma Time-Journal,* October 7, 1963, A1; "Register and Vote Urges Comedian Dick Gregory," A1-2; Height, *Open Wide the Freedom Gates,* 160; Height interview, 2003, 46.

35. Smith, "My Southern Journey"; "Rosa Joyce," obituary, *Selma Times Journal,* August 26, 2009.

36. "Katherine Cothran," obituary, *Selma Times Journal,* March 16, 2010.

37. Smith, "My Southern Journey," 4–5.

38. Cowan, "Chapter 2," 20–22, 23–24, 17; Polly Cowan, "The Freedom to Vote," October 1963, Folder 32, NCNW Papers, 6–8; Polly Cowan, "The Freedom to Vote," confidential memo, October 4–5, 1963, Folder 11, Cowan Papers, 3–4; Smith, "My Southern Journey," 2–6.

39. Cowan, "Chapter 2," 23–24, 17; Cowan, "The Freedom to Vote," NCNW Papers, 6–8; Cowan, "The Freedom to Vote," Folder 11, Cowan Papers, 3–4; Smith, "My Southern Journey," 2–5.

40. Smith, "My Southern Journey," 2–5; Cowan, "Chapter 2," 23–24, 17; Cowan, "The Freedom to Vote," NCNW Papers, 6–8.

41. "Register and Vote urges Comedian Dick Gregory," A1-2; Andrew S. Moore, *The South's Tolerable Alien: Roman Catholics in Alabama and Georgia, 1945–1970* (Baton

Rouge: Louisiana State University Press, 2007), 127–128; "Historic Timeline," Edmundite Missions, www.edmunditemissions.org/history/timeline-30s.asp.

42. "Register and Vote urges Comedian Dick Gregory," A1-2.

43. Stedman interview, 2002, 16; Cowan, "Chapter 2," 17, 21, 23–24; Height, *Open Wide the Freedom Gates*, 162; Polly Cowan, "Freedom to Vote—What does the sending of a team of women to a town like Selma accomplish?" Folder 11, Cowan Papers; Height, *BWOHP*, 79.

44. Height, *Open Wide the Freedom Gates*, 162–164; Polly Cowan, "Women in the Civil Rights Movement: Variations on a Theme," n.d., Folder 2, Cowan Papers, 1; "Inter Organization Women's Committee, Atlanta, Georgia," March 15–16, 1964, Folder 190, NCNW Papers; Stedman interview, 2002, 18.

45. Height, *Open Wide the Freedom Gates*, 164.

46. Stedman interview, 2002, 18–19; Stedman interview, 2008, 01:33:54.

47. Height interview, 2003, 28–29.

48. Height, *Open Wide the Freedom Gates*, 163; Cherisse R. Jones, "'How Shall I Sing the Lord's Song': United Church Women Confront Racial Issues in South Carolina, 1940s–1960s," in *Throwing Off the Cloak of Privilege: White Southern Women Activists in the Civil Rights Era,* ed. Gail S. Murray (Gainesville: University Press of Florida, 2004), 143; "WICS History," Women in Community Service, www.wics.org/history.asp, February 2, 2007.

49. "Inter Organization Women's Committee, Atlanta, Georgia," 2; Height, *Open Wide the Freedom Gates*, 163–164; Stedman interview, 2002, 19.

50. Edith Holbrook Riehm, "The Hope Lies in the Women: White Southern Church-women in the Struggle for Civil Rights and the Quest for Human Rights," presented at Social Science in History Conference, Long Beach, CA, November 2009, in author's possession, 1–3; Edith Holbrook Riehm, "Dorothy Tilly and the Fellowship of the Concerned," in *Throwing Off the Cloak of Privilege*, 23–48.

51. Dorothy Tilly to the Conference and District Secretaries of Christian Social Relations, July 31, 1953, Reel 195, Southern Regional Conference Papers, quoted in Riehm, "The Hope Lies in the Women," 7.

52. Height, *Open Wide the Freedom Gates*, 166; Stedman interview, 2002, 26; "Inter-organization Women's Committee"; Cowan, "Wednesdays in Mississippi—Report" for U.S. Commission on Civil Rights Hearings, 1.

53. Height, *Open Wide the Freedom Gates*, 166; "Wednesdays in Mississippi: Chicago Team, August 11–13," Folder 307, NCNW Papers, 1.

54. Collins Funeral Home, "Our Founders," www.servicebycollins.com/Founders. htm; Mississippi Legislature, Senate Resolution 120, Regular Session 1999, SR No. 120, 99\SS03\R1582, 1–4; Claire Collins Harvey, interview with Gordon Henderson, August 5, 1965 (hereinafter C. Harvey interview, 1965), "Oral History Memoir of Clarie Collins Harvey (Mrs. Martin L.)," Oral History Project—Contemporary Mississippi Life and Viewpoints 1965, Adams Faculty Papers.

55. Dittmer, *Local People*, 98–99.

56. "Inter Organization Women's Committee" 17–18; Stedman interview, 2002, 20; Height, *Open Wide the Freedom Gates,* 164–165.

57. "Consultation Program of Inter-Organization Women's Committee," Folder 190, NCNW Papers, 17; Height, *Open Wide the Freedom Gates,* 165; Stedman interview, 2002, 20–22; "Inter-organization Women's Committee, Atlanta Georgia, Panel Reports from Work Groups," notes, March 15, 1964, Folder 191, NCNW Papers (images 38–39).

58. Height, *Open Wide the Freedom Gates,* 166.

59. Report from Pearl Willen, National Council of Jewish Women Papers, Washington D. C., Office Records, Series III, Box 29, DLC, quoted in Shulman, *National Council of Negro Women,* 16.

60. Stedman interview, 2002, 26; Stedman interview, 2008, WIMS Film, 01:30:51–01:31:58.

CHAPTER THREE

1. "Dorothy Tilly," in *Women and the Civil Rights Movement,* 111.

2. Holly Cowan Shulman, "Wednesdays in Mississippi: Civil Rights as Women's Work," paper presented as part of a panel titled "Voices of Moderation: Jewish Women and the Civil Rights Movement," for the Thirty-first Annual Southern Jewish Historical Society Conference, Little Rock, AR, November 10, 2006, digital recording in author's possession.

3. Polly Cowan, memo to the National Women's Committee for Civil Rights and the National Council of Negro Women, November 14, 1963, Folder 14, Cowan Papers, 2; Cowan, "Chapter I," 24; Height, *Open Wide the Freedom Gates,* 168.

4. Gail S. Murray, *Throwing Off the Cloak of Privilege,* 3; Lynn, *Progressive Women in Conservative Times,* 3, 142.

5. Lynn, *Progressive Women in Conservative Times,* 3–4; Susan Ware, *Beyond Suffrage: Women in the New Deal* (Cambridge: Harvard University Press, 1981), 2.

6. Cowan, "Women in the Civil Rights Movement," 1.

7. Height interview, 2002, 13, 15.

8. Stedman interview, 2008, 01:40:11–01:42:07.

9. Stedman interview, 2002, 25; Cowan interview, 1968, 1, 8; Height, *BWOHP,* 185.

10. Polly Cowan, autobiography fragments, n.d., Folder 97, NCNW Papers, 7.

11. Shirley B. Smith, "Re: Contacts on Jackson, Mississippi Trip—May 7th & 8th," memo to Polly Cowan and Dorothy Height, May 14, 1964, Folder 310, NCNW Papers; "Wednesdays in Mississippi—Chicago Team," August 11–13, 1964, Folder 307, NCNW Papers, 1–2; Height, *Open Wide the Freedom Gates,* 168; Height, *BWOHP,* 186.

12. Polly Cowan, notes of meeting with Jackson women, May 8, 1964, Folder 277, NCNW Papers, 1–2.

13. Cowan, notes of meeting with Jackson women, May 7, 1964, 1–2.

14. Cowan interview, 1968, 12; Cowan, autobiography fragments, Folder 97, 5.

15. National Council of Negro Women, "Wednesdays in Mississippi," 1964, NCNW Papers, Folder 277, 1–2.

16. "Wednesdays in Mississippi—Chicago Team," 1–2; Cowan, interview, 1968, 12; Height, *Open Wide the Freedom Gates,* 168–169; Height, *BWOHP,* 186.

17. White, *Too Heavy a Load,* 177.

18. Height, *BWOHP,* 185.

19. Height, *Open Wide the Freedom Gates,* 168–169; Stedman interview, 2002, 31–33; Height interview, 2003, 5; National Council of Negro Women, "Wednesdays in Mississippi" Proposal, May 22, 1964, Folder 277, NCNW Papers.

20. National Council of Negro Women, "Wednesdays in Mississippi Budget as of 28 September 1964," Folder 42, NCNW Papers; National Council of Negro Women, "Financial Statement—Appendix #1" of the "Financial Statement Wednesday in Mississippi of the Educational Foundation of the National Council of Negro Women, Inc., June–December 1964," Folder 116, NCNW Papers, 5–6.

21. Cowan interview, 1968, 26–28; "Financial Statement—Appendix #1," 5–6.

22. Diane Vivell, "Profile of Diane C. Vivell," Folder 208, NCNW Papers; NCNW, "Wednesdays in Mississippi," 1964, Folder 277; Height, *BWOHP,* 186.

23. Stedman interview, 2002, 5–6, 33–34; Goodwillie interview, "Reminiscences," 3–4, 17–19, 21–22; Shirley B. Smith to Susan Goodwillie and Diane Vivell, May 21, 1964, "Wednesdays in Mississippi: Civil Rights as Women's Work," www.history.eduh.edu/cph/WIMS/; Stedman interview, 2008, 01:02:47–01:03:44, 01:28:57–01:29:55; Height interview, 2002, 20.

24. Stedman interview, 2008, 02:16:30–02:18:08.

25. Doris Wilson, interview with Mary Ann Lawlor, March 9, 2003 (hereinafter Wilson interview, 2003), 1–17, WIMS OH, in the possession of Holly Cowan Shulman, University of Virginia; Nnamdi interview, 2001; Helen Laville, "'If the Time Is not Ripe, Then It Is Your Job to Ripen the Time!' The Transformation of the YWCA in the USA from Segregated Association to Interracial Organization, 1930–1965," *Women's History Review* 15, no. 3: 359–383.

26. Wilson interview, 2003, 1–17; Nnamdi interview, 2001.

27. Stedman interview, 2008, 01:55:51–01:56:44.

28. WIMS Conference, panel with Susie Goodwillie Stedman, Doris Wilson, Josie Johnson, and Erica Poff, March 8, 2003, WIMS OH, in possession of Holly Cowan Shulman, University of Virginia, 14; Nnamdi interview, 2001.

29. Height, *Open Wide the Freedom Gates,* 170; Height interview, 2002, 20; Wilson interview, 2003, 16; Jean Davis, letter to "all of you," 1964, Folder 307, NCNW Files; M. Davis, "Report on Wednesday, August 12, 1964 in Mississippi."

30. Lawson and Payne, *Debating the Civil Rights Movement,* 30, 126; Dittmer, *Local People,* 210, 219.

31. Height interview, 2003, 11.

32. Smith, letter to Goodwillie and Vivell.

33. Shirley B. Smith and Frankie Stein, "Meeting with Justice Department June 10, 1964—Bob Owen, Joan Doar & St. John Barrett," memo to Dorothy Height, Polly Cowan, and Jackson staff, June 12, 1964, Folder 72, NCNW Papers.

34. Smith and Stein, "Meeting with Justice Department"; John Doar, "The Work of the Civil Rights Division in Enforcing Voting Rights under the Civil Rights Act of 1957 and 1960," *Florida State University Law Review* 25 (1991): 1–17.

35. Smith, letter to Goodwillie and Vivell.

36. Height interview, 2003, 11; Height, *Open Wide the Freedom Gates,* 171; Height interview, 2002, 19–20; Stedman interview, 2002, 34–35; Lottie Joiner, "Down in the Delta," *New Crisis* 109 (March/April 2002), 35; Susan Goodwillie, diary, June 30, 1964 (hereinafter Goodwillie diary), Papers of Susan Goodwillie, SSC; Goodwillie interview, "Reminiscences," 15–16; National Council of Negro Women, "Wednesdays in Mississippi," Confidential Report, June 9, 1964, Folder 277, NCNW Papers, 2.

37. Stedman interview, 2002, 36–37; Stedman interview, 2008, 01:49:54–01:55:16, 01:55:51–1:56:44.

38. Shirley B. Smith, "Potpourri," memo to Polly Cowan, June 12, 1964, Folder 72, NCNW Papers.

39. WIMS conference, 19–20; Josie Johnson, interview with Mary Ann Lawlor, March 9, 2003 (hereinafter Johnson interview), 11–12, WIMS OH, in possession of Holly Cowan Shulman, University of Virginia.

40. Sylvia Weinberg Radov, interview with Amy Murrell, June 25, 2002 (hereinafter Radov interview), WIMS OH, SSC. Sylvia Weinberg Radov remarried after her involvement with WIMS and is referred to as Sylvia Weinberg.

41. Cowan, autobiography fragments, NCNW Papers, 9.

42. Stedman interview, 2002, 36–37; Height, *Open Wide the Freedom Gates,* 170; Cowan interview, 1968, 28, 30; Stedman interview, 2008, 01:49:54–01:55:16.

43. "The Dept. of Justice Gave the Following," Memo, July 6, 1964, Series II, Subseries 10, Box 144, Folder 8: Highway Patrol, Johnson Papers.

44. Stedman interview, 2011, 23–24.

45. "Ann Fraser Hewitt," *The Ann Arbor News,* January 31, 2004; Goodwillie diary, June 30, 1964, 1; Stedman interview, 2011, 24, 26.

46. "WIMS Team #1," Debriefing transcript, 1964, NABWH-001-S15-SS5-F17-S2, Folder 17, Side 2, NCNW Papers, Series 15, Subseries 5, 42–43.

47. "WIMS Team #1," Debriefing, Side 2, 35–36.

48. Goodwillie diary, June 30, 1964, 2–4.

49. Schutt interview, 1994, 3–4.

50. "Jane Schutt," in *Women and the Civil Rights Movement,* 217; Peter M. Sussman to Jane Schutt, December 18, 1962, Schutt Papers, Box 1, Folder 17.

51. Miriam Ezelle to Jane Schutt, n.d., Schutt Papers, Box 1, Folder 16.

52. "WIMS Team #1," Debriefing, Side 2, 33.

53. Jean Benjamin, "Mississippi—July 1964," n.d., Folder 269, NCNW Papers, 1.

54. Peggy Roach, interview with Al Chambers, April 18, 2003 (hereinafter Roach interview, 2003) WIMS OH, in possession of Holly Cowan Shulman, University of Virginia, 31–32; Peggy Roach, "Report, Peggy Roach," July 24, 1964, Folder 208, NCNW Papers, 6.

55. Randers-Pehrson, "Report of a Team Member," 7.

56. Stedman interview, 2011, 5.

57. Lillie B. Jones, interviewed by Catherine McMichael, June 20, 1978, Jackson State University Oral History Program, The Farish Street Historic District Project, O.H. 78.11 (hereinafter Jones interview, 1978), 1–2; Irons, "The Shaping of Activist Recruitment and Participation," 698–699; Tiyi Makeda Morris, "Black Women's Civil Rights Activism in Mississippi: The Story of WomanPower Unlimited" (PhD diss., Purdue University, May 2002), 93–94;

58. Itineraries with hostess lists are in Folders 302–308, NCNW Files.

59. Benjamin, "Mississippi—July 1964," 2.

60. Stedman interview, 2011, 3, 5.

61. Stedman interview, 2008, 01:52:01–01:53:07.

62. Lynn Watkins, "She Won't Stop Caring for Her Kids at the Y," *Clarion-Ledger,* December 13, 1982; Lillie B. Jones, interviewed by Catherine McMichael, June 20, 1978, Jackson State University Oral History Program, The Farish Street Historic District Project, O.H. 78.11.

63. Height, *Open Wide the Freedom Gates,* 170; Goodwillie interview, "Reminiscences," 20; Stedman interview, 2002, 35–36.

64. Goodwillie diary, June 30, 1964, 1.

65. Goodwillie diary, June 30, 1964, 1.

66. Polly Cowan, misc. notes, July 4, 1973, Folder 13, Cowan Papers.

67. Height, *BWOHP,* 190.

68. Wilson interview, 2003, 17, 34.

69. Smith, letter to Goodwillie and Vivell.

70. Cowan interview, 1968, 16; National Council of Negro Women, "1964—The Women Who Went to Mississippi," Folder 299, NCNW Papers, 2; Lily D. Geismer, "Don't Blame Us: Grassroots Liberalism in Massachusetts, 1960–1990" (PhD diss., University of Michigan, 2010); Laya Wiesner, "Registration Form for Wednesdays in Mississippi," Folder 13, NCNW Papers.

71. WIMS conference, 18-19; NCNW, "1964—The Women Who Went to Mississippi," 3.

72. Polly Cowan, Registration Form, Folder 12, NCNW Papers; Geraldine Kohlenberg, Registration Form, Folder 13, NCNW Papers; Marian Logan, Registration Form, Folder 12, NCNW Papers.

73. Polly Cowan, Memo Number 3 to Community Coordinators, "Re: Selection of Your Teams and Their Responsibilities," June 15, 1964, Folder 208, NCNW Papers.

74. Height interview, 2002, 16; Cowan interview, 1968, 12, 24, 16–17.

75. Mrs. Kenneth F. (Lucy) Montgomery, Registration Form, Folder 14, NCNW Papers; Wilhelmina Vincel Hetzel, Registration Form, Folder 18, NCNW Papers.

76. Cowan, Memo Number 3.

77. NCNW Education Foundation, "Wednesdays in Mississippi 1964," 10; Joiner, "Down in the Delta," 32; Height, *Open Wide the Freedom Gates,* 175; Cowan interview, 1968, 16; Polly Cowan, "Wednesdays in Mississippi 1964–1965: Final Report," Folder 276, NCNW Papers, 40–43, 50; "Colleges and Universities Attended by Wednesday Ladies," Folder 51, NCNW Papers.

78. Johnson interview, 2003, 17–19.

79. Ruth Batson, interview with Mel King, n.d., Batson Papers, Box 1, Folder 2, 10; Lyndon Johnson to Ruth Batson, April 27, 1962, Batson Papers, Box 3, Folder 8; Ruth Batson, "Wednesday in Mississippi: Chronology," n.d., Batson Papers, Box 6, Folder 3, 1.

80. Johnson interview, 2003, 10.

81. Radov interview part 2, 2002, 4–6; Claudia Heckscher, interview with Mary Ann Lawlor, January 3, 2003, WIMS OH, 6–7.

82. Priscilla Hunt, interview with author, July 6, 2011, OHH, 2–3.

83. Maxine Nathanson, interview with Christie Jones, July 29, 2003, WIMS OH, digital recording in possession of author, 01:12–06:00.

84. Jean Davis, interview with Holly Cowan Shulman, June 27, 2002, WIMS OH, 17.

85. Hunt, Stedman, and Zetzel interview, 2011, 33, 38, 40–41. Geraldine Kohlenberg Zetzel remarried after her involvement with WIMS and is referred to as Geraldine Kohlenberg; interviews and written material are referenced by her name at the time of their creation.

86. Registration Form for Wednesdays in Mississippi, Folder 18, NCNW Papers; Zetzel interview, 2011, 1.

87. "WIMS Team #3," Debriefing, Sides 1, 5, 6–7.

88. Radov interview, 2002, 31–32.

89. Peggy Roach, interview with Al Chambers, April 18, 2003, WIMS OH, in possession of Holly Cowan Shulman, University of Virginia, 2–3, 47.

90. Miriam Davis, interview with Holly Cowan Shulman, November 16, 2002, WIMS OH, in possession of Holly Cowan Shulman, University of Virginia, 26–27.

91. Zetzel interview, 2011, 9–10.

92. Johnson interview, 2003, 38–39.

93. Faith Rogow, *Gone to Another Meeting: The National Council of Jewish Women, 1893–1993* (Tuscaloosa: University of Alabama Press, 1993), 40.

94. Rogow, *Gone to Another Meeting*, 33; Radov interview, 2002, 25, 10–11, 27–29.

95. Cowan interview, 1968, 14; Height, *Open Wide the Freedom Gates*, 170.

96. Polly Cowan, Memo Number 1 to Community Coordinators, "Correspondence Format" June 15, 1964, Folder 208, NCNW Papers.

97. Height, *Open Wide the Freedom Gates*, 170; NCNW, "Wednesdays in Mississippi" Proposal; Cowan, Memo Number 1; Dick Schaap, "Secret Project in Mississippi—Interracial Meetings of Women," *New York Herald Tribune*, August 30, 1964, Folder 232, NCNW Papers; Silver, *Mississippi: The Closed Society*. A copy of Silver's speech is in Folder 197, NCNW Papers.

98. Cowan, Memo Number 3.

99. Polly Cowan, "Wednesdays in Mississippi" Memo Number 6 to Community Coordinators, July 2, 1967, Folder 208, NCNW Papers; NCNW, "Wednesdays in Mississippi" Proposal, 2, 6.

100. WIMS Conference, 19.

101. Cowan, Memo No. 6; Stedman interview, 2002, 32, 50; Cowan, misc. notes, July 4, 1973, Folder 13, Cowan Papers.

102. Stedman interview, 2002, 39, 41; Unita Blackwell with JoAnne Prichard Morris, *Barefootin': Life Lessons from the Road to Freedom* (New York: Crown Publishing Group, 2006), 96.

103. Tracy Sugarman, *Stranger at the Gates: A Summer in Mississippi* (New York: Hill and Wang, 1966), 114; Chana Kai Lee, "Anger, Memory, and Personal Power: Fannie Lou Hamer and Civil Rights Leadership," *Sisters in the Struggle*, 158.

104. Polly Cowan, "Women in Mississippi (WIMS) Preliminary Report," 1964, Folder 280, NCNW Papers, 8; "WIMS Team #2," Debriefing, Subseries 5, 3–4.

105. WIMS Conference, 20.

106. Nathanson, Report, 1.

107. Joiner, "Down in the Delta," 33.

108. Goodwillie diary, June 27, 1964, 2.

CHAPTER FOUR

1. Goodwillie, letter to "Dear Friends far away."

2. Susan Goodwillie, "Letter from Susan Goodwillie—Re: The First Wednesdays in Mississippi—July 7–9," July 1964, Folder 298, NCNW Papers, 1; "Wednesdays in Mississippi—Team #1," July 13, 1964, Folder 302, NCNW Papers.

3. Height, *Open Wide the Freedom Gates*, 171.

4. "Prospectus for the Mississippi Freedom Summer," n.d., Schutt Papers, Box 1, Folder 32, 1.

5. Height interview, 2003, 4.

6. "Prospectus for the Mississippi Freedom Summer," 4.

7. "Prospectus for the Mississippi Freedom Summer," 4; Stedman interview, 2002, 41– 43; Goodwillie, "Letter . . . Re: The First Wednesdays in Mississippi," 2–3; Height interview, 2003, 4; Goodwillie diary, July 8, 1964, 3.

8. Dittmer, *Local People*, 259; Virginia (Mrs. Henry) Bourne, "Report on Wednesdays in Mississippi Project," July 28–30, 1964, Folder 305, NCNW Papers, 1; Hunt, "De-briefing—Wednesdays in Mississippi," 7.

9. Height interview, 2003, 4; Joiner, "Down in the Delta," 37; Stedman interview, 2002, 41–43; Goodwillie, "Letter . . . Re: The First Wednesdays in Mississippi," 2–3; Goodwillie diary, July 15, 1964, 4; Dittmer, *Local People,* 259; Russlyn Ali and Susan Goodwillie., *Wednesdays in Mississippi: The Story* (Washington D.C.: Children's Defense Fund, 2006),18; Alice Ryerson, "Report on Trip to Mississippi July 14–16, 1964," Folder 303, NCNW Papers, 6; Goodwillie diary, July 8, 1964.

10. "WIMS Team #1," Debriefing, Side 1, 32–33.

11. "WIMS Team #7," Team Debriefing transcript, 1964, NABWH-001-S15-SS5-F38-S1, Folder 38, Side 1, NCNW Papers, Series 15, Subseries 39.

12. Geraldine Woods, "Wednesday in Mississippi Report," July 24, 1964, Folder 306, NCNW Papers.

13. "Wednesdays in Mississippi—Team #1," 18; Goodwillie, "Letter . . . Re: The First Wednesdays in Mississippi," 2.

14. "WIMS Team #1," Debriefing, Side 2, 39.

15. "WIMS Team #1," Debriefing, Side 1, 32–33.

16. "Nun Sees U.S. Bettering Itself by Helping Negro," newspaper clipping, *Mississippi Register*, n.d., Schutt Papers, Box 1, Folder 50.

17. Geraldine Kohlenberg, "Comments on the July 15th Wednesdays in Mississippi," 1964, Folder 269, NCNW Papers; "WIMS Team #1," Debriefing, Side 2, 39–40. On the concept of the "white Negro," see Eric J. Sundquist, *Strangers in the Land: Blacks, Jews, Post-Holocaust America* (Cambridge: Belknap Press of Harvard University, 2005).

18. Arnetta Wallace, "Wednesdays in Mississippi, August 11–13, 1964," n.d., Folder 307, NCNW Papers, 2–3.

19. Goodwillie diary, July 15, 1964, 4.

20. "WIMS Team #2," Debriefing, 128–129.

21. Kohlenberg, "Comments on the July 15th Wednesdays in Mississippi," 3.

22. Trude W. Lash, Memo to Polly Cowan, September 8, 1964, Folder 306, NCNW Papers, 3.

23. Goodwillie diary, August 3, 1964.

24. Hunt, Stedman, and Zetzel interview, 2011, OHH, 50; Ryerson, "Report on Trip to Mississippi," 8–9; Kohlenberg, "Comments on the July 15th Wednesdays in Mississippi," 4–5; "WIMS Team #1," Debriefing, Side 2; "WIMS Team #2," Debriefing.

25. Ryerson, "Report on Trip to Mississippi," 8–9; "WIMS Team #2," Debriefing, 10–11, 27–28; Sister Catherine John Flynn, "Report Questionnaire, Wednesdays in Mississippi," n.d., Folder 269, NCNW Papers, 1.

26. Ryerson, "Report on Trip to Mississippi," 8–9; "WIMS Team #2," Debriefing, 10–11, 27–28.

27. "WIMS Team #1," Debriefing, Side 1, 46–47.

28. "Wednesdays in Mississippi—Team #1"; Jean Benjamin, "Wednesdays in Mississippi Answers to Report Questionnaire," July 27, 1964, Folder 269, NCNW Papers, 1–2; Ali and Goodwillie, *Wednesdays in Mississippi*, 20; Polly Cowan, "Women in Mississippi (WIMS) Preliminary Report," 1964, Folder 280, NCNW Papers, 6–7.

29. Ali and Goodwillie, 20; Wilhelmina Hetzel, "Wednesdays in Mississippi Report Questionnaire, Attachment Memo Number 14," n.d., Folder 269, NCNW Papers, 1; Cowan, "Women in Mississippi (WIMS) Preliminary Report," 6–7; Zetzel interview, 2011, OHH, 13.

30. "Wednesdays in Mississippi—New Jersey Team to Hattiesburg," n.d., Folder 308, NCNW Papers, 8.

31. "WIMS Team #7," Debriefing, Side 1, 9–10.

32. Ruth Batson, "Wednesday in Mississippi: Chronology," n.d., Batson Papers, Box 6, Folder 3, 3.

33. "Prospectus for the Mississippi Freedom Summer," 6.

34. "WIMS Team #2," Debriefing, 120–122.

35. Benjamin, "Mississippi—July 1964," 4; Lash, "Project: Wednesdays in Mississippi," 6; "WIMS Team #5," Debriefing, Side 2, 46, 50–51; Wallace, "Wednesdays in Mississippi," 3; "WIMS Team #1," Debriefing, Side 1, 21.

36. Woods, "Wednesday in Mississippi Report"; Benjamin, "Mississippi—July 1964," 4; WIMS Conference, 22.

37. Niles, "Report on Trip to Mississippi," 4–5; Roach interview, 2003, 33–35.

38. Randers-Pehrson, "Report of a Team Member,'" 4.

39. Niles, "Report on Trip to Mississippi," 19.

40. "WIMS Team #6," Team Debriefing transcript, 1964, NABWH-001-S15-SS5-F21-S2, Side 2, Folder 21, NCNW Papers, Series 15, Subseries 5, 32–34; Jean Davis, letter to "all of you," 1964, Folder 307, NCNW Papers.

41. Goodwillie, "Letter . . . Re: The first Wednesdays in Mississippi," 1.

42. Ryerson, "Report on Trip to Mississippi," 7.

43. Randers-Pehrson, "Report of a Team Member 'Wednesdays in Mississippi,'" 5.

44. Hunt, Stedman, and Zetzel interview, 2011, 32; Ryerson, "Report on Trip to Mississippi," 7.

45. Roach, "Report, Peggy Roach," 1.

46. "WIMS Team #2," Debriefing, 69–71.

47. Goodwillie diary, July 15, 1964, 2; "WIMS Team #2," Debriefing, 126–127.

48. Cowan, "Women in Mississippi (WIMS) Preliminary Report," 12; "WIMS Team #6," Team Debriefing transcript, 1964, NABWH-001-S15-SS5-F21-S1, Folder 21, Side 1, NCNW Papers, Series 15, Subseries 5, 43.

49. "Prospectus for the Mississippi Freedom Summer," 3.

50. Newman, *Divine Agitators*, 53.

51. "WIMS Team #2," Debriefing, 139–140.

52. "WIMS Team #6," Debriefing, Side 1, 54.

53. "WIMS Team #2," Debriefing, 139–140.

54. Roach, "Report, Peggy Roach," 3–4.

55. Hetzel, "Wednesdays in Mississippi Report Questionnaire," 1.

56. "WIMS Team #5," Team Debriefing transcript, 1964, NABWH-001-S15-SS5-F18-S1, Side 1, Folder 18, NCNW Papers, Series 15, Subseries 5, 57–58.

57. Frances Haight, "Frances Haight Notes on Trip to Mississippi," August 26, 1964, Folder 306, NCNW Papers, 4–5.

58. "WIMS Team #2," Debriefing, 35–37; Ryerson, "Report on Trip to Mississippi," 3.

59. Cowan, "Women in Mississippi (WIMS) Preliminary Report," 12.

60. Ruth Batson, "Organization Objectives for the Freedom Democratic Party Challenge," n.d., Batson Papers, Box 3, Folder 11, 1.

61. "WIMS Team #2," Debriefing, 143–153.

62. "WIMS Team #2," Debriefing, 150–151.

63. Polly Cowan to Dorothy Height, August 22, 1964, NCNW Papers.

64. Barbara Cunningham, "Report Questionnaire," August 1964, Folder 269, NCNW Papers.

65. Stedman interview, 2002, 39.

66. "WIMS Team #1," Debriefing, Side 1, 26–27.

67. "WIMS Team #6," Debriefing, Side 1, 17–18; Wallace, "Wednesdays in Mississippi," 1.

68. Cowan, "Women in Mississippi (WIMS) Preliminary Report," 9–10; "WIMS Team #1," Debriefing, Side 1, 26–27.

69. Haight, "Frances Haight Notes on Trip to Mississippi"; Lash, "Project: Wednesdays in Mississippi," 2.

70. "WIMS Team #5," Debriefing, Side 2, 18–20.

71. P. Harvey, *Freedom's Coming*, 175.

72. "WIMS Team #6," Debriefing, Side 1,76–78.

73. Ross, *Witnessing and Testifying*, 91.

74. M. Davis, "Report on Wednesday, August 12, 1964 in Mississippi," 3.

75. Batson, "Wednesday in Mississippi: Chronology," 2.

76. Roach, "Report, Peggy Roach," 7; Woods "Wednesday in Mississippi Report," 3.

77. James L. Jones, "King Tours Mississippi, Backs New State Party," July 22, 1964, *The Washington Post, Times Herald*, A-3; "Rev. King May Ask Marshalls," *Clarion-Ledger*, July 23, 1964, 1, 14.

78. "Rev. King May Ask Marshalls," 1.

79. Roach, "Report, Peggy Roach," 7.

80. Randers-Pehrson, "Report of a Team Member," 8.

81. Geraldine Kohlenberg, "Comments on the July 15th Wednesdays in Mississippi," 1964, NCNW Papers Series 19, Folder 269, 6.

82. Kohlenberg, "Comments on the July 15th Wednesdays in Mississippi," 6.

83. Sokol, *There Goes My Everything*, 4.

84. Miriam Davis, interview with Holly Cowan Shulman, November 16, 2002 (hereinafter M. Davis interview, 2002), WIMS OH, in possession of Holly Cowan Shulman, University of Virginia.

85. Helen Meyner, "In and Out of New Jersey: The Miraculous Power of Prayer in Mississippi," Newark, New Jersey, *The Star Ledger*, September 1, 1964, clipping, Folder 232, NCNW Papers.

86. C. Harvey interview, 1965, 16; Matthew 25:35-36 (New Living Translation).

87. Morris, "Black Women's Civil Rights Activism in Mississippi," 65.

88. Morris, "Black Women's Civil Rights Activism in Mississippi," 81, 83.

89. Harvey, "Women in the Civil Rights Movement—Trailblazers and Torchbearers," 8.

90. Benjamin, "Mississippi—July 1964," 6.

91. Schutt interview, 5–6.

92. C. Harvey, "Women in the Civil Rights Movement," 5–6.

93. P. Harvey, *Freedom's Coming*, 1; Wallace, "Wednesdays in Mississippi," 4.

94. M. Davis, "Report on Wednesday, August 12, 1964 in Mississippi," 2–3; "WIMS Team #6," Debriefing, Side 1, 61.

95. Wallace, "Wednesdays in Mississippi," 4.

96. M. Davis, "Report on Wednesday, August 12, 1964 in Mississippi," 3, 6.

97. Schutt interview, 1994, 31, 30.

98. Elaine Crystal, interview with Marlene McCurtis, July 24, 2008 (hereinafter Crystal interview, 2008), WIMS Film, 00:11:28–00:13:15.

99. Katagiri, *The Mississippi State Sovereignty Commission*, 169, quoting the *Meridian Star*, August 26, 1964.

100. Patricia Derian, interview with Marlene McCurtis, January 26, 2008 (hereinafter Derian interview, 2008), WIMS Film, 02:25:27; 02:28:02–02:30:34.

101. Derian interview, 1991, 3.

102. Crystal interview, 2008, 06:46:52–06:48:50.

103. "WIMS Team #6," Debriefing, Side 2, 18-19.

104. Constance Curry, "Wild Geese to the Past," in Constance Curry, Joan C. Browning, Dorothy Dawson Burlage, Penny Patch, Theresa Del Pozzo, Sue Thrasher, Elaine DeLott Baker, Emmie Schrader Adams, and Casey Hayden, *Deep in Our Hearts: Nine White Women in the Freedom Movement* (Athens, GA: University of Georgia Press, 2000), 26.

105. Roach, "Report, Peggy Roach," 2.

106. Lash, "Project: Wednesdays in Mississippi," 16; "WIMS Team #5," Debriefing, Side 1, 46.

107. Randers-Pehrson, "Report of a Team Member," 3; Roach, "Report, Peggy Roach," 2.

108. Derian interview, 1991, 24.

109. "Wake Up Mississippi!" September 13, 1964, clipping, CRMC, Series 1.

110. Roach, "Report, Peggy Roach," 2; Goodwillie diary, June 30, 1964, 3.

111. Haight, "Frances Haight Notes on Trip to Mississippi," 2; "WIMS Team #5," Debriefing, Side 1, 43–45.

112. Hunt, "De-briefing—Wednesdays in Mississippi," 3; Priscilla Hunt, interview with author, July 6, 2011 (hereinafter Hunt interview, 2011), OHH, 15, 37, 48.

113. Olive Noble, "Wednesdays in Mississippi Report of Mrs. Joseph V. Noble," August 19, 1964, Folder 308, NCNW Papers, 3.

114. Census 1960, General Population Characteristics, Mississippi, 26–38, www.census.gov; Henrietta Moore to Polly Cowan, October 6, 1964, Folder 307, NCNW Papers, 1.

115. WIMS Conference, 17; Height, *Open Wide the Freedom Gates*, 183.

116. Virginia Bourne to Polly Cowan, August, 12, 1964, Folder 305, NCNW Papers; Johnson interview, 2003, WIMS OH, 30–31.

117. WIMS Conference, 23; Maxine Nathanson, interview with Christie Jones, July 29, 2003 (hereinafter Nathanson interview, 2003), WIMS OH, digital recording in possession of author, 26:20–29:00; Nathanson, Report, 5.

118. United States Commission on Civil Rights, letter to Mrs. Lewis [sic] Cowan, July 28, 1964, Folder 48, NCNW Papers.

119. C. Harvey interview, 1965, 7.

120. Polly Cowan, "Wednesdays in Mississippi—Report from Polly Cowan, Project Coordinator," for the U.S. Commission on Civil Rights Hearings, August 1964, Folder 48, NCNW Papers.

121. "WIMS Team #3," Team Debriefing transcript, 1964, NABWH-001-S15-SS5-F42-S2, Side 2, Folder 42, NCNW Papers, Series 15, Subseries 5, 46.

122. Johnson interview, 2003, 26–27; Zetzel interview, 2011, 4.

123. "WIMS Team #2," Debriefing, 5–6; Zetzel interview, 2011, 8.

124. Batson, "Wednesday in Mississippi: Chronology," 1.

125. Benjamin, "Mississippi—July 1964," 1.

126. Zetzel interview, 2011, 4, 8.

127. Johnson interview, 2003, 24.

128. Zetzel, "Wednesdays in Mississippi"; Edith Savage Jennings, interview with Christie Jones, July 26, 2003, (hereinafter Jennings interview, 2003) WIMS OH, digital recording in possession of author, 14:50–16:00; Edith M Savage, "Report on Wednesdays in Mississippi Project" August 18–20, 1964, Folder 308, NCNW Papers, 1; "WIMS Team #2," Debriefing, 117–118; Cowan, "Women in Mississippi (WIMS) Preliminary Report," 8–9.

129. Randers-Pehrson, "Report of a Team Member,'" 1, 8.

130. Alice Ryerson-Hayes, interview with Christie Jones, July 27, 2003, WIMS OH, digital recording in possession of author, 23:30.

131. Marjorie (Mrs. Richard) Dammann, "And What Will Prevail?" Folder 306, NCNW Papers, 10.

132. Zetzel, "Wednesdays in Mississippi," 3; Zetzel interview, 2011, 8.

133. Roach interview, 2003, 38.

134. Hunt interview, 2011, 14.

135. Batson, "Wednesday in Mississippi: Chronology," 5.

136. Sokol, *There Goes My Everything*, 197; Claude Sitton, "3 Hotels Register Negroes in Peaceful Jackson Test," July 6, 1964, *New York Times*, 1.

137. Jerry DeLaughter, "Robert E. Lee Shut: New CR Act Blamed," July 7, 1964, *Clarion-Ledger*, 1; Polly Cowan, Memo Number 11 to Community Coordinators, "Re: Safety Precautions," July 17, 1964, Folder 208, NCNW Papers.

138. "WIMS Team #1," Debriefing, Side 1, 11–12, 36–37.

139. Polly Cowan to Doris Wilson, Susan Goodwillie, and Diane Vivell, July 11, 1964, Folder 72, NCNW Papers.

140. Cowan, Memo Number 11.

141. Polly Cowan to Doris Wilson, August 1, 1964, Folder 72, NCNW Papers.

142. Polly Cowan, "Wednesdays in Mississippi: A Story of 92 Women," n.d., Folder 7, Cowan Papers, 16; Polly Cowan, "synopsis" autobiography fragment notes, n.d., Folder 7, Cowan Papers, 2; "WIMS Team #5," Debriefing, Side 1, 21–23.

143. Goodwillie, "Letter . . . Re: The First Wednesdays in Mississippi," 4; Polly Cowan, notes on Team 1 trip, n.d., Folder 182, NCNW Papers, 28. Height's autobiography indicates that this incident occurred at Morningstar Church; however, Cowan's notes at the time explain that the team visited Mt. Zion in the morning, then went to Morningstar, and returned for lunch at Mt. Zion, where the Molotov cocktail was thrown.

144. Height, *BWOHP*, 189; Cowan interview, 1968, 19–20, 27; Stedman interview, 2002, 55, 57; Height, *Open Wide the Freedom Gates*, 173–174; Benjamin, "Wednesdays in Mississippi Answers to Report Questionnaire," 3; "Wednesdays in Mississippi—Team #1," 7; "WIMS Team #1," Debriefing, Side 1, 36–37.

145. WIMS Conference, 34.

146. Cowan interview, 1968, 19–20; Cowan, letter to Wilson, Goodwillie, and Vivell.

147. "WIMS Team #3," Debriefing, Side 2, 37–38, 46.

148. Hunt, "De-briefing—Wednesdays in Mississippi," 5; Polly Cowan, misc. notes, July 4, 1973, Folder 13, Cowan Papers.

149. "WIMS Team #2," Debriefing, 165.

150. Cowan interview, 1968, 19–20; Height, *Open Wide the Freedom Gates,* 170; Height, *BWOHP,* 190.

151. Although copies of the correspondence alerting Mississippi law enforcement of the details of all the team trips are in the WIMS files, only the memos for Team 1 and Team 7 appear in the Highway Patrol archival files, making it impossible to know if the highway patrol received the communication regarding the other teams. Series II, Subseries 10, Box 144, Folder 8, Johnson Papers; "Information Received from Bill Cullen of F.B.I.," memo to Highway Patrol, August 17, 1964, Series II, Subseries 10, Box 144, Folder 9, Johnson Papers.

152. Zetzel interview, 2011, 3; Roberts and Klibanoff, *The Race Beat,* 359.

153. Goodwillie diary, July 15, 1964; Zetzel interview, 2011, 3.

154. Zetzel interview, 2011, 8; Hunt, Stedman, and Zetzel interview, 2011, 45–46.

155. "WIMS Team #3," Debriefing, Side 2, 86–89; Woods "Wednesday in Mississippi Report," 3; Niles, "Report on Trip to Mississippi," 11.

156. "Wednesdays in Mississippi, Minneapolis-St. Paul," August 7, 1964, Folder 305, NCNW Papers, 4.

157. Goodwillie interview, "Reminiscences," 20–21; Stedman interview, 2002, 21.

158. Wallace, "Wednesdays in Mississippi," 2; Hunt interview, 2011, 5; Noble, "Wednesdays in Mississippi Report," 5; "WIMS Team #7," Debriefing, 9.

159. "WIMS Team #6," Debriefing, Side 1, 9.

160. J. Davis, letter to "all of you," 2.

161. "WIMS Team #2," Debriefing, 14.

162. "WIMS Team #3," Debriefing, Side 1, 82–84; Randers-Pehrson, "Report of a Team Member," 7–8.

163. WIMS Conference, 24.

164. Stedman interview, 2011, 40, 16.

165. "Wednesdays in Mississippi—New Jersey Team to Hattiesburg," 11–12; "Wednesdays in Mississippi—Boston Team July 14–16," 1964, Folder 307, NCNW Papers, 8; Stedman interview, 2011, 7, 11.

166. Goodwillie, letter to Gwen, July 7, 1964, in possession of Susan Goodwillie Stedman.

167. Goodwillie diary, July 27, 1964; Stedman interview, 2011, 8.

168. Goodwillie diary, August 1, 1964.

169. Goodwillie diary, July 21, 1964.

170. Goodwillie diary, June 27, 1964, 2.

171. Goodwillie diary, July 5, 1964.

172. Goodwillie, letter to "Dear Friends far away."

173. Goodwillie diary, July 9, 1964, August 4, 1964; Stedman interview, 2011, 8, 10.

174. Goodwillie diary, June 30, 1964, July 2, 1964.

175. Goodwillie diary, August 16, 1964.

176. Niles, "Report on Trip to Mississippi—July 21–23, 1964," Folder 279, NCNW Paper, 2.

177. Wilson interview, 2003, 7, 9, 13–14; Nnamdi interview, 2001.

178. Stedman interview, 2011, 5–6, 46, 59.

179. Kohlenberg, "Comments on the July 15th Wednesdays in Mississippi," 1.

180. M. Davis, "Report on Wednesday, August 12, 1964 in Mississippi," 1.

181. Savage, "Report on Wednesdays in Mississippi Project," 1.

182. Zetzel interview, 2011, 6, 13.

183. "WIMS Team #1," Debriefing, Side 1, 25.

184. Hunt, Stedman, and Zetzel interview, 2011, 25.

CHAPTER FIVE

1. Geraldine Kohlenberg Zetzel, personal conversation with author, January 24, 2008.

2. Stedman interview, 2002, 44.

3. Cowan interview, 1968, 20.

4. Height interview, 2003, 6.

5. Stedman interview, 2002, 21; Wilson interview, 2003, 23–24; Goodwillie, "Reminiscences," 4–5; Nnamdi interview, 2001; "Wednesdays in Mississippi—Team #1," 14.

6. Stedman interview, 2011, 16.

7. Goodwillie diary, July 5, 1964.

8. Crystal interview, 2008, 00:17:48–00:18:28.

9. Goodwillie diary, July 4, 1964.

10. Derian interview, 2008, 01:51:06–01:52:09.

11. "WIMS Team #1," Debriefing, Side 2, 38–40; "WIMS Team #2," Debriefing, 20; Cowan, "Women in Mississippi (WIMS) Preliminary Report," 9.

12. "WIMS Team #2," Debriefing, 52–53; Zetzel interview, 2011, 3–5.

13. "Team #5," Debriefing, Side 1, 18.

14. "Church Women United President's Meeting in Lexington, Kentucky," 1981, 1223-5-3:75, CWU Records, 9–10.

15. David L. Chappell, *Inside Agitators: White Southerners in the Civil Rights Movement* (Baltimore: The Johns Hopkins University Press, 1994), 214.

16. "Wednesdays in Mississippi, Minneapolis-St. Paul, August 7, 1964, Folder 305, NCNW Papers, 5.

17. "WIMS Team #5," Debriefing, Side 2, 81–82.

18. Nathanson, Report, 3.

19. M. Davis, "Report on Wednesday, August 12, 1964," 6.

20. Noble, "Wednesdays in Mississippi Report," 4; "WIMS Team #7," Debriefing, Side 1, 8–9.

21. Marjorie (Mrs. Richard) Dammann, "And What Will Prevail?" Folder 306, NCNW Papers, 9–10.

22. Henrietta Moore to Polly Cowan, October 6, 1964, Folder 307, NCNW Papers, 1.

23. Moore, letter to Polly Cowan, 1.

24. Ryerson-Hayes interview, 18:31.

25. Zetzel interview, 2011, 5–6.

26. Ryerson, "Report on Trip to Mississippi," 2.

27. "WIMS Team #6," Debriefing, Side 1, 11.

28. J. Davis, letter to "all of you," 2.

29. "Wednesdays in Mississippi—Chicago Team," August 11–13, 1964, Folder 307, NCNW Papers 12–13.

30. "WIMS Team #6," Debriefing, Side 1, 83–85.

31. Henrietta B. Moore, "Wednesdays in Mississippi: The Chicago Team's Trip—August 11th to 13th, 1964," Folder 307, NCNW Papers, 1.

32. "WIMS Team #6," Debriefing, Side 1, 89.

33. Moore, "Wednesdays in Mississippi: The Chicago Team's Trip," 1.

34. "WIMS Team #6," Debriefing, Side 1, 3–5; M. Davis, "Report on Wednesday, August 12, 1964," 6.

35. M. Davis, "Report on Wednesday, August 12, 1964, 6.

36. M. Davis interview, 2002, 17–18.

37. J. Davis, letter to "all of you," 2–3.

38. M. Davis, "Report on Wednesday, August 12, 1964," 6.

39. Cunningham, *Agony at Galloway*, 39–40.

40. Cunningham, *Agony at Galloway*, 39–40; Mississippi Association of Methodist Ministers and Laymen, "Information Bulletin," 1:7, July 1964, Series 2, CRMC; Newman, *Divine Agitators*, ix, 4, 7–8, 12, 14, 31.

41. "WIMS Team #6," Debriefing, Side 1, 83–88; M. Davis, "Report on Wednesday, August 12, 1964"; Miriam Davis, "The 'Rules' in Ruleville," August 1964, Folder 307, NCNW Papers, 1–2.

42. Cunningham, *Agony at Galloway*, 3–4

43. King interview, 1980, 142.

44. Miriam J. Ezelle to A. D. Beittel, May 23, 1963, Owens Papers, Box 2, Folder 1 .

45. A. D. Beittel to Miriam J. Ezelle, May 30, 1963, Owens Papers, Box 2, Folder 1.

46. J. Davis, letter to "all of you," 3.

47. Miriam Ezelle to Jean Davis, October 21, 1964, www.history.uh.edu/cph/WIMS/.

48. Miriam J. Ezelle to George A. Owens, November 22, 1965, Owens Papers, Box 2, Folder 1.

49. Miriam J. Ezelle to George A. Owens, November 22, 1965, George A. Owens Papers, Box 2, Folder 1.

50. J. Davis, letter to "all of you," 3.

51. Geraldine Kohlenberg Zetzel, "Wednesdays in Mississippi," April 2001, 1.

52. "WIMS Team #5," Debriefing, Side 2, 48.

53. "WIMS Team #2," Debriefing, 46; Stedman interview, 2011, 7–8.

54. Hunt, Stedman, and Zetzel interview, 2011, 21.

55. "WIMS Team #3," Debriefing, Side 1, 80–81.

56. Niles, "Report on Trip to Mississippi," 6; Randers-Pehrson, "Report of a Team Member," 5.

57. "WIMS Team #5," Debriefing, Side 1, 69–70.

58. Cowan, "Women in Mississippi (WIMS) Preliminary Report," 21.

59. Cowan, "Women in Mississippi (WIMS) Preliminary Report," 16.

60. Ryerson, "Report on Trip to Mississippi," 10.

61. Benjamin, "Mississippi—July 1964," 3.

62. Hunt, Stedman, and Zetzel interview, 2011, 21–22; Kohlenberg, "Comments on the July 15th Wednesdays in Mississippi,"1964, 6.

63. "WIMS Team #5," Debriefing, Side 2, 72.

64. Lash, "Project: Wednesdays in Mississippi," 15–16.

65. "WIMS Team #5," Debriefing, Side 2, 74–76, 14–15, 77–78.

66. Goodwillie diary, August 7, 1964, 3–4.

67. Goodwillie diary, August 7, 1964, 3–4.

68. Roberts and Klibanoff, *The Race Beat*, 359.

69. Zetzel, "Wednesdays in Mississippi," 1.

70. Team Debriefing transcript, 1964, NABWH-001-S15-SS5-F18-S1, Folder 18, Side 1, NCNW Papers, Series 15, Subseries 5, 10–11.

71. Florence Mars, interview with Thomas F. Healy, January 5, 1978 (hereinafter Mars interview, 1978), F341.5.M57, vol. 179, COHCH, 24–25.

72. Trude W. Lash, memo to Polly Cowan, September 8, 1964, Folder 306, NCNW Papers, 1–2.

73. Eli N. Evans, *The Provincials: A Personal History of Jews in the South*, revised edition (Chapel Hill, NC: University of North Carolina Press, 2005), 290; Lash, "Project: Wednesdays in Mississippi," 15, 18.

74. Lash, "Project: Wednesdays in Mississippi," 15, 18.

75. Haight, "Frances Haight Notes on Trip to Mississippi," 3.

76. Lash, "Project: Wednesdays in Mississippi," 14; Haight, "Frances Haight Notes on Trip, 8.

77. Haight, "Frances Haight Notes on Trip," 7–8; "WIMS Team #5," Debriefing, Side 1, 163–164.

78. "Wednesdays in Mississippi—Team #1,"13.

79. "Wednesdays in Mississippi—Minneapolis-St. Paul"; Joiner, "Down in the Delta," 37.

80. "WIMS Team #2," Debriefing, 21–23.

81. "WIMS Team #6," Debriefing, Side 2, 28.

82. "WIMS Team #6," Debriefing, Side 2, 3–10; Stedman interview, 2002, 21–22; Reed, *Simple Decency & Common Sense*, 158; Sokol, *There Goes My Everything*, 87–88; B. E. Smith, *Neither Separate nor Equal*, 17–18; Dittmer, *Local People*, 64–66.

83. "WIMS Team #2," Debriefing, 21–23.

84. Roach interview, 2003, 41.

85. Schutt interview, 1994, 24; Sokol, *There Goes My Everything*, 3–4; Crystal interview, 2008, 00:18:28–00:20:26; Barbara Brinson and Elaine Crystal, interview with Marlene McCurtis, July 24, 2008, transcript (hereinafter Brinson and Crystal interview), WIMS Film, 06:12:50–06:13:35; Webb, *Fight against Fear*, 80–81.

86. Crystal interview, 2008, 00:18:28–00:20:26; Brinson and Crystal interview, 2008, 06:12:50–06:13:35.

87. Dorothy Stewart, interview with Marlene McCurtis, July 23, 2008 (hereinafter Stewart interview, 2008), WIMS Film, Tape 1, 00:57:19:07–00:59:40:25.

88. Zetzel interview, 2011, 5.

89. Stedman interview, 2008, 03:01:21:09–03:02:54:02.

90. Cowan interview, 1968, 20.

91. Height, *Open Wide the Freedom Gates*, 165.

92. "Wednesdays in Mississippi, Minneapolis-St. Paul," August 7, 1964, Folder 305, NCNW Papers, 7–8.

93. "Wednesdays in Mississippi, Minneapolis-St. Paul," August 7, 1964, Folder 305, NCNW Papers, 8.

94. Lash, "Project: Wednesdays in Mississippi," 13.

95. Hunt interview, 2011, 16.

96. "WIMS Team #2," Debriefing, 30, 24–25.

97. "WIMS Team #2," Debriefing, 97–98.

98. Willen, letter to Cowan.

99. Goodwillie diary, July 15, 1964.

100. Ryerson, "Report on Trip to Mississippi," 1–2.

101. Kohlenberg, "Comments on the July 15th Wednesdays in Mississippi," 1–2

102. "WIMS Team #2," Debriefing, 60–62.

103. "WIMS Team #2," Debriefing, 64-65.

104. Zetzel interview, 2011, 5.

105. Lash, memo to Polly Cowan, 3.

106. Goodwillie diary, July 28, 1964.

107. Goodwillie, "Reminiscences," 18–19; Stedman interview, 2008, Tape 2, 02:23:35–02:38:12; Goodwillie diary August 17, 1964.

108. "WIMS Team #5," Debriefing, Side 1, 47–48.

109. "Wednesdays in Mississippi—Fact Sheet," n.d., Folder 32, NCNW Paper, 2; Patt Derian to Polly Cowan, n.d., Folder 278, NCNW Papers, 3.

110. Cowan, "Women in the Civil Rights Movement."

111. Lash, memo to Polly Cowan, 2; Stedman interview, 2008, Tape 2, 02:31:36–02:32:34; NCNW Education Foundation, "Wednesdays in Mississippi 1964"; Geraldine Kohlenberg Zetzel, phone interview with author, January 24, 2008; Hunt, Stedman, and Zetzel interview, 2011, 39.

112. Hunt, Stedman, and Zetzel interview, 2011, 46.

113. Stedman, interview, 2011, 35.

114. Hunt, Stedman, and Zetzel interview, 2011, 39, 24; Zetzel interview, 2011, 22; Stedman interview, 2011, 25.

115. Stedman interview, 2011, 25; Zetzel interview, 2011, 2; Zetzel, personal conversation with author, 2008.

116. Radov interview, 2002, 32.

117. Ryerson, "Report on Trip to Mississippi," 7.

118. Polly Cowan, "Wednesdays in Mississippi—Report from Polly Cowan, Project Coordinator," 1964, Folder 277, NCNW Papers, 4.

119. Hunt, Stedman, and Zetzel interview, 2011, 22, 63.

120. Stedman interview, 2011,14.

121. Joiner, "Down in the Delta," 37; Height interview, 2003, 1–2.

122. Height, interview, 2003,1–2.

123. Hunt, Stedman, and Zetzel interview, 2011, 17. The "rapport vs. report" theory was advanced by sociolinguist Deborah Tannen, who argued that men report information while women develop a rapport in their communication, which is less direct and incorporates feelings.

124. Mary M. Talbot, *Language and Gender: An Introduction* (Cambridge, UK: Polity Press, 2005), 98–99. See, Deborah Tannen, *That's Not What I Meant* (New York: Dent, 1986); Deborah Tannen, *You Just Don't Understand* (London, England: Virago, 1991); and Deborah Tannen, *Talking from 9 to 5* (London, England: Virago, 1995). Later, feminist linguists discounted Tannen's theory. Nevertheless, the WIMS experience validated the use of such communication techniques between the northern and southern women in the era to open dialogue and generate understanding.

125. Zetzel interview, 2011, 3.

126. Benjamin, "Wednesdays in Mississippi Answers to Report Questionnaire," 1.

127. Lash, "Project: Wednesdays in Mississippi," 9.

128. Woods, "Wednesday in Mississippi Report," 2.

129. Niles, "Report on Trip to Mississippi," 8.

130. Niles, "Report on Trip to Mississippi," 7; Randers-Pehrson, "Report of a Team Member," 6; "WIMS Team #3," Debriefing, Side 1, 5, 51.

131. Woods, "Wednesday in Mississippi Report," 2; "WIMS Team #3," Debriefing, Side 1, 57–58.

132. Roach, "Report, Peggy Roach,"1.

133. Randers-Pehrson, "Report of a Team Member," 6.

134. Randers-Pehrson, "Report of a Team Member," 6.

135. "WIMS Team #1," Debriefing, Side 1, 5, 21–22.

136. "WIMS Team #1," Debriefing, Side 1, 5, 27–29.

137. Lash, memo to Polly Cowan, 3; Height interview, 2003, 6; Stedman interview, 2002, 49; Joiner, "Down in the Delta," 37; Derian interview, 2008, Tape 4, 04:20:22–04:21:50.

138. Woods, "Wednesday in Mississippi Report," 2–3.

139. Denomme, "'To End This Day of Strife,'" quoting Cynthia Wedel; Clarie Collins Harvey, interviewed by Margaret Shannon, Lexington, KY, ca. 1980, Box 56, File 52, 23 CWU General Commission on Archives and History, 240–241.

140. Stewart interview, 2008, Tape 1, 00:57:19:07–00:59:40:25, 00:35:03:29–00:36:33:00, 00:51:42:22.

141. Cowan interview, 1968, 21; Clopton and Shands interview, 2008, 15:19:38:56–15:25:09:01; Stewart interview, 2008, Tape 1, 00:33:38:29–00:36:33; Purvis interview, 2008, Tape 2, 10:20:37:10–10:21:07:11; Burnstein interview, 06:57:16–06:58:12.

142. Edith Savage Jennings, interview with Christie Jones, July 26, 2003 (hereinafter Jennings interview, 2003), WIMS OH, digital recording in possession of author, 17:15–19:56; Hunt interview, 2011, 14.

143. Johnson interview, 2003, 37; Harvey interview, 1965, 22.

144. Cowan, "'Wednesdays in Mississippi'—Report from Polly Cowan, Project Coordinator," Folder 277, 4; Stedman interview, 2002, 48; Height, *BWOHP*, 240; Purvis interview, 2008, Tape 2, 10:05:54:23–10:06:56:20; Crystal interview, 2008, 00:11:28–00:12:28.

145. "WIMS Team #2," Debriefing, 50–51.

146. Moore, "Wednesdays in Mississippi," 1–2.

147. Moore, "Wednesdays in Mississippi," 1.

148. "WIMS Team #6," Debriefing, Side 2, 7–9

149. Noble, "Wednesdays in Mississippi Report," 6; "WIMS Team #7," Debriefing, Side 1, 44–45.

150. "WIMS Team #7," Debriefing transcript, 1964, Side 1, 5; Edith M Savage, "Report on Wednesdays in Mississippi Project," August 18–20, 1964, Folder 308, NCNW Papers, 1.

151. "WIMS Team #1," Debriefing, Side 1, 6–7; Shulman, *Wednesdays in Mississippi: The National Council of Negro Women and the Civil Rights Movement*, 5.

152. Frances Hennessy to Peggy Roach, June 23, 1964, Folder 304, NCNW Papers.

153. Height, *Open Wide the Freedom Gates*, 177–178.

154. Chappell, *Inside Agitators*, 214.

155. Miriam Ezelle to Polly Cowan, n.d., Folder 201, NCNW Papers, 1–2.

156. Florence Gooch to Susan Goodwillie, August 28, 1965, Folder 201, NCNW Papers, 1.

157. Polly Cowan, memo to all team members, August 22, 1964, Folder 264, NCNW Papers, 1; "Yankee Women Visit State on CR Mission," *Clarion-Ledger*, September 4, 1964, B-2, clipping, Folder 232, NCNW Papers.

158. "Voice of the People," written to the 48 Northern women, *Clarion-Ledger*, n.d., clipping, Folder 232, NCNW Papers.

159. "Voice of the People," *Clarion-Ledger*.

160. "WIMS Team #2," Debriefing, 4–5; "WIMS Team #1," Debriefing, Side 1, 25; Sister Catherine John Flynn, "Report Questionnaire, Wednesdays in Mississippi," n.d., Folder 269, NCNW Papers, 3; Randers-Pehrson, "Report of a Team Member," 2; Zetzel, "Wednesdays in Mississippi," 2.

161. Ethel Haserodt to Dorothy Height, February 5, 1965, Folder 60, NCNW Papers.

162. Priscilla Hunt interview, audio recording in possession of author, 2008; "Wednesdays in Mississippi—New Jersey Team to Hattiesburg," n.d., Folder 308, NCNW Papers, 8–9; "WIMS Team #7," Debriefing, Side 2, 1–3; Cowan, "Wednesdays in

Mississippi—Report from Polly Cowan, Project Coordinator," Folder 277, NCNW Papers, 4; Height, *Open Wide the Freedom Gates,* 183.

163. Miriam Davis, "Thoughts after Being the Guest of a Woman Who Cares," 1964, Folder 307, NCNW Papers, 2.

164. Denomme, "'To End This Day of Strife,'" quoting Harvey, interview, 240–241.

165. Roach interview, 2003, 47.

166. Jennings interview, 2003, 40:37–43:00.

167. Johnson interview, 2003, 35–36.

168. Virginia (Mrs. Henry) Bourne, "Report on Wednesdays in Mississippi Project," July 28–30, 1964, Folder 305, NCNW Papers, 3.

169. J. Davis, letter to "all of you," 2.

170. Randers-Pehrson, "Report of a Team Member," 3.

171. Woods, "Wednesday in Mississippi Report," 3.

172. Hunt interview, 2011, 6, 27–28, 39.

173. Noble, "Wednesdays in Mississippi Report," 3.

174. "WIMS Team #2," Debriefing transcript, 19.

175. Ryerson, "Report on Trip to Mississippi," 11.

176. Zetzel, "Wednesdays in Mississippi," 3.

177. Zetzel interview, 2011, 9–10.

178. Narcissa King to Polly Cowan, November 17, 1964, Folder 307, NCNW Papers, 2.

179. Cowan interview, 1968, 28.

180. Nathanson, Report, 8; Nathanson interview, 38:39–39:19.

181. Nathanson, Report, 1964, 8.

182. Ryerson, "Report on Trip to Mississippi," 11.

183. Kohlenberg, "Comments on the July 15th Wednesdays in Mississippi," 1964, 1.

184. Joiner, "Down in the Delta," 36.

185. "WIMS Team #7," Debriefing, Side 1, 36.

186. Sister Catherine John Flynn, "Report Questionnaire, Wednesdays in Mississippi," n.d., Folder 269, NCNW Papers, 3; Hunt, Stedman, and Zetzel interview, 2011, 50–51.

187. Flynn, "Report Questionnaire"

188. Nathanson interview, 2003, 12.

189. "WIMS Team #2," Debriefing, 4–5.

190. Haserodt, letter to Height.

191. Susan Goodwillie, "Thoughts on Leaving Mississippi," August 20, 1964, in possession of Susan Goodwillie Steadman, 2.

192. Height, *Open Wide the Freedom Gates,* 145.

193. Olson, *Freedom's Daughters,* 125, 223; Belinda Robnett, "African-American Women in the Civil Rights Movement, 1954–1965: Gender, Leadership, and Micromobilization," *The American Journal of Sociology* 101 no. 6 (May 1996), 1661–1693; Belinda Robnett, *How Long? How Long?: African-American Women in the Struggle for Civil Rights* (New York: Oxford University Press, 1997), 121.

194. Stedman interview, 2008, 04:35:08–04:35:18.

195. Cowan, "Wednesdays in Mississippi—Report from Polly Cowan, Project Coordinator," Folder 277, 2.

196. Irons, "The Shaping of Activist Recruitment and Participation," 699.

197. NCNW, "Wednesdays in Mississippi," 2.

198. WIMS Conference, 44–45.

199. Benjamin, "Wednesdays in Mississippi Answers to Report Questionnaire," 1.

200. Lash, memo to Polly Cowan, 1.

201. "WIMS Team #1," Debriefing, Side 1, 35–36.

202. Clopton and Shands interview, 2008, 16:59:26.

203. Purvis interview, 2008, 10:05:54–10:06:59.

204. Gooch, letter to Goodwillie.

CHAPTER SIX

1. Hope Ackerman and Polly Cowan, "Wednesdays in Mississippi: Report on Trip to Jackson, Mississippi, March 2–7, 1965," n.d., Folder 220, NCNW Papers, 6.

2. Polly Cowan, "Wednesdays in Mississippi Report from Polly Cowan, Team No. 1—July 6–9, 1965," 1965, Folder 310, NCNW Papers, 1.

3. Kay Mills, *This Little Light of Mine: The Life of Fannie Lou Hamer* (New York: Dutton, 1993), 196; Height, *Open Wide the Freedom Gates,* 178–179, 184–185; "Wednesdays in Mississippi—Fact Sheet," 1.

4. Derian interview, 2008, 04:17:58; Ackerman and Cowan, "Wednesdays in Mississippi: Report on Trip to Jackson, Mississippi," 9.

5. K. Mills, *This Little Light of Mine,* 196.

6. "Wednesdays in Mississippi—Fact Sheet," 1; Stedman interview, 2002, 51, 52–53.

7. "Excerpts from Letters from Mississippi Friends," Folder 201, NCNW Papers, 4; Derian, letter to Cowan, n.d., 1.

8. Derian interview, 2008, 02:15:15–02:21:40.

9. Dittmer, *Local People,* 341, 343, 346–347.

10. David Zarefsky, *President Johnson's War on Poverty: Rhetoric and History* (University, AL: University of Alabama Press, 1986), 47.

11. Zarefsky, *President Johnson's War on Poverty,* xiii.

12. John A. Andrew III, *Lyndon Johnson and the Great Society* (Chicago: Ivan R. Dee, Inc., 1998), 64–65; Randall B. Woods, *LBJ: Architect of American Ambition* (New York: Free Press, 2006), 453–458.

13. Kenneth T. Andrews, "Social Movements and Policy Implementation: The Mississippi Civil Rights Movement and the War on Poverty, 1965 to 1971," *American Sociological Review* 66 (February 2001): 77.

14. Dittmer, *Local People,* 363.

15. "Wednesdays in Mississippi—Fact Sheet," 3; Cowan interview, 1968, 15; Stedman interview, 2002, 52–53. The WIMS records indicate that seven regular teams, plus a team of art teachers, traveled to Mississippi in 1965. Although the NCNW did not assign that

team a number or count it in its number of teams, the participants were included in the total of number of women taking part.

16. Dittmer, *Local People*, 341, 343, 346–347, 408.

17. Although the acronym for Workshops in Mississippi remained the same as its predecessor, to avoid confusion, WIMS refers only to Wednesdays in Mississippi in this text.

18. Height interview, 2003, 8–10, 14–16; Height, *Open Wide the Freedom Gates*, 189–192.

19. Cowan, "Wednesdays in Mississippi 1964–1965: Final Report," 4.

20. Derian interview, 2008, 03:41:19–03:43:25.

21. Ackerman and Cowan, "Wednesdays in Mississippi: Report on Trip to Jackson," 18, 11.

22. Height interview, 2003, 9.

23. Ackerman and Cowan, "Wednesdays in Mississippi: Report on Trip to Jackson, 1–16."

24. Polly Cowan, "WIMS Newsletter," n.d., Folder 23, NCNW Papers, 1; National Council of Negro Women, "Tentative Budget for WIMS 1965," Folder 42, NCNW Papers; National Council of Negro Women; "January 1, 1965–December 31, 1965 Contributions," Folder 116, NCNW Papers.

25. Polly Cowan to Mr. Bingham, January 8, 1965, Folder 33, NCNW Papers; Jean Benjamin and Marian Logan, "Wednesdays in Mississippi"; (WIMS) Benefit, letter to Polly Cowan, January 8, 1965, Folder 33, NCNW Papers; Polly Cowan, form letter regarding New Jersey benefit, January 8, 1965, Folder 34, NCNW Papers; Edith Savage to Polly Cowan, November 10, 1965, Folder 60, NCNW Papers; "Mrs. Martin Luther King, Jr. (Mrs. Coretta Scott King)—Soprano—in a Freedom Concert," October 14, 1965, Folder 34, NCNW Papers.

26. Cowan, "Wednesdays in Mississippi 1964–1965: Final Report," 6, 7, 45–48.

27. "Wednesdays in Mississippi—Fact Sheet," 2; Cowan, "Wednesdays in Mississippi 1964–1965: Final Report," 7.

28. "WIMS Newsletter," July 1965, Folder 233, NCNW Papers.

29. Cowan, "Wednesdays in Mississippi 1964–1965: Final Report," 7.

30. Ellen Craft Dammond, "Report on the 'Wednesdays in Mississippi' (WIMS) Team Visit of July 7–9, 1965," Folder 310, NCNW Papers, 1–2.

31. Dammond, "Report on the 'Wednesdays in Mississippi,'" 1–2; Wednesdays in Mississippi, form letter to Mississippi contacts, June 10, 1965, Folder 60, NCNW Papers.

32. Carol Guyer, "Wednesdays in Mississippi Report from Carol Guyer, Team #1, New York, July 6–8, 1965," 1965, Folder 310, NCNW Papers, 2.

33. Florence Mars to Caroline Smith, July 17, 1965, Folder 311, NCNW Papers.

34. "WIMS—Selected Debriefing and Discussion Segments," 1965, NABWH-001-S15-SS5-F36-S1, Folder 36, Side 1, NCNW Papers, Series 15, Subseries 5, 13.

35. "WIMS—Selected Debriefing and Discussion Segments," 13.

36. Guyer, "Wednesdays in Mississippi Report from Carol Guyer," 3–4, 5.

37. Cowan, "Wednesdays in Mississippi 1964–1965: Final Report," 32.

38. Height, *Open Wide the Freedom Gates,* 184; Cowan, "Wednesdays in Mississippi Report from Polly Cowan, Team No. 1—July 6–9, 1965," 23–24; Cowan interview, 1968, 24.

39. Cowan interview, 1968, 21–22.

40. Flaxie Pinkett, "Wednesdays in Mississippi, August 3–5, 1965, inclusive," 1965, Folder 314, NCNW Papers, 4.

41. Lorna Scheide, "Wednesdays in Mississippi, Report from Loran Scheide, Team #3—New Jersey, July 20–22, 1965," 1965, Folder 312, NCNW Papers, 2.

42. Cowan, "Wednesdays in Mississippi 1964–1965: Final Report," 37.

43. "WIMS—Selected Debriefing and Discussion Segments," Side 1, 13–14.

44. Guyer, "Wednesdays in Mississippi Report from Carol Guyer," 7.

45. Ackerman and Cowan, "Wednesdays in Mississippi: Report on Trip to Jackson," 6.

46. Mars, *Witness in Philadelphia,* 182; Dittmer, *Local People,* 341, 345, 356.

47. Guyer, "Wednesdays in Mississippi Report from Carol Guyer," 2.

48. Marguerite Cassell, "Report to 'Wednesdays in Mississippi' Chicago Team—July 27, 28 and 29, 1965," 1965, Folder 313, NCNW Papers, 1.

49. "Danelle K. Vockroth v. George B. Vockroth," Find a Case, June 5, 1967, http://ms.findacase.com/research/wfrmDocViewer.aspx/xq/fac.19670605_40170.MS.htm/qx.

50. Dittmer, *Local People,* 356.

51. Cowan, "Wednesdays in Mississippi 1964–1965: Final Report," 1965, 32.

52. Gladys Zales, "Journey into Fear: My Jackson Episode," 1965, Folder 310, NCNW Papers, 1.

53. Hannah Levin, "Wednesdays in Mississippi, Report from Hannah Levin, New Jersey Team—July 20–22, 1965," 1965, Folder 312, NCNW Papers, 1.

54. "Wednesdays in Mississippi Transcript of De-briefing: Team #2—Philadelphia," August 5, 1965, Folder 310, NCNW Papers, 13; Cunningham, *Agony at Galloway,* 120–123; William L. Chaze, "Mayor Asks Compliance," newspaper clipping, n.d., Schutt Papers, Box 1, Folder 55.

55. Chaze, "Mayor Asks Compliance"; Sokol, *There Goes My Everything,* 197; Niles, "Report on Trip to Mississippi," 14.

56. Josie Harbison, "Wednesdays in Mississippi, Report from Josie Harbison, New Jersey Team—July 20–22, 1965," 1965, Folder 312, NCNW Papers, 3.

57. The White House, "Remarks of the President, Operation Head Start, The Rose Garden," May 18, 1965, Folder 183, NCNW Papers; Zarefsky, *President Johnson's War on Poverty,* 137.

58. Cowan interview, 1968, 22; Cowan, "Wednesdays in Mississippi 1964–1965: Final Report," 8.

59. Polly Cowan, writings, n.d., Folder 97, NCNW Papers, 11.

60. Cowan, "Wednesdays in Mississippi 1964–1965: Final Report," 9.

61. Maris A. Vinovskis, *The Birth of Head Start: Preschool Education Policies in the Kennedy and Johnson Administrations* (Chicago: University of Chicago Press, 2005), 25.

62. Dittmer, *Local People,* 368–369; James F. Findlay, "The Mainline Churches and Head Start in Mississippi: Religious Activism in the Sixties," *Church History* 64, no. 2 (June 1995), 239, 242; Dittmer, *Local People,* 369.

63. Dittmer, *Local People,* 369.

64. Payne, *I've Got the Light of Freedom,* 329.

65. Dittmer, *Local People,* 369, 371; Zales, "Journey into Fear," 3; Dammond, "Report on the 'Wednesdays in Mississippi,'" 5; Cowan, "Wednesdays in Mississippi 1964–1965: Final Report," 8–9.

66. Dittmer, *Local People,* 371; Payne, *I've Got the Light of Freedom,* 329.

67. Cowan, "Wednesdays in Mississippi 1964–1965: Final Report," 8.

68. "Mississippi Tapes—Team 00, Boston Art Team, June 27–July 1, 1965," Folder 309, NCNW Papers, 2.

69. Rita DeLisi, "Wednesdays in Mississippi Cambridge Group, June 27th–July 1st, 1965," Folder 309, NCNW Papers, 1.

70. Guyer, "Wednesdays in Mississippi Report from Carol Guyer," 9.

71. Cowan, "Wednesdays in Mississippi 1964–1965: Final Report," 18–19.

72. Cowan, "Wednesdays in Mississippi 1964–1965: Final Report," 9.

73. Esther H. Cooke, "Wednesdays in Mississippi—New Jersey Team Report: Impressions and Observations," 1965, Folder 312, NCNW Papers, 8.

74. Cooke, "Wednesdays in Mississippi—New Jersey Team Report," 8.

75. Derian interview, 1991, 15.

76. Stewart interview, 2008, 40:36:08–42:54:09.

77. Cowan, "Wednesdays in Mississippi 1964–1965: Final Report," 10–11.

78. Dittmer, *Local People,* 368, 373; Findlay, "The Mainline Churches and Head Start," 239; Rebecca Sharpless, *Cooking in Other Women's Kitchens: Domestic Workers in the South, 1865–1960* (Chapel Hill: University of North Carolina Press, 2010), 186–187; "Given a Chance," *America's War on Poverty,* PBS Video, 1995.

79. Derian interview, 1991, 14.

80. Stewart interview, 2008, 40:36–42:54:00.

81. Findlay, "The Mainline Churches and Head Start," 240.

82. Vinovskis, *The Birth of Head Start,* 97.

83. Dittmer. *Local People,* 370–372; Vinovskis, *The Birth of Head Start,* 97.

84. Andrew, *Lyndon Johnson and the Great Society,* 77–78.

85. Andrews, "Social Movements and Policy Implementation," 80.

86. Joseph Crespino, *In Search of Another Country: Mississippi and the Conservative Counterrevolution* (Princeton, NJ: Princeton University Press, 2007), 135.

87. Derian interview, 1991, 11.

88. Edward Zigler and Susan Muenchow, *Head Start: The Inside Story of America's Most Successful Educational Experiment* (New York: Basic Books, 1992), 133–134. Marian Wright married Peter Edelman in 1968 and is referred to as Marian Wright Edelman in this text.

89. Andrew, *Lyndon Johnson and the Great Society,* 78.

90. Derian interview, 1991, 18.

91. Andrew, *Lyndon Johnson and the Great Society,* 78.

92. Findlay, "The Mainline Churches and Head Start," 242, 243; Dittmer, *Local People,* 370–372.

93. Stewart interview, 2008, 40:36:08–42:54:09.

94. Derian interview, 1991, 22.

95. Cowan, "Wednesdays in Mississippi Report from Polly Cowan, Team No. 1—July 6–9, 1965," 1.

96. Cowan, writings, n.d., Folder 97, 11.

97. Cowan, "Wednesdays in Mississippi 1964–1965: Final Report," 11–12.

98. Height, *Open Wide the Freedom Gates,* 180–181. 99. Height, *Open Wide the Freedom Gates,* 180–182.

100. Height, *Open Wide the Freedom Gates,* 183.

101. Height, *Open Wide the Freedom Gates,* 183.

102. Roscoe A. Boyer to Polly Cowan, August 18, 1965, Folder 329, NCNW Papers.

103. J. D. Williams to Polly Cowan, August 21, 1965, Folder 329, NCNW Papers.

104. Boyer, letter to Cowan, August 18, 1965.

105. Lee interview, 15, 28, 27, 37; Mars, *Witness in Philadelphia,* 200.

106. "The United States Section of WILPF," the Women's International League for Peace and Freedom, www.wilpf.org/US_WILPF.

107. Mars, *Witness in Philadelphia,* 200.

108. Cowan, "WIMS Newsletter." Although they joined the Philadelphia, Pennsylvania, teams, three team members were from other communities: Oakland, California; Roslyn Heights, New York; and Omaha, Nebraska.

109. Mars interview, 35–36.

110. Margery Gross, "Wednesday in Mississippi Report from Margery Gross, Team #2—Philadelphia—July 12–16, 1965," 1965, Folder 311, NCNW Papers, 6.

111. Mars interview, 1978, 35–36.

112. Marjorie Duckrey, "Wednesdays in Mississippi, Report from Marjorie Duckrey, Team #6—Philadelphia," 1965, Folder 315, NCNW Papers, 7.

113. Cowan, "Wednesdays in Mississippi 1964–1965: Final Report," 13–15.

114. Cowan, "Wednesdays in Mississippi 1964–1965: Final Report," 14.

115. "WIMS—Selected Debriefing and Discussion Segments," 20, 24–25.

116. Mars, letter to Caroline Smith; "Wednesdays in Mississippi Transcript of Debriefing: Team #2," 10.

117. Gross, "Wednesday in Mississippi Report from Margery Gross," 7.

118. "Wednesdays in Mississippi Transcript of De-briefing: Team #2—Philadelphia," 13.

119. Mars, *Witness in Philadelphia,* 201; Cowan, "Wednesdays in Mississippi 1964–1965: Final Report," 13.

120. Susan Goodwillie to Sister Catherine John, April 9, 1965, Folder 308, NCNW Papers.

121. Paul T. Murray, "Father Nathaniel and the Greenwood Movement," *Journal of Mississippi History* 72, no. 3 (Fall 2010), 278–280.

122. Murray, "Father Nathaniel and the Greenwood Movement," 280.

123. Cowan, "Wednesdays in Mississippi 1964–1965: Final Report," 15; Jane McIlvaine McClary, "Pax Christi," Folder 314, NCNW Papers, 1; Murray, "Father Nathaniel and the Greenwood Movement," 281.

124. McClary, "Pax Christi," 1.

125. Murray, "Father Nathaniel and the Greenwood Movement," 283–285.

126. Namorato, *The Catholic Church in Mississippi*, 83; Murray, "Father Nathaniel and the Greenwood Movement," 277–278, 308–310.

127. Cowan, "Wednesdays in Mississippi 1964–1965: Final Report," 17, 24; Namorato, *The Catholic Church in Mississippi*, 199; Flaxie M. Pinkett, "Wednesdays in Mississippi: August 3–5, 1965," Folder 314, NCNW Papers, 3.

128. Cowan, "Wednesdays in Mississippi 1964–1965: Final Report," 18–19.

129. Frances J. Perkins, "Wednesdays in Mississippi, Report from Frances J. Perkins, Team #7—Boston, August 17–20, 1965, Folder 316, NCNW Papers, 3–4.

130. Mary Cannady, "Team Member Report," 1965, Folder 316, NCNW Files, 3–4.

131. Curry, "Wild Geese to the Past," 27.

132. Cowan, "Wednesdays in Mississippi 1964–1965: Final Report," 20.

133. "Wednesdays in Mississippi Transcript of De-briefing: Team #1—New York," August 4, 1965, Folder 310, NCNW Papers, 8.

134. Sue Miller, "Report to WIMS, Trip to Oxford, Mississippi, March 27, 28, 29," Folder 312, NCNW Papers, 4–5.

135. "Wednesdays in Mississippi Transcript of De-briefing: Team #1—New York," August 4, 1965, Folder 311, NCNW Papers, 5; Cowan, "Wednesdays in Mississippi 1964–1965: Final Report," 20–21.

136. "Wednesdays in Mississippi Transcript of De-briefing: Team #7—Boston, August 17–20, 1965," 1965, Folder 316, NCNW Files, 1.

137. "Wednesdays in Mississippi Transcript of De-briefing: Team #7—Boston, August 17–20, 1965," 2–4; Cowan, "Wednesdays in Mississippi 1964–1965: Final Report," 1965, Folder 276, NCNW Papers, 21.

138. "Wednesdays in Mississippi Transcript of De-briefing: Team #7—Boston, August 17–20, 1965," 5.

139. "Wednesdays in Mississippi Transcript of De-briefing: Team #2—Philadelphia," 1, 3.

140. "Wednesdays in Mississippi Transcript of De-briefing: Team #3—New Jersey," 1965, Folder 312, NCNW Files, 8.

141. Zarefsky, *President Johnson's War on Poverty*, 42; Caryn E. Neumann, "Enabled by the Holy Spirit: Church Women United and the Development of Ecumenical Christian Feminism," in *Feminist Coalitions: Historical Perspectives on Second-Wave Feminism in the United States*, with a foreword by Sara M. Evans, Stephanie Gilmore, ed. (Urbana: University of Illinois Press, 2008), 125.

142. Josephine Weiner, *The Story of WICS* (Washington, DC: Women in Community Service, Inc., 1979); "WICS History," Women in Community Service, www.wics.org/history.asp (accessed February 2, 2007).

143. Neumann, "Enabled by the Holy Spirit," 125.

144. Cooke, "Wednesdays in Mississippi—New Jersey Team Report," 5–6.

145. Scheide, "Wednesdays in Mississippi, Report from Loran Scheide," 1.

146. Cowan, "synopsis," 2.

147. Stedman interview, 2008, 04:34:15–04:34:52; Cowan, "Wednesdays in Mississippi 1964–1965: Final Report," 29.

148. Cowan, "Wednesdays in Mississippi 1964–1965: Final Report," 30.

149. Ellen Tarry, *The Third Door: The Autobiography of an American Negro Woman* (Tuscaloosa, AL: University of Alabama Press, 1992); Cowan, "Wednesdays in Mississippi Report from Polly Cowan, Team No. 1—July 6–9, 1965," 2.

150. Charles W. Eagles, *The Price of Defiance: James Meredith and the Integration of Ole Miss* (Chapel Hill: University of North Carolina, 2009), 179.

151. Cowan, "Wednesdays in Mississippi 1964–1965: Final Report," 30–31.

152. Florence Gooch to Susan Goodwillie, August 28, 1965, Folder 201, NCNW Papers; Cassell, "Report to 'Wednesdays in Mississippi' Chicago Team," 1.

153. "Wednesdays in Mississippi Transcript of De-briefing: Team #6—Philadelphia," 1.

154. "WIMS—Selected Debriefing and Discussion Segments," Side 1, 11–12, 14.

155. Elizabeth Haselden, "Addition to Report from Elizabeth Haselden, Team #4—Chicago, July 27–29, 1965," 1965, Folder 313, NCNW Papers.

156. Cowan, "Wednesdays in Mississippi 1964–1965: Final Report," 25.

157. "Wednesdays in Mississippi Transcript of De-briefing: Team #3—New Jersey," 5; Cowan, "Wednesdays in Mississippi 1964–1965: Final Report," 24; Caroline Smith, "WIMS Conclusions and Recommendations," October 29, 1965, Folder 282, NCNW Papers, 2.

158. "Wednesdays in Mississippi Transcript of De-briefing: Team #6—Philadelphia," 1.

159. "Wednesdays in Mississippi Transcript of De-briefing: Team #1—New York," 7–8.

160. Cowan, "Wednesdays in Mississippi Report from Polly Cowan, Team No. 1—July 6–9, 1965," 4.

161. Cowan, "Wednesdays in Mississippi 1964–1965: Final Report," 24–25.

162. Buddy Mayer, "Report of Mrs. Robert B. Mayer as a Member of the Chicago Team of WIMS, July 27–29, 1965," 1965, Folder 313, NCNW Papers, 2; Selma Taub, "Wednesdays in Mississippi Report from Selma Taub, Chicago Team #4, July 27–29, 1965," 1965, Folder 313, NCNW Papers, 1–2; Cowan, "Wednesdays in Mississippi 1964–1965: Final Report," 24–25.

163. Cowan, "Wednesdays in Mississippi 1964–1965: Final Report," 25.

164. "Wednesdays in Mississippi Transcript of De-briefing: Team #6—Philadelphia," 15.

165. Shirley Lipsey, interview with Christie Jones, July 28, 2003 (hereinafter Lipsey interview, 2003), WIMS OH, digital recording in possession of author, 28:53.

166. Smith, "WIMS Conclusions and Recommendations," 2.

167. "Violence in Jackson," Civil Rights: Reflections of Public Ministry at Harvard Divinity School, www.hds.harvard.edu/library/exhibits/online/hdspublicministry/2 .html; "Wednesdays in Mississippi Transcript of De-briefing: Team #5—Washington/Virginia—August 3–5, 1965," 1965, Folder 314, NCNW Files, 13.

168. "WIMS—Selected Debriefing and Discussion Segments," 8–10.

169. Cowan, "Wednesdays in Mississippi 1964–1965: Final Report," 32.

170. Ester Sampson to Polly Cowan, 1965, Folder 201, NCNW Papers.

171. "Wednesdays in Mississippi Transcript of De-briefing: Team #1—New York," 16.

172. Smith, "WIMS Conclusions and Recommendations," 1-3.

173. Children's Defense Fund, "Marian Wright Edelman, " www.childrensdefense .org/about-us/leadership-staff/marian-wright-edelman/; Children's Defense Fund, *Holding Children in Prayer: An Advent Guide,* 2005, www.childrensdefense.org/child -research-data-publications/data/holding-children-prayer-advent-guide.pdf; Children's Defense Fund, *Kinship Care Resource Kit: Helping Grandparents and Other Relatives Raising Children,* www.childrensdefense.org/child-research-data-publications/data/ kinship-care-organization-resource-kit.pdf.

174. Karen Trendell, "Student Group Makes Members Effective Advocates for Child Welfare," *Syracuse University News,* December 4, 2002, http://suews.syr.edu/story_de tails.cfm?id=1255 (accessed May 16, 2006).

175. K. Mills, *This Little Light of Mine,* 197.

176. Height, *Open Wide the Freedom Gates,* 189.

177. Height interview, 2003, 9, 16.

178. Census 1960, General Population Characteristics, Mississippi, and General Social and Economic Characteristics, www.census.gov.

179. Height, interview, 2003, 19–20.

180. Height, *Open Wide the Freedom Gates,* 189; National Council of Negro Women, "Mississippi Women's Planning Session, November 18–19, 1966," Folder 221, NCNW Papers, 2.

181. K. Mills, *This Little Light of Mine,* 196–197.

182. National Council of Negro Women, "Consultants and Staff at Mississippi Women's Workshop," 1967, Folder 226, NCNW Papers; Annie Devine and Jesse Mosley, form letter, January 9, 1967, Folder 226, NCNW Papers.

183. National Council of Negro Women, "Participants at Mississippi Women's Workshop," 1967, Folder 226, NCNW Papers.

184. Height, *Open Wide the Freedom Gates,* 190; K. Mills, *This Little Light of Mine,* 197.

185. Dittmer, *Local People,* 382–383; Crespino, *In Search of Another Country,* 136; "Children in Mississippi: Statement of the United States Subcommittee on Manpower and Development," July 11, 1967, quoted in Dittmer, *Local People,* 505 n49.

186. Cathy Aldridge, "Mississippi Women Seek Better Homes, Miss. Ladies Here for Summer Plans," *New York Amsterdam News,* April 15, 1967, newspaper clipping, Folder 232, NCNW Papers.

187. Height, *Open Wide the Freedom Gates,* 190.

188. Height interview, 2002, 1; National Council of Negro Women, "Contributions—WIMS," December 11, 1967-January 23, 1968, Folder 116, NCNW Papers; National Council of Negro Women, ledger book, December 1967, Folder 118, NCNW Files, 7.

189. Newman, *Divine Agitators,* 163; Dittmer, *Local People,* 384–386; Cowan, "synopsis," 3–4.

190. Cowan, "synopsis," 3–4.

191. Office of Economic Opportunity, *Rural Opportunities* 2, no. 8 (August 1967), Folder 235, NCNW papers, 3; K. Mills, *This Little Light of Mine*, 197, quoting Polly Cowan conversation with William, Seaborn of the Department of Agriculture, April 18, 1967.

192. Cowan, "synopsis," 4.

193. Rebecca Marie Kluchin, *Fit to be Tied: Sterilization and Reproductive Rights in America, 1950–1980* (New Brunswick, NJ: Rutgers University Press, 2011), 177.

194. Height interview, 2002, 5; Height interview, 2003, 8–10, 14–16; Height, *Open Wide the Freedom Gates*, 193; Charlotte Lewis, Office of Economic Opportunity, letter to Polly Cowan, October 2, 1967, Folder 67, NCNW Papers.

195. Height, *Open Wide the Freedom Gates*, 188.

196. National Council of Negro Women, "A Report on Operation Daily Bread," October 1968, Folder 245, NCNW Papers, 3.

197. Height, *Open Wide the Freedom Gates*, 188; NCNW, "A Report on Operation Daily Bread," 4.

198. Height, *Open Wide the Freedom Gates*, 188; NCNW, "A Report on Operation Daily Bread," 4, 5.

199. NCNW, "A Report on Operation Daily Bread," 7.

200. Chana Kai Lee, *For Freedom's Sake: The Life of Fannie Lou Hamer* (Urbana, IL: University of Illinois Press, 1999), 148.

201. Height, *Open Wide the Freedom Gates*, 188–189.

202. NCNW, "A Report on Operation Daily Bread," 1; Robert F, Wagner, Jr., "Black 'Grow Power' in South, *New York Post*, August 23, 1968, newspaper clipping, Folder 232, NCNW Papers.

203. NCNW, "A Report on Operation Daily Bread," 1.

204. NCNW, "A Report on Operation Daily Bread," 9; Robert F, Wagner, Jr., "Black 'Grow Power' in South," newspaper clipping, *New York Post*, August 23, 1968, Folder 232, NCNW Papers; Lee, *For Freedom's Sake*, 148–162.

205. Lee, *For Freedom's Sake*, 149; NCNW, "A Report on Operation Daily Bread," 9–10.

206. National Council of Negro Women, "Progress Report: Self-help Campaign Against Hunger," June 1969, Mississippi Council on Human Relations, Folder: National Council of Negro Women, Box 37, MDAH, 13; Rodney E. Leonard to Polly Cowan, March 9, 1967, Folder 67, NCNW Papers.

207. K. Mills, *This Little Light of Mine*, 293. Hamer was paid by the NCNW until she ran for the state senate in 1971.

208. K. Mills, *This Little Light of Mine*, 260; Height interview, 2003, 19–20, Height interview, 2002, 10.

209. Leola G. Williams to Dorothy Height, July 26, 1967, Folder 70, NCNW Papers.

210. Height interview, 2003, 14.

211. Blackwell, *Barefootin'*, 128, 177–178.

212. Height, *Open Wide the Freedom Gates*, 195–196.

213. Blackwell, *Barefootin'*, 183, 180; National Council of Negro Women, "Workshops in Mississippi Newsletter," June 1968, NCNW Papers, Folder 233, 2; Height, *Open Wide the Freedom Gates*, 196.

214. NCNW, "Wednesdays in Mississippi Newsletter," June 1968, 2; Height interview, 2003, 10.

215. National Association of Housing, "Home Ownership through Public Housing," n.d., reprint from *Journal of Housing*, National Council of Negro Women.

216. Blackwell, *Barefootin'*, 184–185; "A Look Back at Hurricane Camille," May 3, 2005, *USA Today*, www.usatoday.com/weather/wcamille.htm; Height, *Open Wide the Freedom Gates*, 197.

217. Dorothy Height, personal conversation with author, October 16, 2006.

218. Height, *Open Wide the Freedom Gates*, 197, 196; Blackwell, *Barefootin'*, 178–180; National Council of Negro Women, "NCNW Awarded $750,000 from Bush-Clinton Katrina Fund," Washington D.C., December 2006, www.ncnw.org/about/news.htm.

219. Dittmer, *Local People*, 408–409, 411; Sokol, *There Goes My Everything*, 273; Penny Patch, "Sweet Tea at Shoney's," in *Deep in Our Hearts*; Sara Evans, *Personal Politics: The Roots of Women's Liberation in the Civil Rights Movement and the New Left* (New York: Vintage Books, 1979), 163–164.

220. "Negro Women's Chief Raps 'Black Power,'" *New York Post*, December 20, 1966, clipping, Folder 232, NCNW Papers.

221. Paul Cowan, *An Orphan in History: One Man's Triumphant Search for His Jewish Roots*, with an afterword by Rachel Cowan (Woodstock, VT: Jewish Lights Publishing, 2002), 101–102.

222. Polly Cowan, autobiography notes, July 4, 1973, Folder 13, Cowan Papers, 1.

223. Hunt, Stedman, and Zetzel interview, 2011, 16, 66–69.

224. Dittmer, *Local People*, 363; Weiner, *The Story of WICS*, 7–8, 13–14, 15–17.

225. Height interview, 2003, 18–19. In January 1966, Fannie Lou Hamer wrote a poignant letter to Ruth Batson after the WIMS team member sent toys and dolls to Ruleville for Christmas. "We are very grateful to you for them Mrs. Batson. So many people said they would send toys but you are the only person did it." After telling Batson how monetary donations they had received went to buy food and that many people had left their children in Mississippi to look for seasonal work in Florida, she asked Batson to send fabric scraps so the women could earn extra money making quilts. Hamer closed by saying, "Mrs. Batson thank you again and I'll never forget you as long as I live and a whole lot of other people say they hope one day they can see you and thank you in person. . . . Yours for God and justice for all men." Fannie Lou Hamer to Ruth Batson, January 10, 1966, Box 3, Folder 8, Batson Papers.

CONCLUSION

1. Cowan, "Why Me?" Folder 7, Cowan Papers, 1.

2. Shulman, *Wednesdays in Mississippi: The National Council of Negro Women and the Civil Rights Movement*, 2.

3. Stedman interview, 2008, 04:38:47–04:39:49.

4. Blackwell, *Barefootin'*, 138.

5. Miller, "Mississippi Musings," 46–61.

6. Stewart interview, 2008, 02:10:52:08–02:14:00:27.

7. Cowan, "Wednesdays in Mississippi—Report From Polly Cowan Project Coordinator," Folder 277, 2.

8. Shulman, "Polly Spiegel Cowan."

9. Liza Cowan, "Liza Cowan Remembers Her Mother, Polly Cowan," n.d., www.history.uh.edu/cph/WIMS/effects/LizaCowan.html.

10. Zetzel interview, 2011, 14.

11. Radov interview, 2002, 49.

12. Hunt, Stedman, and Zetzel interview, 2011, 61–62, 63–64.

13. Johnson, interview, 2003, 40–41.

Bibliography

ARCHIVES

ALBERT AND SHIRLEY SMALL SPECIAL COLLECTIONS LIBRARY, UNIVERSITY OF VIRGINIA.
Papers of Marguerite Cassell
Papers of Polly Cowan
Papers of Claudia Heckscher
Papers of Jean S. Davis
Papers of Susan Goodwillie, 1964
Papers of Sylvia Weinberg
Wednesdays in Mississippi Papers
GENERAL COMMISSION ON ARCHIVES AND HISTORY: THE UNITED METHODIST CHURCH, MADISON, NEW JERSEY.
Church Women United Records, 1902–2004
J. B. CAIN ARCHIVES OF MISSISSIPPI METHODISM, MILLSAPS-WILSON LIBRARY, MILLSAPS COLLEGE.
Dr. Sam E. and Ann Lewis Ashmore Papers: 1960–1966, 2007, M100
Robert Bergmark Papers
Local Churches: Galloway UMC
MCCAIN LIBRARY AND ARCHIVES, UNIVERSITY OF SOUTHERN MISSISSIPPI.
Johnson (Paul B.) Family Papers, M 191, Series II
Rabbi Charles Mantinband Papers, M 327
MILLSAPS COLLEGE ARCHIVES, MILLSAPS-WILSON LIBRARY, MILLSAPS COLLEGE.
John Quincy Adams Faculty Papers
MISSISSIPPI DEPARTMENT OF ARCHIVES AND HISTORY.
Civil Rights and Methodism (Jackson, Mississippi)
Ed King Collection
Mississippi Freedom Summer Project Collection
Mississippi Sovereignty Commission Online
Jane M. Schutt Papers
NATIONAL ARCHIVES FOR BLACK WOMEN'S HISTORY, MARY MCLEOD BETHUNE COUNCIL HOUSE, WASHINGTON, D.C.
Polly Cowan Papers
National Council of Negro Women Papers

SCHLESINGER LIBRARY, RADCLIFFE INSTITUTE, HARVARD UNIVERSITY.
  Ruth Batson Papers, 1919–2003, MC 590
  Florynce Kennedy Papers, 1915–2004, MC 555
SMITHSONIAN ARCHIVES CENTER INSTITUTION, NATIONAL MUSEUM OF AMERICAN
  HISTORY.
  Moses Moon Collection Audio Tapes, 1963–1964, Collection #AC0556
TOUGALOO COLLEGE ARCHIVES, L. ZENOBIA COLEMAN LIBRARY, DIGITAL LIBRARY.
  Adam Daniel Beittel Papers
  George A. Owens Papers

                        INTERVIEWS BY AUTHOR

UH—ORAL HISTORY OF HOUSTON, HOUSTON HISTORY PROJECT, M. D. ANDERSON LIBRARY,
  UNIVERSITY OF HOUSTON, HOUSTON, TEXAS.
  Priscilla Hunt
  Susan Goodwillie Stedman
  Geraldine Kohlenberg Zetzel
  Priscilla Hunt, Susan Goodwillie Stedman, and Geraldine Zetzel

                          ORAL HISTORIES

AMERICAN JEWISH ARCHIVES, CINCINNATI, OHIO.
  Perry E. Nussbaum
BLACK WOMEN ORAL HISTORY PROJECT FROM THE ARTHUR AND ELIZABETH SCHLESINGER
  LIBRARY ON THE HISTORY OF WOMEN IN AMERICA, RADCLIFF COLLEGE
  Dorothy Boulding Ferebee
  Dorothy I. Height
CENTER FOR ORAL HISTORY AND CULTURAL HERITAGE, MCCAIN LIBRARY AND ARCHIVES,
  UNIVERSITY OF SOUTHERN MISSISSIPPI.
  W. J. Cunningham
  Julian Beck Feibelman
  Clay F. Lee
  Florence Mars
  Peter Oliver Quinn
  Jane M. Schutt
JACKSON STATE UNIVERSITY ORAL HISTORY PROGRAM, THE FARISH STREET HISTORIC DIS-
  TRICT PROJECT.
  Lillie B. Jones
JOHN C. STENNIS COLLECTION, CONGRESSIONAL AND POLITICAL RESEARCH CENTER, MIS-
  SISSIPPI STATE UNIVERSITY LIBRARIES.
  Patricia Derian

KOJO NNAMDI, "WEDNESDAYS IN MISSISSIPPI: AN INTERVIEW WITH GUESTS SUSAN GOOD-
WILLIE, PRISCILLA HUNT, MILDRED PITT GOODMAN, DORIS V. WILSON, AND RUSSLYN ALI,"
PUBLIC INTEREST, WAMU, AMERICAN UNIVERSITY RADIO, WASHINGTON, DC, 2001.

LOWENSTEIN ORAL HISTORY PROJECT, ORAL HISTORY RESEARCH OFFICE, COLUMBIA
UNIVERSITY.
   Susan Goodwillie

MISSISSIPPI DEPARTMENT OF ARCHIVES AND HISTORY.
   Ed King

ORAL HISTORY PROJECT—CONTEMPORARY MISSISSIPPI LIFE AND VIEWPOINTS 1965, JOHN
QUINCY ADAMS FACULTY PAPERS, MILLSAPS COLLEGE ARCHIVES, MILLSAPS-WILSON
LIBRARY, MILLSAPS COLLEGE.
   Claire Collins Harvey

RALPH J. BUNCHE COLLECTIONS, FORMERLY THE CIVIL RIGHTS DOCUMENTATION PROJ-
ECT; MANUSCRIPT DIVISION, MOORLAND SPINGARN RESEARCH CENTER, HOWARD
UNIVERSITY.
   Pauline Cowan

WEDNESDAYS IN MISSISSIPPI FILM PROJECT UNDER THE DIRECTION OF MARLENE MCCURTIS,
DEAN SCHRAMM, JOY SILVERMAN, AND CATHEE WEISS, WWW.WIMSFILMPROJECT.ORG.
   Barbara Brinson
   Lillian Burnstein
   Wilma Clopton
   Elaine Crystal
   Patt Derian
   Janet Purvis
   Jay Shands
   Susan Goodwillie Stedman
   Dorothy Stewart
   Doris Wilson

WEDNESDAYS IN MISSISSIPPI ORAL HISTORY, ALBERT AND SHIRLEY SMALL SPECIAL COL-
LECTIONS LIBRARY, UNIVERSITY OF VIRGINIA.
   Marguerite Cassell
   Jean Davis
   Miriam Davis
   Susan Goodwillie
   Faith Griefen
   Claudia Heckscher
   Dorothy Height
   Edith Savage Jennings
   Josie Johnson
   Shirley Lipsey
   Beatrice "Buddy" Mayer
   Maxine Nathanson
   Sylvia Weinberg Radov
   Peggy Roach

Alice Judson Ryerson-Hayes
Susan Goodwillie Stedman
Ellen Tarry
Doris Wilson

NEWSPAPERS

Ann Arbor News
Birmingham News
Clarion-Ledger
Jackson Daily News
Los Angeles Sentinel
Meridian Star
Minneapolis Morning Tribune
Mississippi Free Press
Mississippi Methodist Advocate
New York Amsterdam News
New York Herald Tribune
New York Post
New York Times
Selma Times-Journal
The "Queens Voice"
The Star Ledger
USA Today
Washington Post

MAGAZINES AND ORGANIZATIONAL PUBLICATIONS

Ali, Russlyn and Susan Goodwillie. *Wednesdays in Mississippi: The Story*. Washington D.C.: Children's Defense Fund, 2006.
Joiner, Lottie. "Down in the Delta." *New Crisis* 109, March/April 2002.
Lurie, Jess Zel. "Kol Nidre in Mississippi." *American Judaism*, Winter 1964–1965:15.
Mantinband, Charles. "From the Diary of a Mississippi Rabbi." *American Judaism*, Winter 1962–1963: 8–9, 51.
———. "Rabbi in the Deep South: A Mississippian Shows the Way; How to Be True to One's Belief—and Survive—in an Area of Racial Tension." *Anti-defamation League of B'nai B'rith Bulletin*, May 1962.
Office of Economic Opportunity. *Rural Opportunities* 2 no. 8, August 1967.
National Association of Housing. "Home Ownership through Public Housing." Reprint from *Journal of Housing*.

Shulman, Holly Cowan. *Wednesdays in Mississippi: The National Council of Negro Women and the Civil Rights Movement in Mississippi during Freedom Summer, 1964.* Washington, D.C.: National Park Service, Mary McLeod Bethune Council House, forthcoming.

VIDEOS

"Given a Chance." *America's War on Poverty.* PBS Video, 1995.
The Life and Surprising Times of Dr. Dorothy Height, National Visionary Leadership Project. 2002.

GOVERNMENT DOCUMENTS

Census 1900, Social Explorer Dataset (SE), Census 1900, Digitally transcribed by the Inter-university Consortium for Political and Social Research. Edited, verified by Michael Haines. Compiled, edited, and verified by Social Explorer.
Census 1960, General Population Characteristics, Mississippi. www.census.gov.
Civil Rights Act of 1964, Pub. L. No. 88–352, 88th Congress, H.R. 7152, July 2, 1964.
Kennedy, John F. "Radio and Television Address to the American People on Civil Rights, June 11, 1963," John F. Kennedy Presidential Library and Museum.
Mississippi Legislature. Regular Session 1999, SR No. 120, 99\SS03\R1582, 1–4.
The White House. "Executive Order Establishing the President's Committee on Rural Poverty and the National Advisory Commission of Rural Poverty." September 28, 1966.
——. "Remarks of the President, Operation Head Start, The Rose Garden." May 18, 1965.

BOOKS

Andrew, John A. III. *Lyndon Johnson and the Great Society.* Chicago: Ivan R. Dee, Inc., 1998.
Bauman, Mark K. and Berkley Kalin, eds. *The Quiet Voices: Southern Rabbis and Black Civil Rights, 1880s–1990s.* Tuscaloosa, AL: University of Alabama Press, 1997.
Blackwell, Unita with JoAnne Prichard Morris. *Barefootin': Life Lessons from the Road to Freedom.* New York: Crown Publishing Group, 2006.
Branch, Taylor. *Parting the Waters: America in the King Years, 1954–1963.* New York: Simon & Schuster Paperbacks, 1988.
——. *Pillar of Fire: America in the King Years, 1963–1968.* New York: Simon & Schuster Paperbacks, 1998.

Carter, Hodding. *So the Heffners Left McComb.* Garden City, NY: Doubleday & Company, Inc., 1965.

Chappell, David L. *A Stone of Hope.* Chapel Hill: University of North Carolina Press, 2004.

———. *Inside Agitators: White Southerners in the Civil Rights Movement.* Baltimore: The Johns Hopkins University Press, 1994.

Clark, Robert F. *The War on Poverty: History Selected Programs and Ongoing Impact.* Lanham, MD: University Press of American, Inc., 2002.

Classen, Steven D. *Watching Jim Crow: The Struggles Over Mississippi TV, 1955–1969.* Durham, NC: Duke University Press, 2004.

Collier-Thomas, Bettye. *Jesus, Jobs, and Justice: African American Women and Religion.* New York: Alfred A. Knopf, 2010.

Collier-Thomas, Bettye and V.P. Franklin, eds. *Sisters in the Struggle: African American Women in the Civil Rights-Black Power Movement.* New York: New York University Press, 2001.

Cowan, Paul. *An Orphan in History: One Man's Triumphant Search for His Jewish Roots* with afterword by Rachel Cowan. Woodstock, VT: Jewish Lights Publishing, 2002.

Crawford, Vicki L., Jacqueline Anne Rouse, and Barbara Woods, eds. *Women in the Civil Rights Movement: Trailblazers and Torchbearers, 1941–1965.* Bloomington: Indiana University Press, 1990.

Crespino, Joseph. *In Search of Another Country: Mississippi and the Conservative Counterrevolution.* Princeton, NJ: Princeton University Press, 2007.

Cunningham, W. J. *Agony at Galloway: One Church's Struggle with Social Change.* Jackson, MS: University Press of Mississippi, 1980.

Curry, Constance, Joan C. Browning, Dorothy Dawson Burlage, Penny Patch, Theresa Del Pozzo, Sue Thrasher, Elaine DeLott Baker, Emmie Schrader Adams, and Casey Hayden. *Deep in Our Hearts: Nine White Women in the Freedom Movement.* Athens, GA: University of Georgia Press, 2000.

DeYoung, Curtiss Paul, Michael O. Emerson, George Yancey, and Karen Chai Kim. *United by Faith: The Multiracial Congregation as an Answer to the Problem of Race.* New York: Oxford University Press, 2003.

Dittmer, John. *Local People: The Struggle for Civil Rights in Mississippi.* Champaign, IL: University of Illinois Press, 1995.

Eagles, Charles W. *The Price of Defiance: James Meredith and the Integration of Ole Miss.* Chapel Hill, NC: University of North Carolina, 2009.

Evans, Eli N. *The Provincials: A Personal History of Jews in the South,* revised edition. Chapel Hill, NC: University of North Carolina Press, 2005.

Evans, Sara. *Personal Politics: The Roots of Women's Liberation in the Civil Rights Movement and the New Left.* New York: Vintage Books, 1979.

Evers, Myrlie B. with William Peters and introduction by Willie Morris. *For Us, the Living.* Garden City, NY: Doubleday, 1967.

Giddings, Paula. *When and Where I Enter: The Impact of Black Women on Race and Sex in America.* New York: Quill William Morrow, 1984.

Gilmore, Stephanie, ed. with a foreword by Sara M. Evans. *Feminist Coalitions: Historical Perspectives on Second-Wave Feminism in the United States*. Urbana: University of Illinois Press, 2008.

Greenberg, Polly. *The Devil has Slippery Shoes: A Biased Biography of the Child Development Group of Mississippi*. London: The Macmillan Company, 1969.

Hampton, Henry and Steve Fayer with Sarah Flynn, ed. *Voices of Freedom: An Oral History of the Civil Rights Movement from the 1950s through the 1980s*. New York: Bantam Books, 1990.

Harvey, Paul. *Freedom's Coming: Religious Culture and the Shaping of the South from the Civil War through the Civil Rights Era*. Chapel Hill, NC: University of North Carolina Press, 2005.

Height, Dorothy. *Open Wide the Freedom Gates: A Memoir*. New York: Public Affairs, 2003.

Higgenbotham, Evelyn Brooks. *Righteous Discontent: The Women's Movement in the Black Baptist Church, 1880–1920*. Cambridge, MA: Harvard University Press, 1993.

Hill, Samuel S. Jr. with Edgar T. Thompson, Anne Firor Scott, Charles Hudson, and Edwin S. Gaustad. *Religion and the Solid South*. Nashville, TN: Adingdon Press, 1972.

Holsaert, Faith S., Martha Prescod Norman Noonan, Judy Richardson, Betty Garman Robinson, Jean Smith Young, and Dorothy M. Zellner, eds. *Hands on the Freedom Plow: Personal Account by Women in SNCC*. Urbana, IL: University of Illinois Press, 2010.

Houck, Davis W. and David E. Dixon, eds. *Women and the Civil Rights Movement, 1954–1965*. Jackson, MS: University Press of Mississippi, 2009.

Jacobson, Matthew Frye. *Whiteness of a Different Color: European Immigrants and the Alchemy of Race*. Cambridge, MA: Harvard University Press, 1998.

Johnson, Douglas W., Paul R. Picard, and Bernard Quinn. *Churches & Church Membership in the United States: An Enumeration by Region, State and Country*. Glenmary Research Center: Washington, D.C., 1971.

Katagiri, Yasuhiro. *The Mississippi State Sovereignty Commission: Civil Rights and States' Rights*. Jackson, MS: University Press of Mississippi, 2001.

Kluchin, Rebecca Marie. *Fit to be Tied: Sterilization and Reproductive Rights in America, 1950-1980*. New Brunswick, NJ: Rutgers University Press, 2011.

Lawson, Steven F. and Charles Payne with an introduction by James T. Patterson. *Debating the Civil Rights Movement, 1945–1968*. Lanham, MD: Rowan & Littlefield Publishers, Inc., 1998.

Lee, Chana Kai, *For Freedom's Sake: The Life of Fannie Lou Hamer*. Urbana, IL: University of Illinois Press, 1999.

Lynn, Susan. *Progressive Women in Conservative Times: Racial Justice, Peace, and Feminism, 1945 to the 1960s*. Brunswick, NJ: Rutgers University Press, 1992.

Mars, Florence. *Witness in Philadelphia* with Lynn Eden and foreword by Turner Catledge. Baton Rouge, LA: Louisiana State University, 1977.

McLemore, Richard Aubrey and Nannie Pitts McLemore. *The History of the First Baptist Church of Jackson, Mississippi*. Jackson, MS: Hederman Brothers, 1976.

Michel, Gregg L. *Struggle for a Better South: The Southern Student Organizing Committee, 1964-1969*. New York: Palgrave McMillan, 2004.

Mills, Kay. *This Little Light of Mine: The Life of Fannie Lou Hamer*. New York: Dutton, 1993.

Mills, Nicholas. *Like a Holy Crusade: Mississippi 1964—The Turning of the Civil Rights Movement in America*. Chicago: Ivan R. Dee, Publisher, 1992.

Moody, Anne. *Coming of Age in Mississippi*. New York: Bantam Dell, 1968.

Moore, Andrew S. *The South's Tolerable Alien: Roman Catholics in Alabama and Georgia, 1945-1970*. Baton Rouge: Louisiana State University Press, 2007.

Murray, Gail S., ed. *Throwing Off the Cloak of Privilege: White Southern Women Activists in the Civil Rights Era*. Gainesville: University Press of Florida, 2004.

Namorato, Michael V. *The Catholic Church in Mississippi, 1911-1984: A History*. Westport, CT: Praeger, 1998.

Newman, Mark. *Divine Agitators: The Delta Ministry and Civil Rights in Mississippi*. Athens, GA: The University of Georgia Press, 2004.

O'Brian, Michael. *John F. Kennedy: A Biography*. New York: Thomas Dunne Books, 2005.

Olson, Lynne. *Freedom's Daughters: The Unsung Heroines of the Civil Rights. Movement from 1830-1970*. New York: Touchstone, 2001.

Osborne, William A. *The Segregated Covenant: Race Relations and American Catholics*. New York: Herder and Herder, 1967.

Payne, Charles M. *I've Got the Light of Freedom: The Organizing Tradition and the Mississippi Freedom Struggle*. Berkley: University of California Press, 1995.

Phillips, Winnie. *A History of Methodist Women: Mississippi Conference Southeastern Jurisdiction The Methodist Church 1928-1968*. Clinton, MS: United Methodist Women The Methodist Church Mississippi Conference, 1980.

Ransby, Barbara. *Ella Baker and the Black Freedom Movement: A Radical Democratic Vision*. Chapel Hill, NC: University of North Carolina Press, 2003.

Reed, Linda. *Simple Decency & Common Sense: The Southern Conference Movement, 1938-1963*. Bloomington, IN: Indiana University Press, 1991.

Roberts, Gene and Hank Klibanoff. *The Race Beat: The Press, the Civil Rights Struggle, and the Awakening of a Nation*. New York: Alfred A. Knopf, 2007.

Robnett, Belinda. *How Long? How Long?: African-American Women in the Struggle for Civil Rights*. New York: Oxford University Press, 1997.

Roediger, David R. *Working toward Whiteness: How America's Immigrants Became White, The Strange Journey from Ellis Island to the Suburbs*. New York: Basic Books, 2005.

Rogow, Faith. *Gone to Another Meeting: The National Council of Jewish Women, 1893-1993*. Tuscaloosa: University of Alabama Press, 1993.

Ross, Rosetta E. *Witnessing and Testifying: Black Women, Religion, and Civil Rights*. Minneapolis: Fortress Press, 2003.

Rothenberg, Paula S. ed. *White Privilege: Essential Readings on the Other Side of Racism*, 2d ed. New York: Worth Publishers, 2005.

Schultz, Debra L. *Going South: Jewish Women in the Civil Rights Movement*. New York: New York University Press, 2001.

Schweiger, Beth Barton and Donald G. Mathews, eds. *Religion in the American South: Protestants and Others in History and Culture.* Chapel Hill, NC: University of North Carolina Press, 2004.

Sharpless, Rebecca. *Cooking in Other Women's Kitchens: Domestic Workers in the South, 1865–1960.* Chapel Hill: University of North Carolina Press, 2010.

Silver, James W. *Mississippi: The Closed Society.* New York: Harcourt, Brace & World, 1964.

Smith, Barbara Ellen, ed. *Neither Separate nor Equal: Women, Race, and Class in the South.* Philadelphia: Temple University Press, 1999.

Sokol, Jason. *There Goes My Everything: White Southerners in the Age of Civil Rights, 1945–1975.* New York: Alfred A. Knopf, 2006.

Sparks, Randy J. *Religion in Mississippi,* Heritage of Mississippi Series Vol. II. Jackson, MS: University Press of Mississippi, 2001.

Sugarman, Tracey. *Stranger at the Gates: A Summer in Mississippi.* New York: Hill and Wang, 1966.

Sundquist, Eric J. *Strangers in the Land: Blacks, Jews, Post-Holocaust America.* Cambridge, MA: Belknap Press of Harvard University, 2005.

Talbot, Mary M. *Language and Gender: An Introduction.* Cambridge, UK: Polity Press, 2005.

Tannen, Deborah. *Talking from 9 to 5.* London, England: Virago, 1995.

———. *You Just Don't Understand.* London, England: Virago, 1991.

Tarry, Ellen. *The Third Door: The Autobiography of an American Negro Woman.* Tuscaloosa, AL: University of Alabama Press, 1992.

Thornton, J. Mills, III, *Dividing Lines: Municipal Politics and the Struggle for Civil Rights in Montgomery, Birmingham, and Selma.* Tuscaloosa: University of Alabama Press, 2002.

Vinovskis, Maris A. *The Birth of Head Start: Preschool Education Policies in the Kennedy and Johnson Administrations.* Chicago: University of Chicago Press, 2005.

Ware, Susan. *Beyond Suffrage: Women in the New Deal.* Cambridge, MA: Harvard University Press, 1981.

Watson, Bruce. *Freedom Summer: The Savage Season that Made Mississippi Burn and Made America a Democracy.* New York: Viking Adult, 2010.

Webb, Clive. *Fight Against Fear: Southern Jews and Black Civil Rights.* Athens, GA: University of Georgia Press, 2003.

Weiner, Josephine. *The Story of WICS.* Washington, DC: Women in Community Service, Inc., 1979.

White, Deborah Gray. *Too Heavy a Load: Black Women in Defense of Themselves, 1894–1994.* New York: W. W. Norton & Company, 1999.

Woods, Randall B. *LBJ: Architect of American Ambition.* New York: Free Press, 2006.

Zarefsky, David. *President Johnson's War on Poverty: Rhetoric and History.* University, AL: University of Alabama Press, 1986.

Zigler, Edward and Susan Muenchow. *Head Start: The Inside Story of America's Most Successful Educational Experiment.* New York: Basic Books, 1992.

JOURNAL ARTICLES

Andrews, Kenneth T. "Social Movements and Policy Implementation: The Mississippi Civil Rights Movement and the War on Poverty, 1965 to 1971." *American Sociological Review* 66 (February 2001): 71–95.

Doar, John. "The Work of the Civil Rights Division in Enforcing Voting Rights under the Civil Rights Act of 1957 and 1960." *Florida State University Law Review* 25 (1991): 1–17.

Findlay, James F. "The Mainline Churches and Head Start in Mississippi: Religious Activism in the Sixties." *Church History* 64 no. 2 (June 1995): 237–250.

Harwell, Debbie Z. "Wednesdays in Mississippi: Uniting Women across Regional and Racial Lines, Summer 1964." *Journal of Southern History* 76, no. 3 (August 2010): 617–654.

Irons, Jenny. "The Shaping of Activist Recruitment and Participation: A Study of Women in the Mississippi Civil Rights Movement." *Gender and Society* 12, no. 6, Special Issue. *Gender and Social Movements*, Part 1 (December 1998): 692–709.

Laville, Helen. "'If the Time Is Not Ripe, Then It Is Your Job to Ripen the Time!' The Transformation of the YWCA in the USA from Segregated Association to Interracial Organization, 1930–1965." *Women's History Review* 15, no. 3: 359–383.

Miller, Mike. "Mississippi Musings: Freedom Summer Revisited (Civil Rights Movement in the 1960s)." *Social Policy* 25 no. 1 (Fall 1994): 46–61.

Murray, Paul T. "Father Nathaniel and the Greenwood Movement." *Journal of Mississippi History* 72, no. 3 (Fall 2010): 277–311.

Rachal, John R. "'The Long Hot Summer': The Mississippi Response to Freedom Summer, 1964." *The Journal of Negro History* 84, no. 4 (Autumn 1999): 315–339.

Reiff, Joseph T. "Conflicting Convictions in White Mississippi Methodism: The 1963 'Born of Conviction' Controversy." *Methodist History* 49:3 (April 2011): 162–178.

Robnett, Belinda. "African-American Women in the Civil Rights Movement, 1954–1965: Gender, Leadership, and Micromobilization." *The American Journal of Sociology* 101 no. 6 (May 1996): 1661–1693.

Ssewamala, Fred M. "Expanding Women's Opportunities: The Potential of Heifer Projects in Sub-Saharan Africa. *Development in Practice* 14 no. 4 (June 2004).

PAPER PRESENTATIONS

Riehm, Edith Holbrook. "The Hope Lies in the Women: White Southern Churchwomen in the Struggle for Civil Rights and the Quest for Human Rights." Social Science in History Conference, Long Beach, CA, November 2009.

Shulman, Holly Cowan. "Wednesdays in Mississippi: Civil Rights as Women's Work." Thirty-first Annual Southern Jewish Historical Society Conference, Little Rock, AR, November 10, 2006.

THESES AND DISSERTATIONS

Denomme, Janine Marie. "'To End This Day of Strife': Churchwomen and the Campaign for Integration, 1920–1970." PhD diss., University of Pennsylvania, 2001.

Geismer, Lily D. "Don't Blame Us: Grassroots Liberalism in Massachusetts, 1960–1990." PhD diss., University of Michigan, 2010.

Harwell, Debbie Z. "'Like a Long-handled Spoon': How Wednesdays in Mississippi United Women across Regional, Racial, and Religious Lines." PhD diss., University of Houston, 2012.

———. "Wednesdays in Mississippi: Women as a Catalyst for Change, Summer 1964." M.A. thesis, University of Memphis, May 2007.

Krause, Allen. "The Southern Rabbi and Civil Rights." M.A. thesis, Hebrew Union College—Jewish Institute of Religion, Cincinnati, Ohio, 1967.

Mantinband, Charles. "The Church and Race Relations." PhD diss., Burton College and Seminary, 1958.

Morris, Tiyi Makeda. "Black Women's Civil Rights Activism in Mississippi: The Story of WomanPower Unlimited." PhD diss., Purdue University, May 2002.

Nichols, Kimberly E. "'Service for All Citizens': Operation Compliance and the '*Opening of Public Accommodations to All*,' 1964." M.A. thesis, University of Memphis, May 1997.

WEBSITES

Children's Defense Fund. *Holding Children in Prayer: An Advent Guide,* 2005. www.chil drensdefense.org/child-research-data-publications/data/holding-children-prayer -advent-guide.pdf.

———. *Kinship Care Resource Kit: Helping Grandparents and Other Relatives Raising Children.* www.childrensdefense.org/child-research-data-publications/data/kinship -care-organization-resource-kit.pdf.

———. "Marian Wright Edelman." www.childrensdefense.org/about-us/leadership-staff/ marian-wright-edelman/.

Collins Funeral Home. "Our Founders." www.servicebycollins.com/Founders.htm.

Cowan, Liza. "Liza Cowan Remembers Her Mother, Polly Cowan." www.history.uh.edu/ cph/WIMS/effects/LizaCowan.html.

"Hazel Brannon Smith." Encyclopedia of Alabama. www.encyclopediaofalabama.org/ face/Article.jsp?id=h-1826.

"Lynchings, by State and Race, 1882–1968." The Charles Chesnutt Digital Archives. www .chesnuttarchive.org/classroom/lynchings_table_state.html.

"Our History." Straus News. April 29, 2004. www.strausnewscom/articles/2004/05/18/ about_us/history/about01.txt.

Shulman, Holly C. "Polly Spiegel Cowan: Civil Rights Activist, 1913–1976." Jewish Women's Archive. 2004. http://jwa.org/weremember/cowan.

"The United States Section of WILPF," The Women's International League for Peace and Freedom, www.wilpf.org/US_WILPF.

Trendell, Karen. "Student Group Makes Members Effective Advocates for Child Welfare." Syracuse University News, December 4, 2002. http://suews.syr.edu/story_details.cfm?id=1255.

"Violence in Jackson." Civil Rights: Reflections of public Ministry at Harvard Divinity School. www.hds.harvard.edu/library/exhibits/online/hdspublicministry/2.html.

"Wednesdays in Mississippi: Civil rights as Women's Work." www.history.uh.edu/cph/WIMS/.

"WICS History." Women in Community Service. www.wics.org/history.asp.

Index